IMAGES
of America

SAN DIMAS

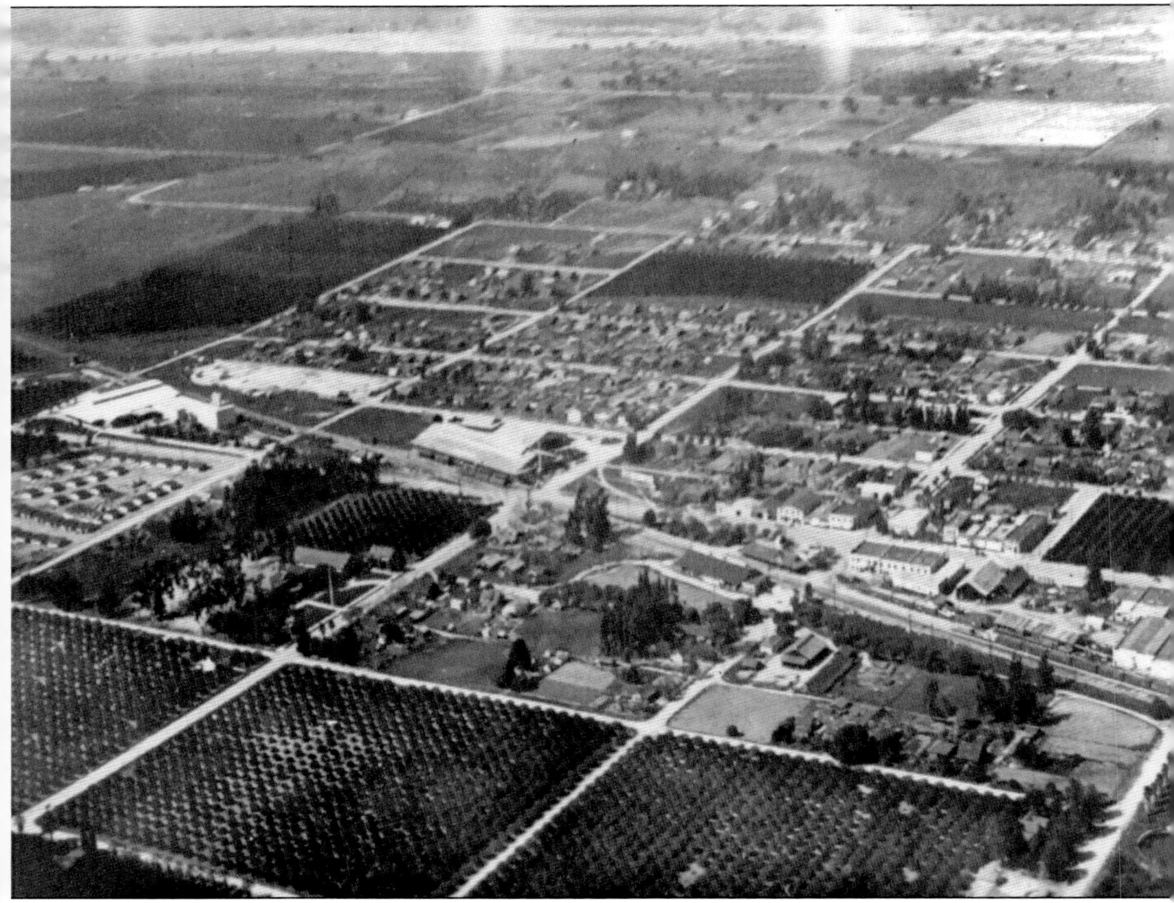

This aerial view depicts the town of San Dimas among the citrus groves of the early 1920s. The large buildings on the left side of the picture are the orange and lemon packinghouses. The citrus industry made the town grow and supported that growth into the 1950s. Today the groves are gone, replaced by homes and businesses, another example of the changing times.

On the Cover: Early residents of San Dimas gather in front of the A. A. Neher Building, constructed in 1911. The building replaced another Neher Building that was moved to make way for the new building. (Courtesy San Dimas Historical Society.)

IMAGES
of America

SAN DIMAS

Paul Rippens and
the San Dimas Historical Society

ARCADIA
PUBLISHING

ISBN 978-0-7385-5934-6

Published by Arcadia Publishing
Charleston, South Carolina

Printed in the United States of America

Library of Congress Catalog Card Number: 2008921577

For all general information contact Arcadia Publishing at:
Telephone 843-853-2070
Fax 843-853-0044
E-mail sales@arcadiapublishing.com
For customer service and orders:
Toll-Free 1-888-313-2665

Visit us on the Internet at www.arcadiapublishing.com

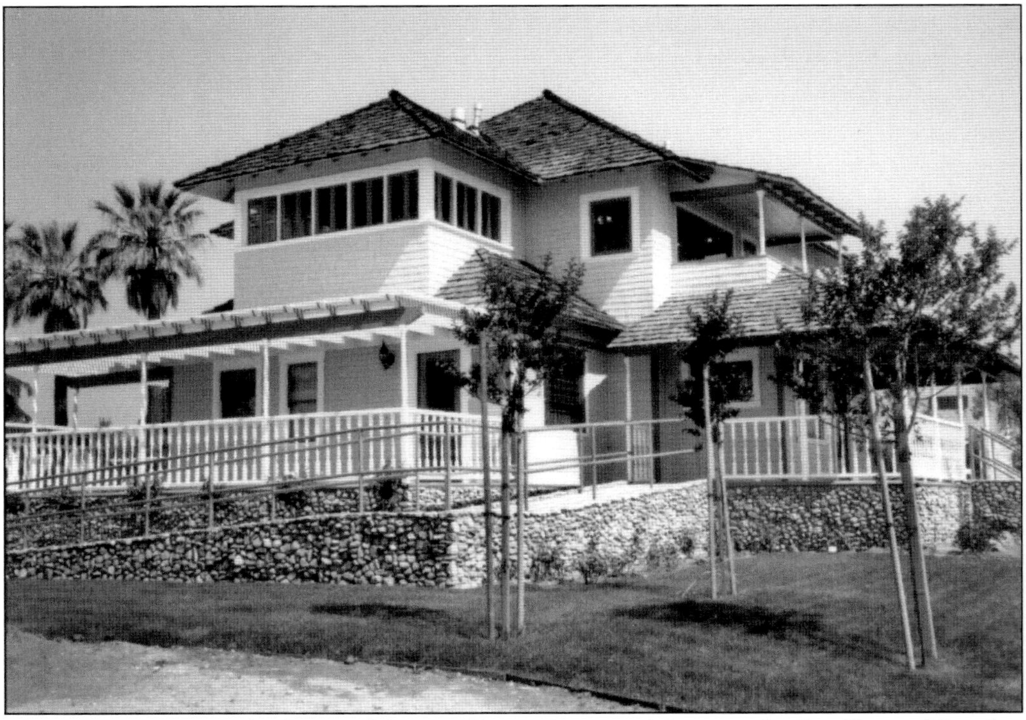

The Martin House is the home of the San Dimas Historical Society, the San Dimas Chamber of Commerce, and the Festival of Arts. Built in 1901 by William Martin as his family residence, the home was relocated to this site in 1987. It is owned by the City of San Dimas.

Contents

Acknowledgments

San Dimas is fortunate to have a wonderful collection of writings and photographs of its early history. Much of this collection was the work of Genevieve Walker, who came to town on her honeymoon in 1894 and lived out her life here. Many of her collection of photographs are included in this book.

Most of the work on this book can be credited to one person, Paul Rippens, who serves as the archivist for the San Dimas Historical Society. His knowledge of San Dimas and his dedication to this project made it happen, pure and simple. Paul took over the maintenance of the archives in 2000 following Martha Glauthier and Roberta Yoder, the two ladies who put the archives together. Paul is assisted by Susan Davis, whom he could not do without and who helped with the captions, proof reading, and the selection of pictures for the book. Susan's son, Nick, assisted with the scanning on the photographs. Their help was invaluable. All of the photographs in the book are from the archives of the San Dimas Historical Society.

This is a labor of love and we hope you enjoy the efforts put forth to allow more people to enjoy the history of San Dimas, California.

Introduction

Long before the town of San Dimas began, a *cienega* existed in the area that drew Native Americans and travelers to enjoy one of the few places with shade and water. This area, known as Mud Springs, saw such early visitors as Juan Bautista DeAnza in 1774 and Jedediah Strong Smith in 1826.

In 1837, a land grant was given to Ygnacio Palomares and Ricardo Vejar by Gov. Juan Bautista Alvarado, governor of California. The 23,000-acre grant included the *cienega*. Palomares gave part of the land to Saturino Carrion, and the Mud Springs part of the land was purchased by the San Jose Ranch Company in 1887. The Ranch Company laid out the town of San Dimas and changed its name that same year. The first home in the fledgling town was constructed in 1887 for the Ranch Company's land agent, E. M. Marshall, and his family. That home still stands as of 2008.

The area began to grow, albeit slowly, until the planting of citrus trees started. San Dimas became part of the citrus belt that extended along the foothills of the San Gabriel Mountains for 60 miles. Almost the entire area that encompassed San Dimas was citrus trees, with navel oranges planted in the lower elevations and lemons in the higher elevations to ward off the cold winter nights. For many years, the area was thought to be frost free, but that came to a dramatic change in 1913 when extremely cold weather settled over the area, damaging much of the citrus crop.

The citrus industry made the town grow until housing developments forced many of the growers out of the area. The Lemon Association Packinghouse was the last to close in 1963. Part of the complex, once the largest lemon packinghouse in the world, still exists in 2008.

The citrus industry gave way to homes and businesses. The once small, quiet town has given way to light industry and 36,000 residents. Incorporated in 1960, the city of San Dimas is still able to maintain that small-town feeling and is a much desired place to live in Los Angeles County.

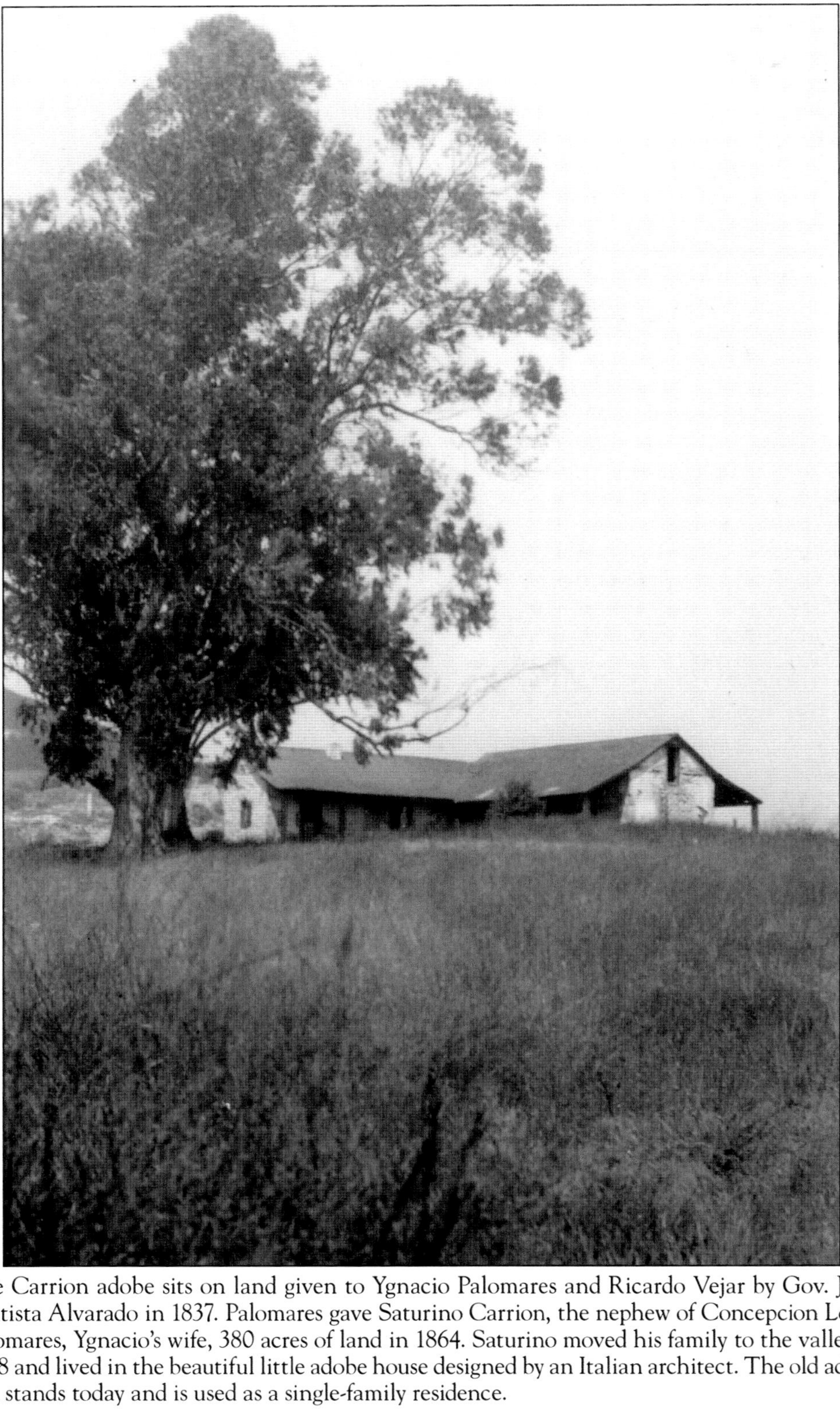

The Carrion adobe sits on land given to Ygnacio Palomares and Ricardo Vejar by Gov. Juan Bautista Alvarado in 1837. Palomares gave Saturino Carrion, the nephew of Concepcion Lopez Palomares, Ygnacio's wife, 380 acres of land in 1864. Saturino moved his family to the valley in 1868 and lived in the beautiful little adobe house designed by an Italian architect. The old adobe still stands today and is used as a single-family residence.

One

The Early Days
Mud Springs to San Dimas

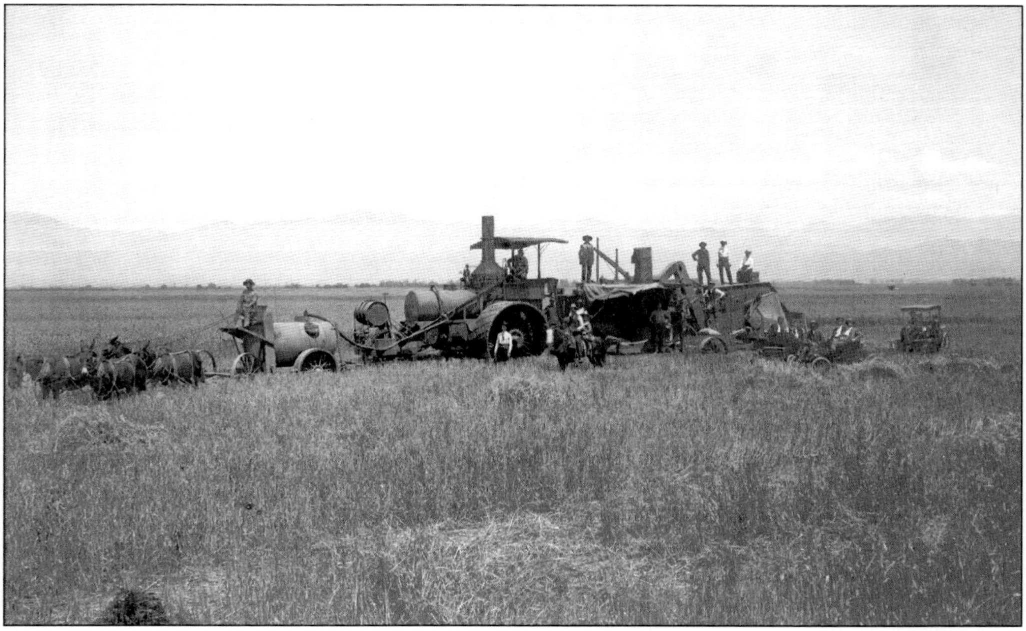

Early settlers in San Dimas tried their hand at raising wheat but soon found that the climate in the area would not support their crops. They decided to change to citrus trees, which required a large amount of water. The citrus industry made San Dimas grow as it did to communities from Pasadena to the San Bernardino and Riverside area. The growth of orange and lemon groves spread across land now occupied by homes and businesses, which started taking over the area following World War II when many of the troops returning from the war decided to stay in warm Southern California.

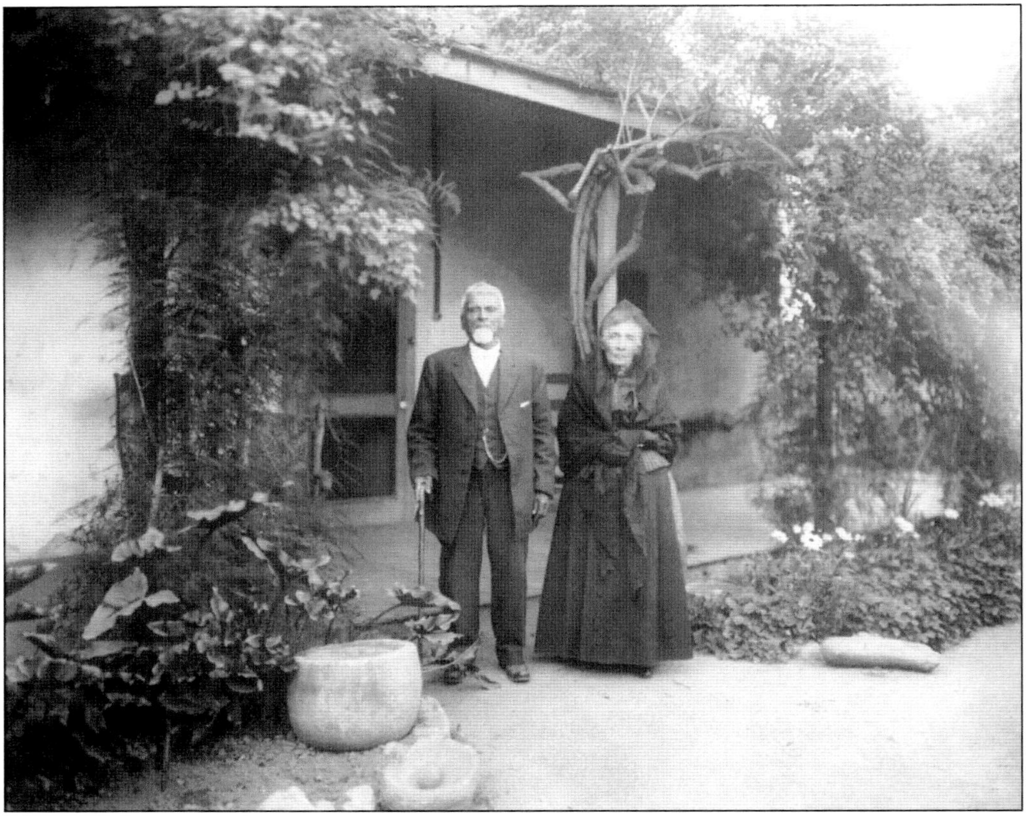

This photograph shows Ramon and Teresa Vejar in front of an adobe, possibly their home. The Vejar and Palomares families were the owners of Rancho San Jose. The two families divided the rancho, with the Palomareses taking the northern part of the land and the Vejars taking the southern part.

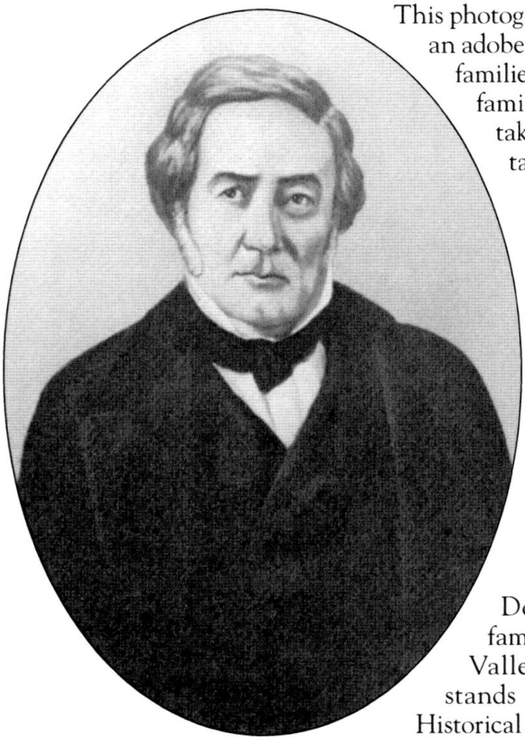

Don Ygnacio Palomares settled with his family on the Rancho San Jose of the Pomona Valley and built his adobe home, which still stands today and is owned and maintained by the Historical Society of Pomona Valley.

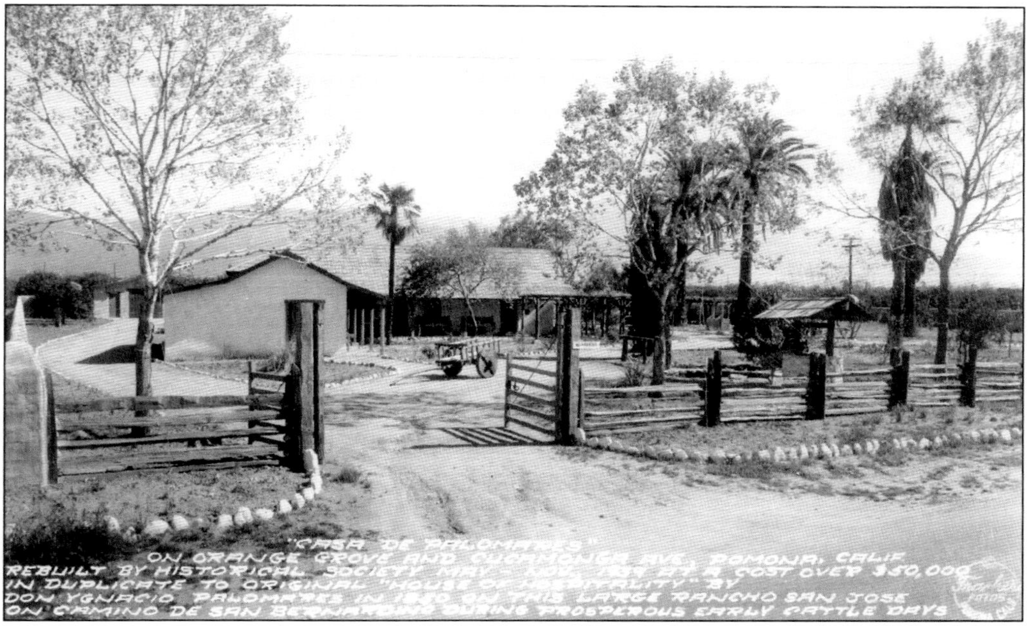

Casa de Palomares, the home of Don Ygnacio Palomares, was restored in 1939 by the Historical Society of Pomona Valley at a cost of $50,000. The adobe still stands as a fine example of what life was like during the days of the Spanish land grants and before the white men came to the area and purchased the land for future development. The adobe is open to the public.

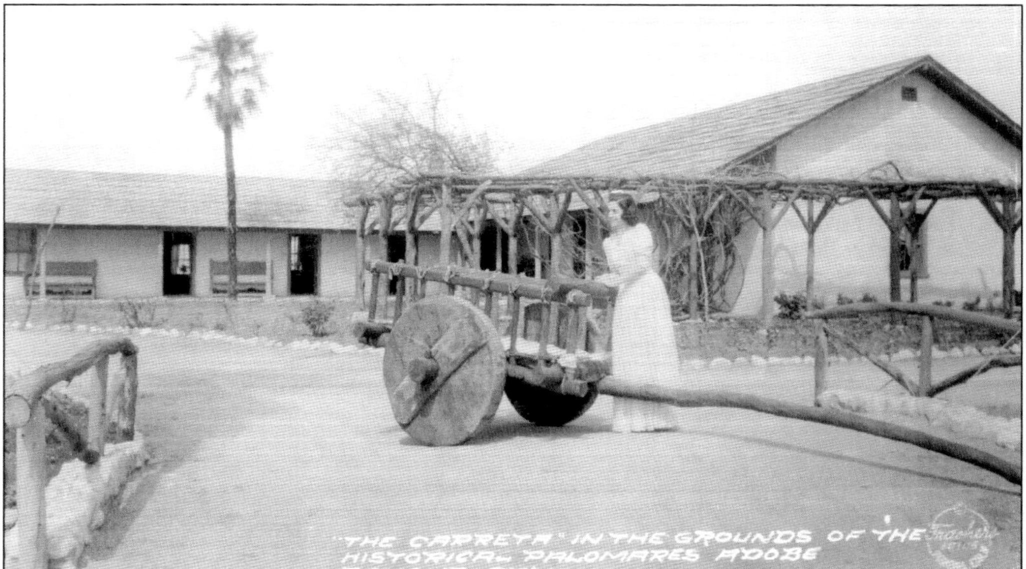

In the days when the Palomares adobe was the home of Don Ygnacio and Concepcion Palomares, the *carreta* was used to transport everything from people to animals along San Bernardino Road, which ran in front of the adobe.

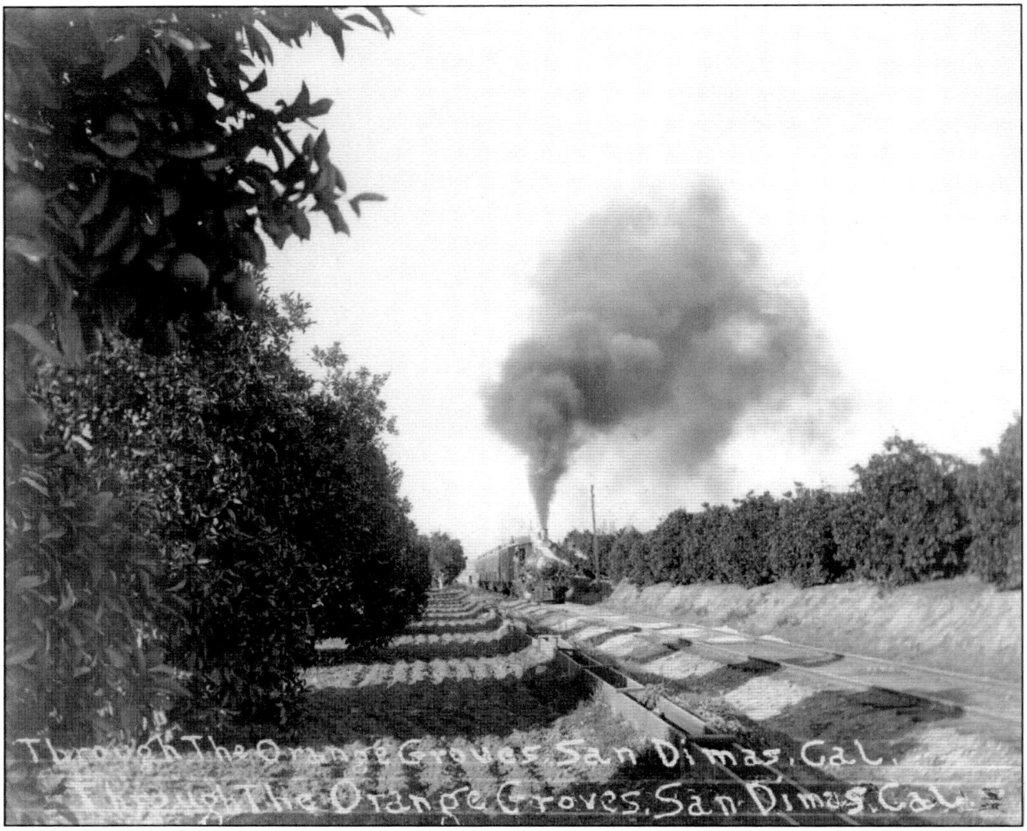

The early trains traveling through the San Dimas area were surrounded by citrus groves. The Santa Fe and Southern Pacific Railways opened the area to settlers and future business opportunities.

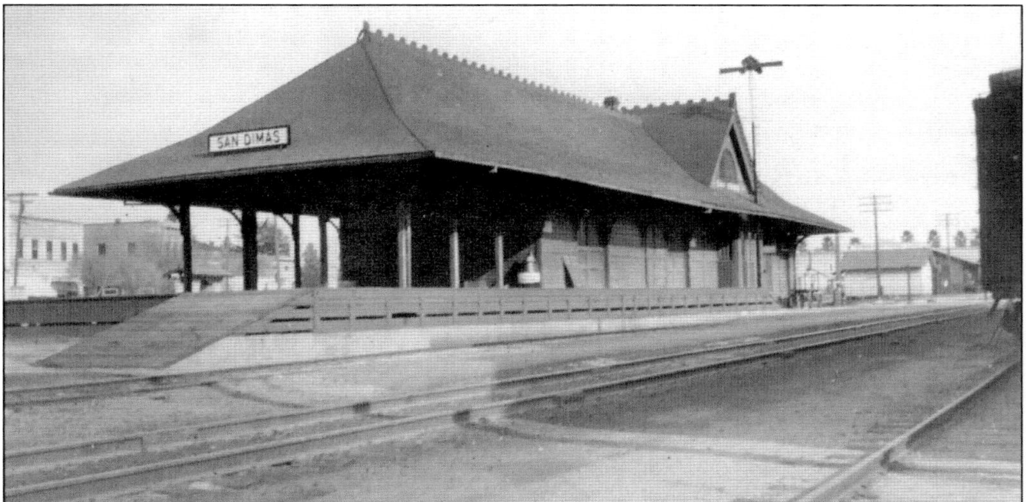

The coming of the Santa Fe Railroad was the emphasis for starting San Dimas. Built from the east and west, the railway met in San Dimas in 1887, with the first train coming into San Dimas on April 30 of that year.

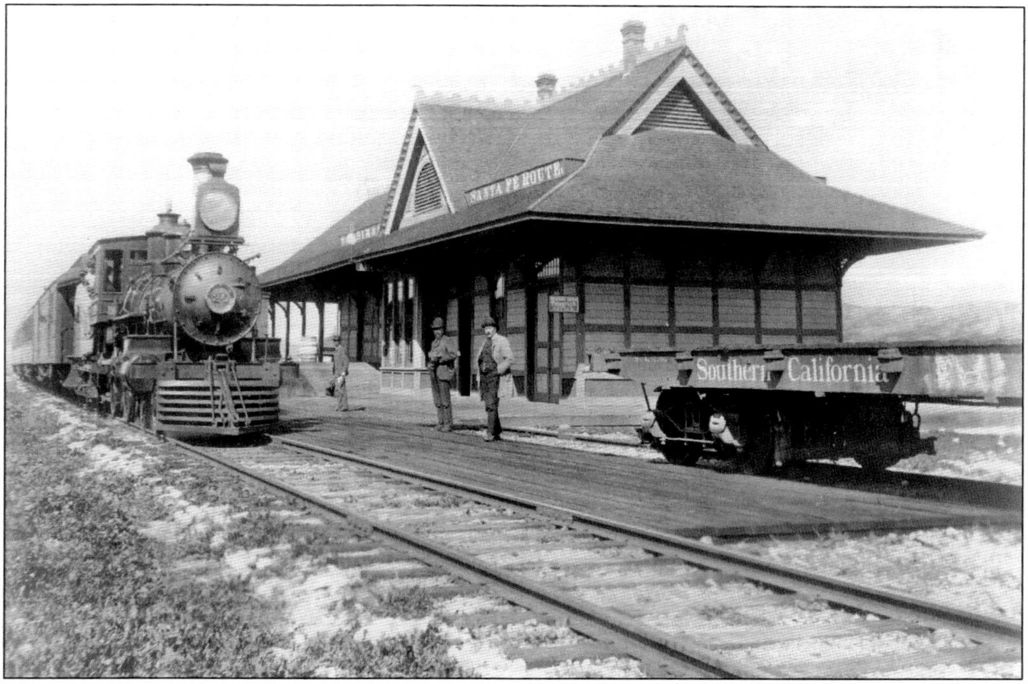

This photograph shows the Santa Fe Railway station, completed in 1889 and lasting until 1933, when it burned to the ground. It was soon replaced with a "modern" station.

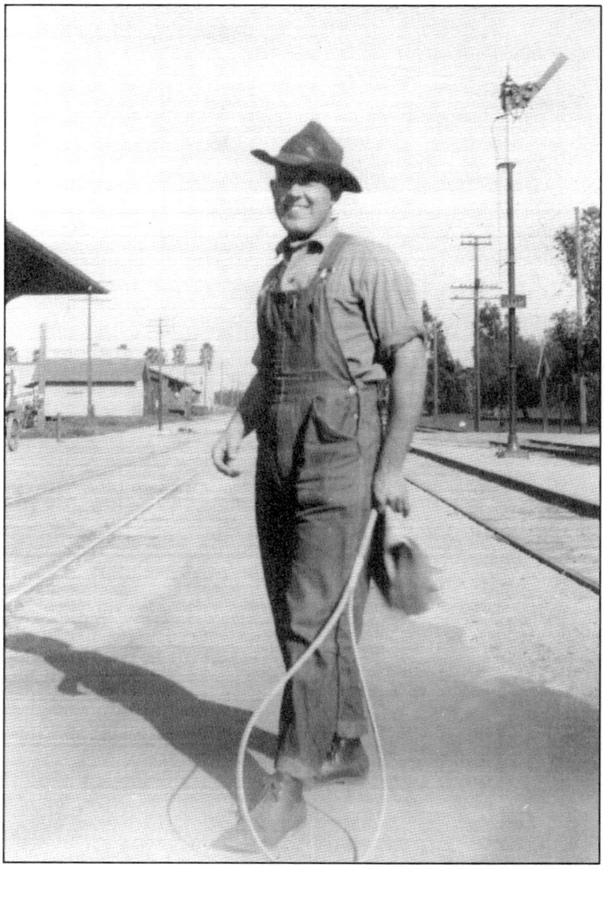

C. L. Slossen waits to catch the mail from a passing train. This photograph was taken outside the original San Dimas Santa Fe station on April 14, 1922.

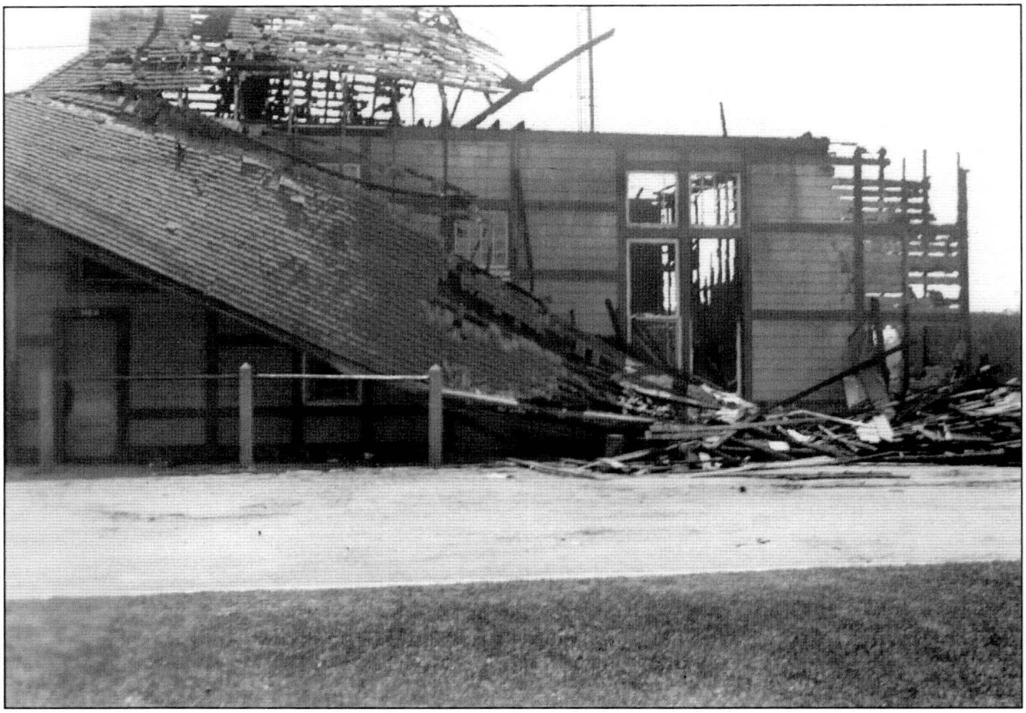

The 1933 fire destroyed the wooden station along with a small citrus packinghouse on the south side of the train tracks, behind the station. At the time of the fire, the town had only one fire truck, which would not have been able to handle a fire of this size.

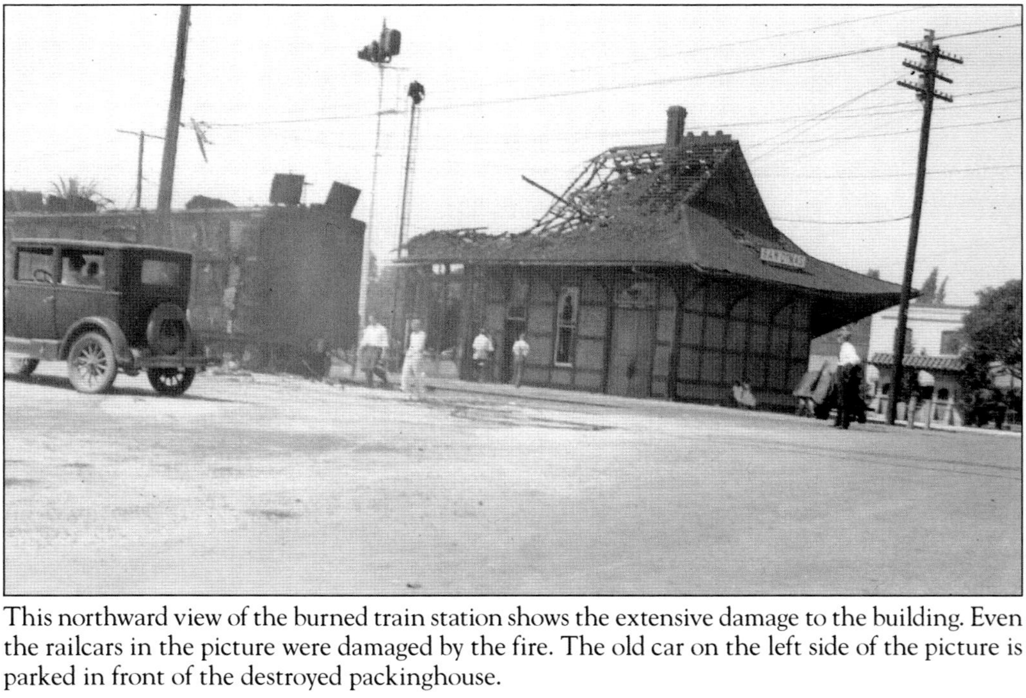

This northward view of the burned train station shows the extensive damage to the building. Even the railcars in the picture were damaged by the fire. The old car on the left side of the picture is parked in front of the destroyed packinghouse.

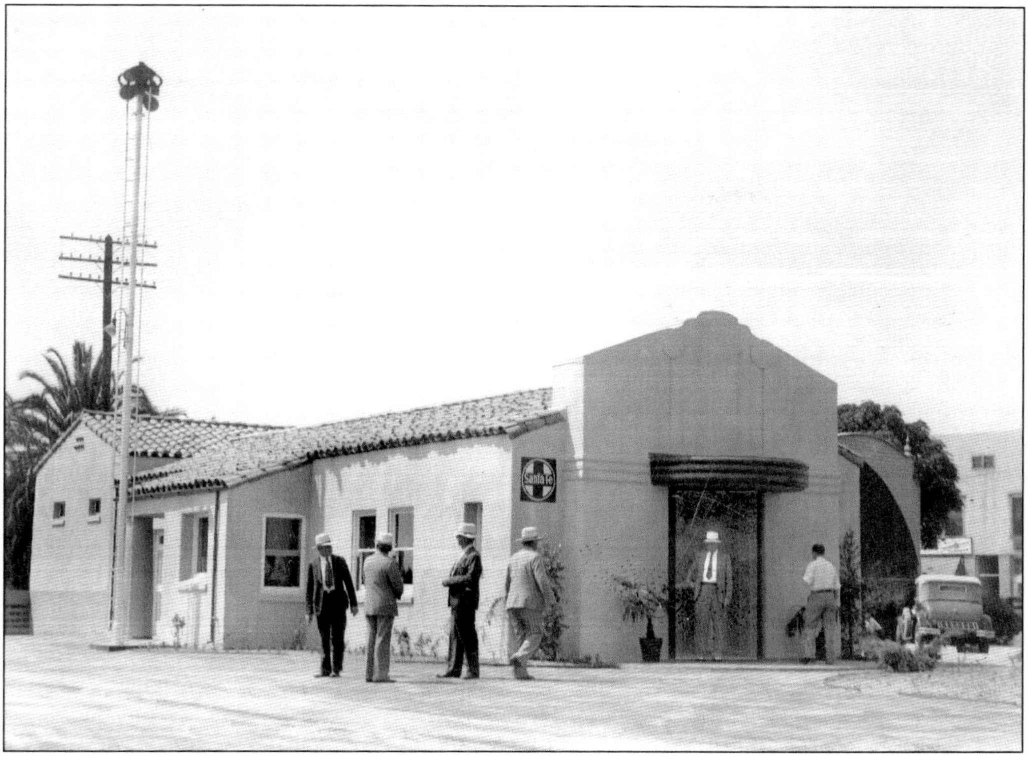

The second Santa Fe Railroad Station in San Dimas was completed in 1934 and still exists. It houses a fine exhibit of early railroad memorabilia and a library for railroad research and is operated by the Pacific Railroad Society. The San Dimas Historical Society maintains a small museum in the west end of the station.

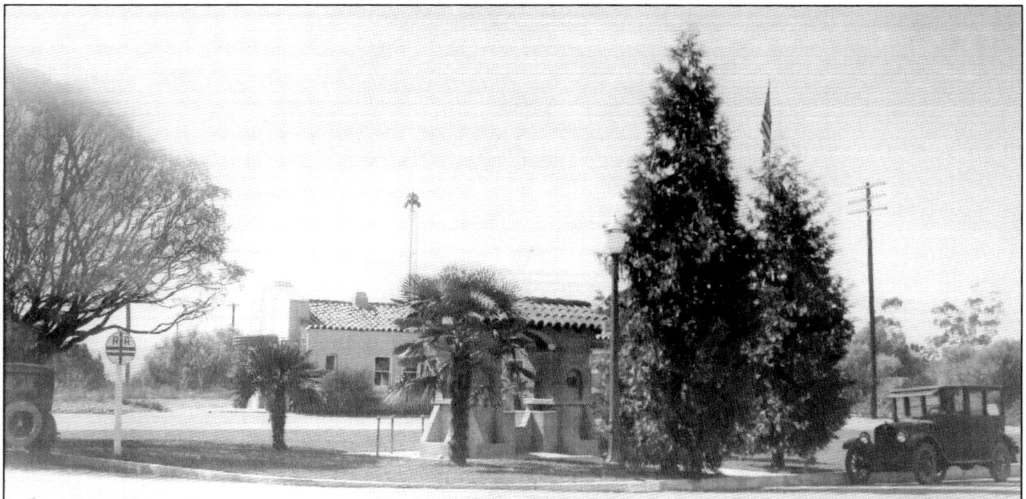

Another view of the Santa Fe station was taken from the corner of Bonita Avenue and Depot Street, today's Monte Vista Avenue. The small structure in the foreground is a drinking fountain "for man and beast."

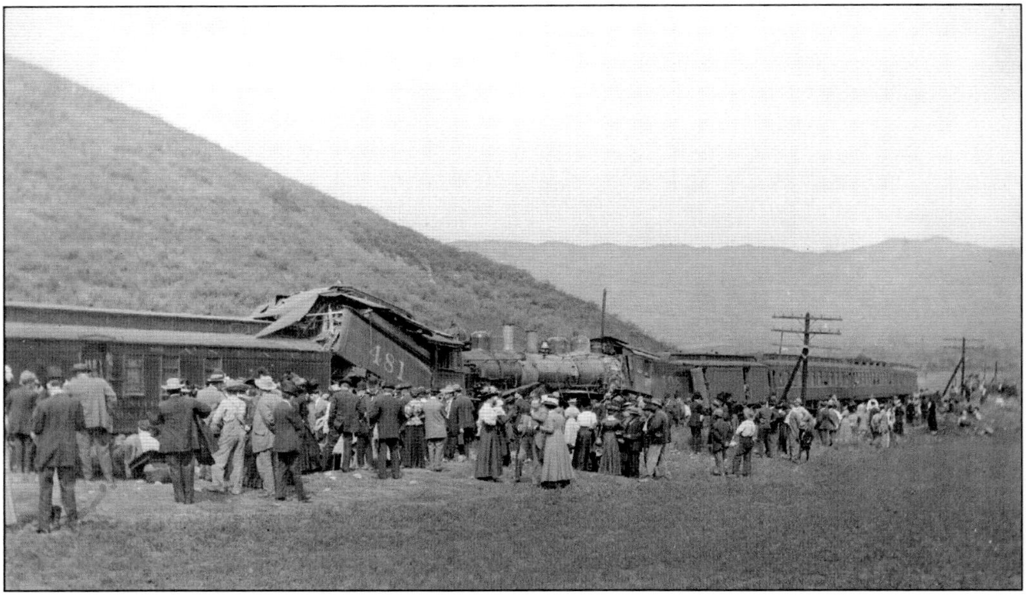

Railroad accidents were a common occurrence during the early days. This accident in 1911 occurred between the towns of San Dimas and Glendora when the train station operator in San Dimas fell asleep and allowed the westbound train to continue.

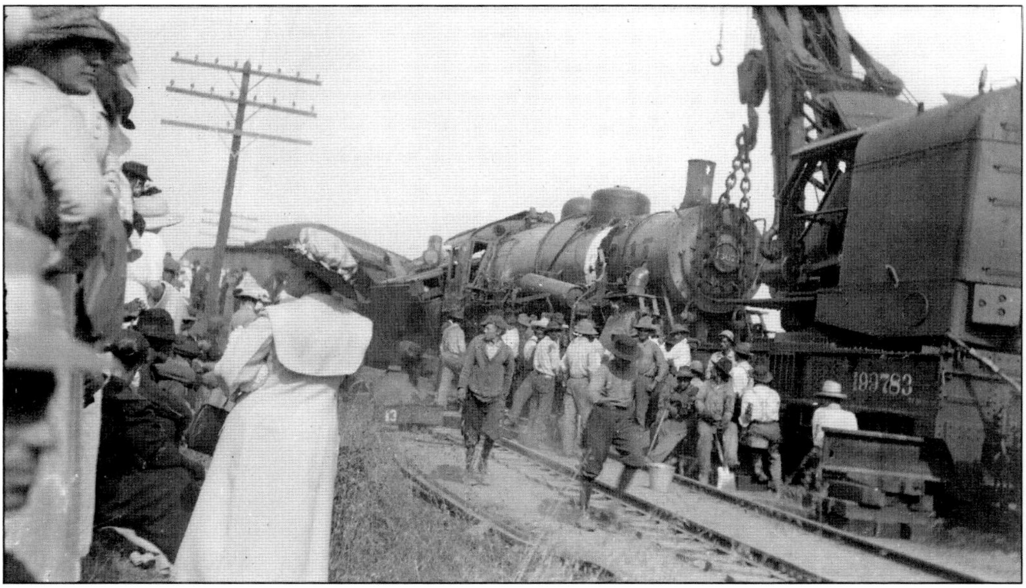

This picture is another view of the 1911 railroad accident between San Dimas and Glendora. This rail line still exists but is used only to transfer freight to manufacturers located west of San Dimas.

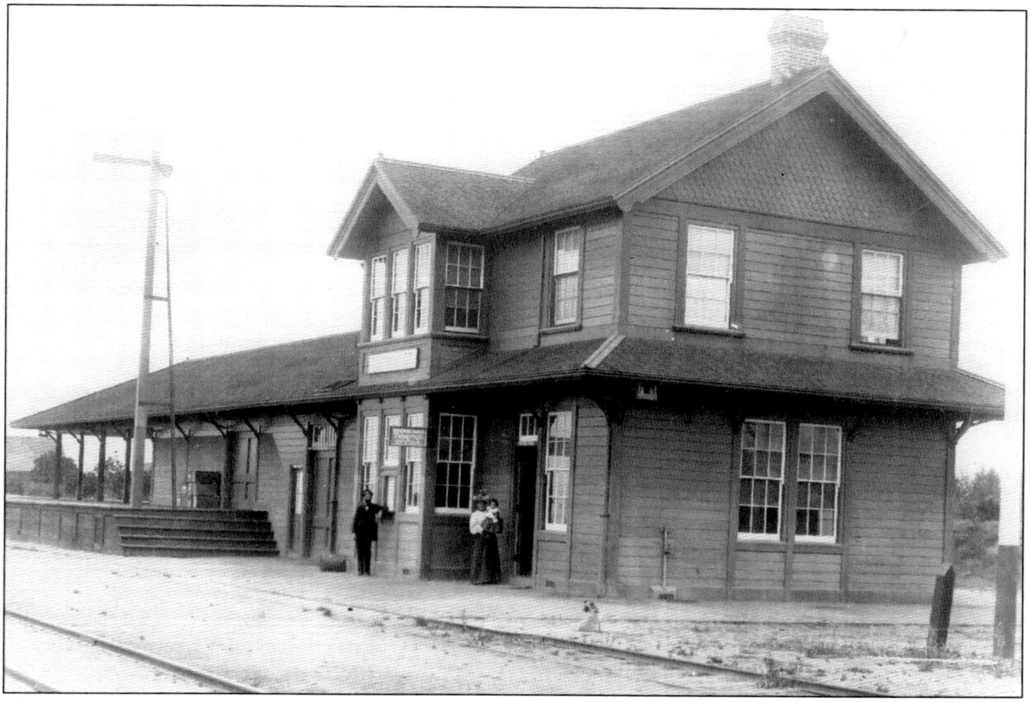

The Southern Pacific Railroad completed its line through San Dimas in 1895. The first station featured second-story living quarters for the station agent, Tom Gore. The second story was later removed.

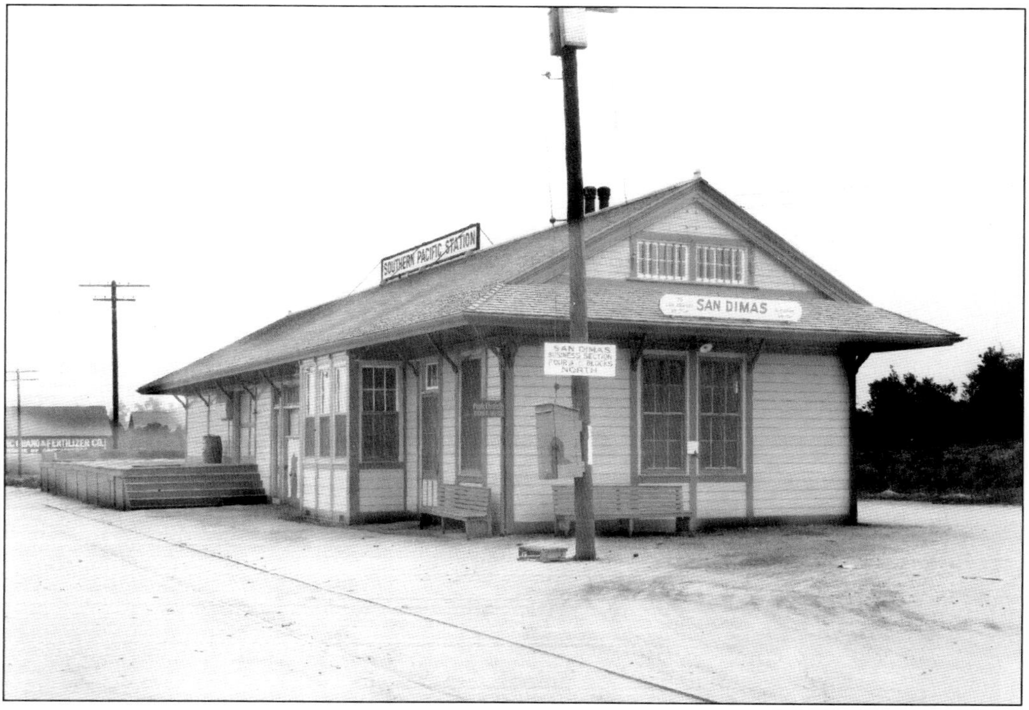

The Southern Pacific Railroad station with its new look is shown after the removal of the second-story living quarters. The building lasted 60 years until it was destroyed by fire.

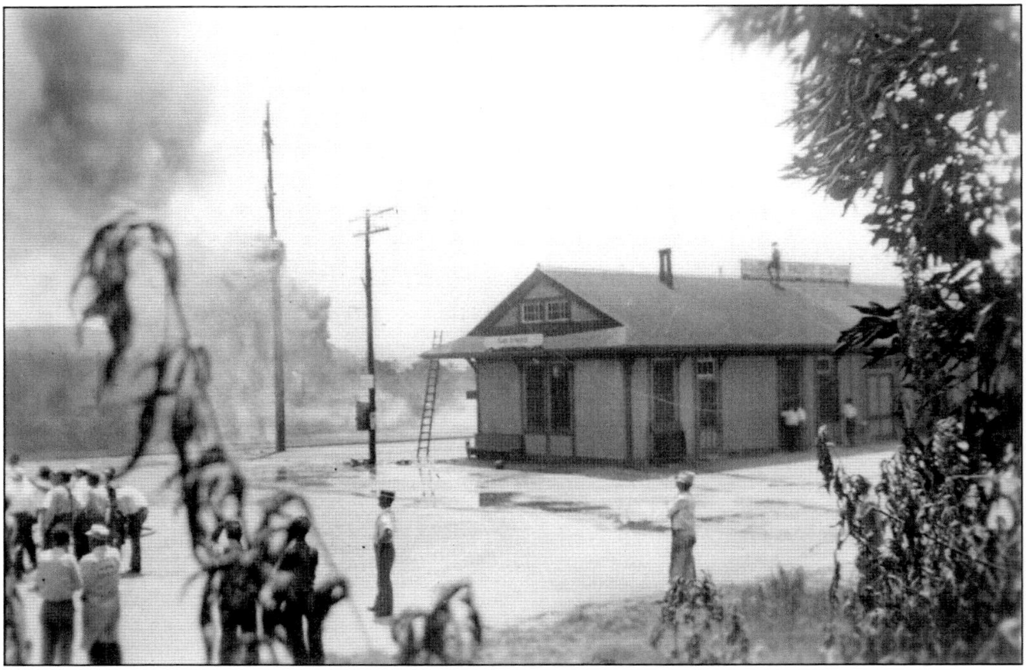

The old Southern Pacific station was destroyed during a large wildfire that roared through the southern part of San Dimas on September 1, 1955. The fire, started by boys playing with matches, burned during 106-degree weather and destroyed several homes.

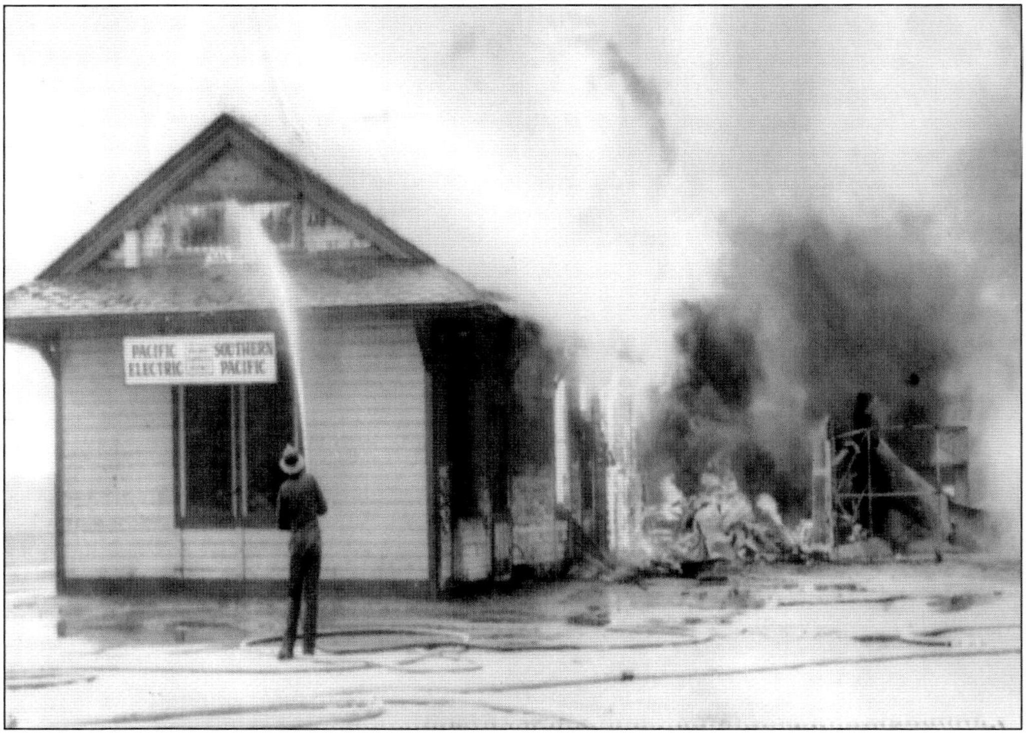

Despite the efforts of the Los Angeles County Fire Department, who fought the fire in extreme heat, the old wooden building was lost to the fast-moving fire. The building was never rebuilt.

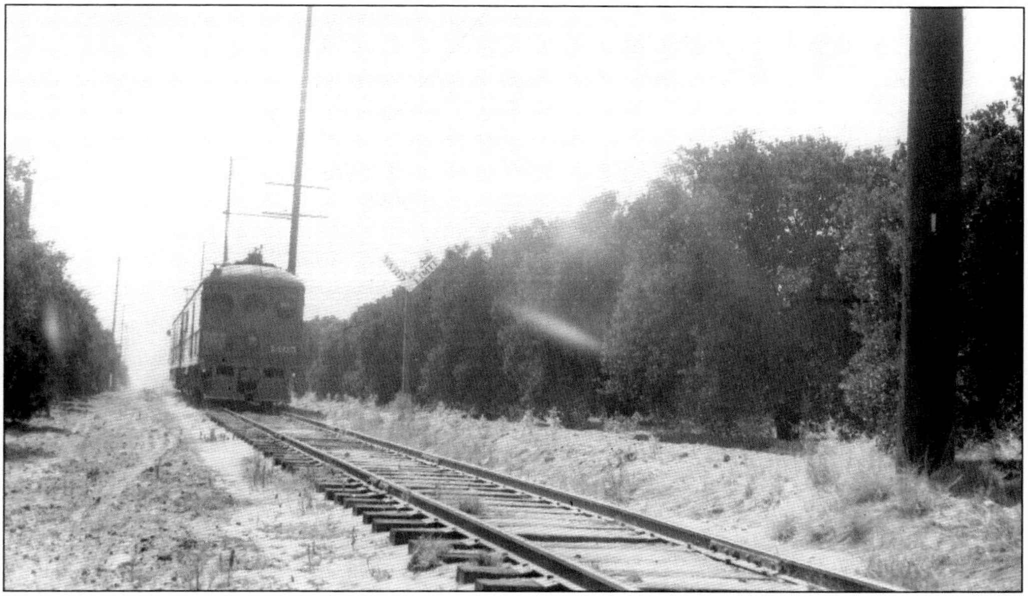

The Pacific Electric Railway Cars, or Red Cars, made their way into San Dimas through the orange groves to the station located north of the main part of town. The line continued into Sycamore Canyon, where the San Dimas Rock Quarry loaded rock onto cars to be used as road base in many area cities.

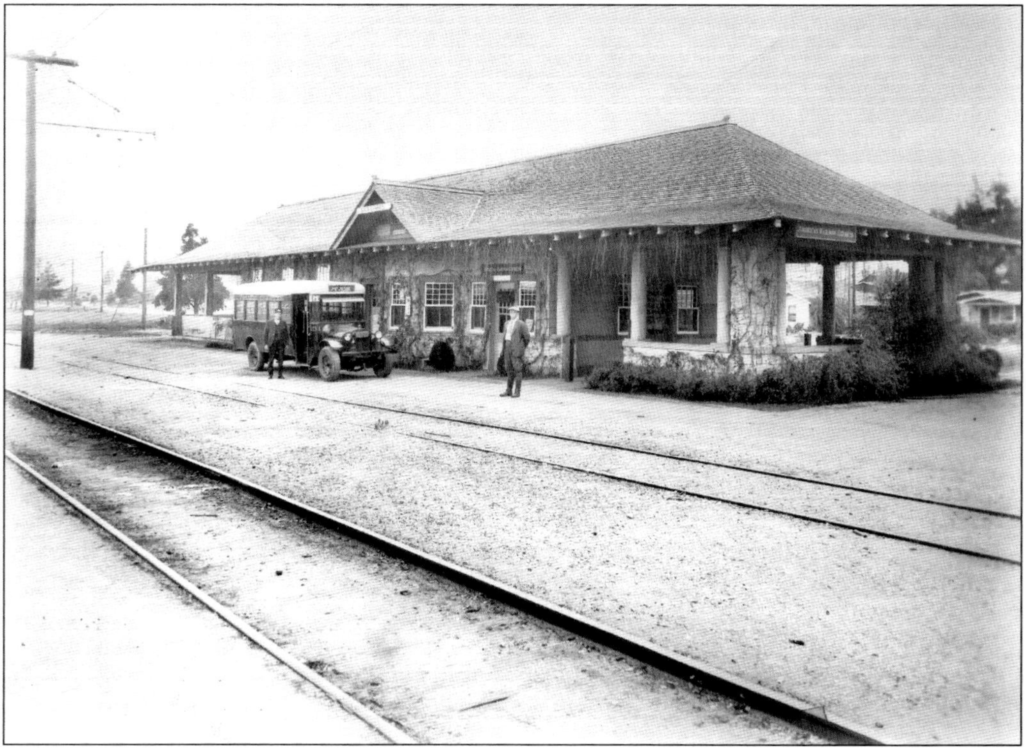

The San Dimas Pacific Electric station located at the corner of San Dimas Avenue and Fourth Street was the end of the line for passengers. The line continued into San Dimas Canyon, where a rock quarry was located. Cars would transport the rock from the canyon to various projects.

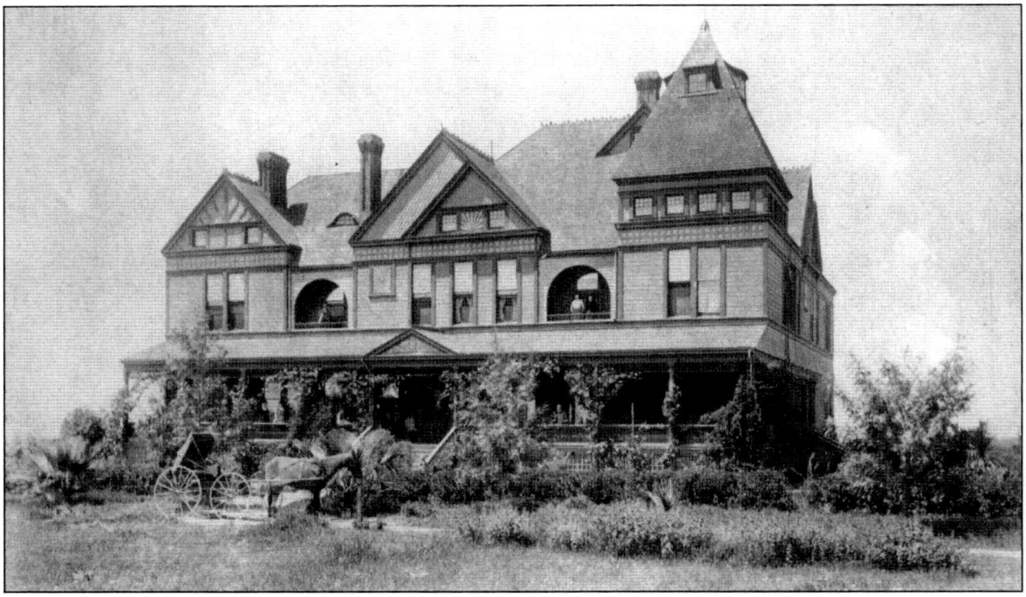

With the advent of the railroad coming into San Dimas, the San Jose Ranch Company, under the direction of Moses Wick, decided to construct a hotel for the expected land boom. However, when that land boom did not happen, they were left with a nearly 15,000-square-foot hotel that never had a paying guest. The building and 40 acres of land were sold to James and Sue Walker in 1889 for $25,000. The building still stands and is an outstanding example of early Southern California architecture. When new, it had 30 bedrooms, 4 bathrooms, and 14 fireplaces.

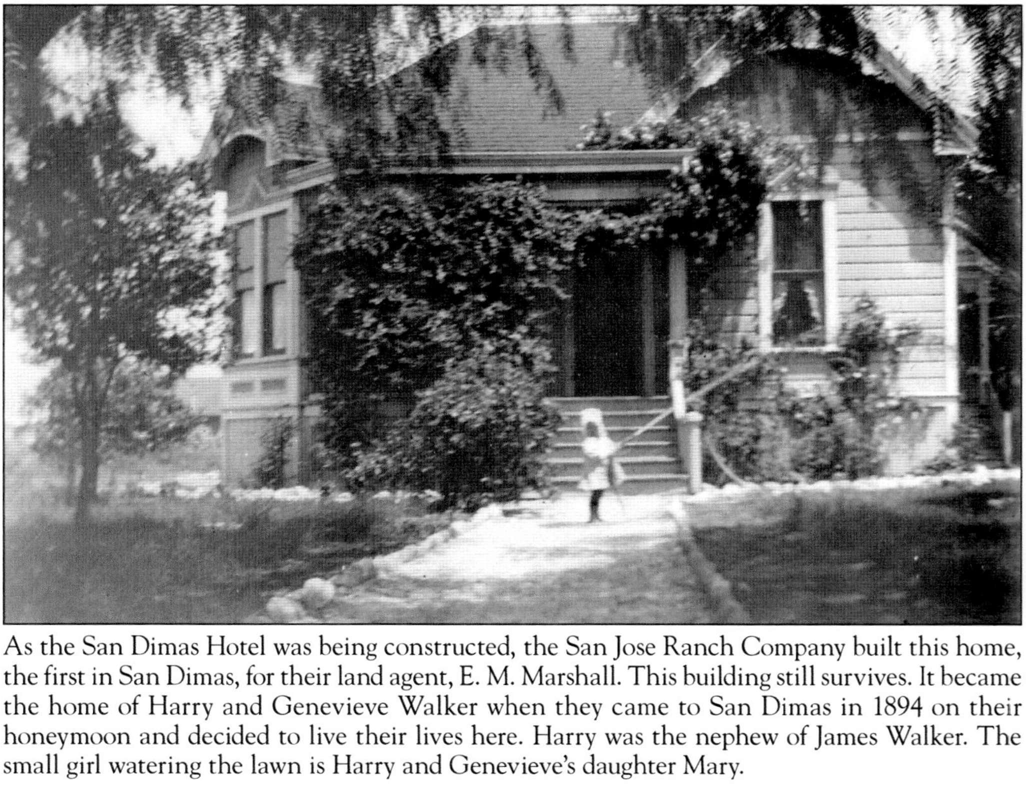

As the San Dimas Hotel was being constructed, the San Jose Ranch Company built this home, the first in San Dimas, for their land agent, E. M. Marshall. This building still survives. It became the home of Harry and Genevieve Walker when they came to San Dimas in 1894 on their honeymoon and decided to live their lives here. Harry was the nephew of James Walker. The small girl watering the lawn is Harry and Genevieve's daughter Mary.

James W. Walker and his wife, Sue, of Covington, Kentucky, bought the San Dimas Hotel in 1889. "Uncle Jimmy" and "Aunt Sue" were gracious Southerners and shared their home with the little community. Many parties and meetings were held there. The first school classes met in the basement, and churches held their first worship services in the parlor. Six generations of the Walker family lived in the hotel/home before it was leased as a restaurant in 1978. The building is listed on the National Register of Historic Places.

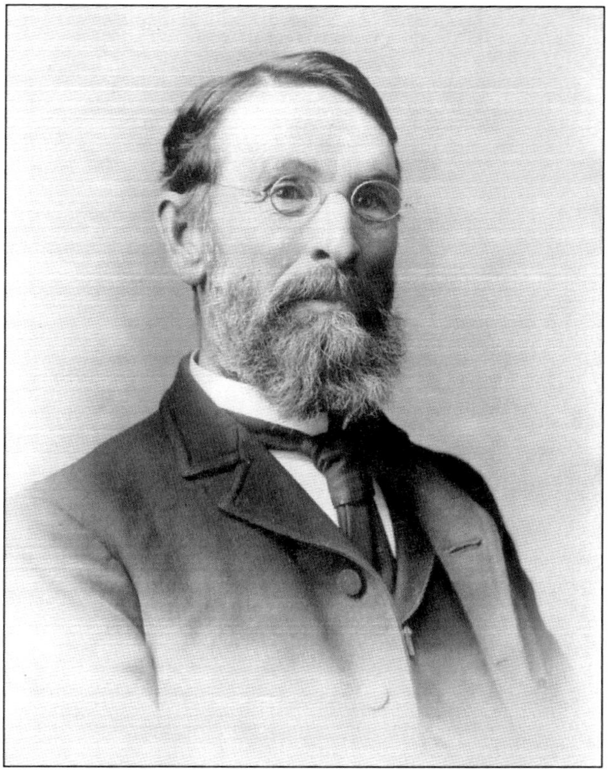

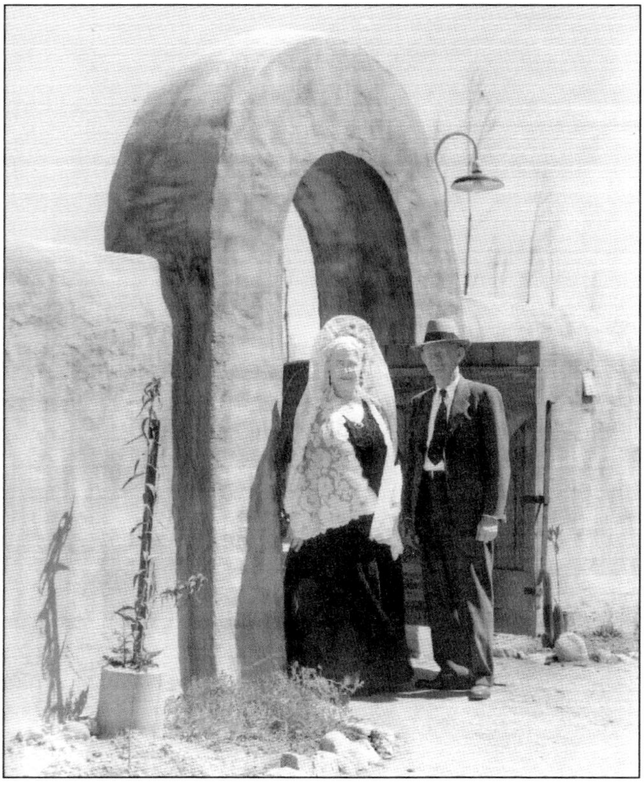

Harry and Genevieve Walker lived their entire adult lives in San Dimas and were very involved in the town's activities. Harry was a member of the board of the Historical Society of Pomona Valley, and Genevieve was the first unofficial historian of San Dimas. She kept records on everything that went on in town, even who moved in and out. She was active in the restoration of the Carrion adobe and the Palomares adobe. This picture was taken at the rededication of the Palomares adobe in 1939.

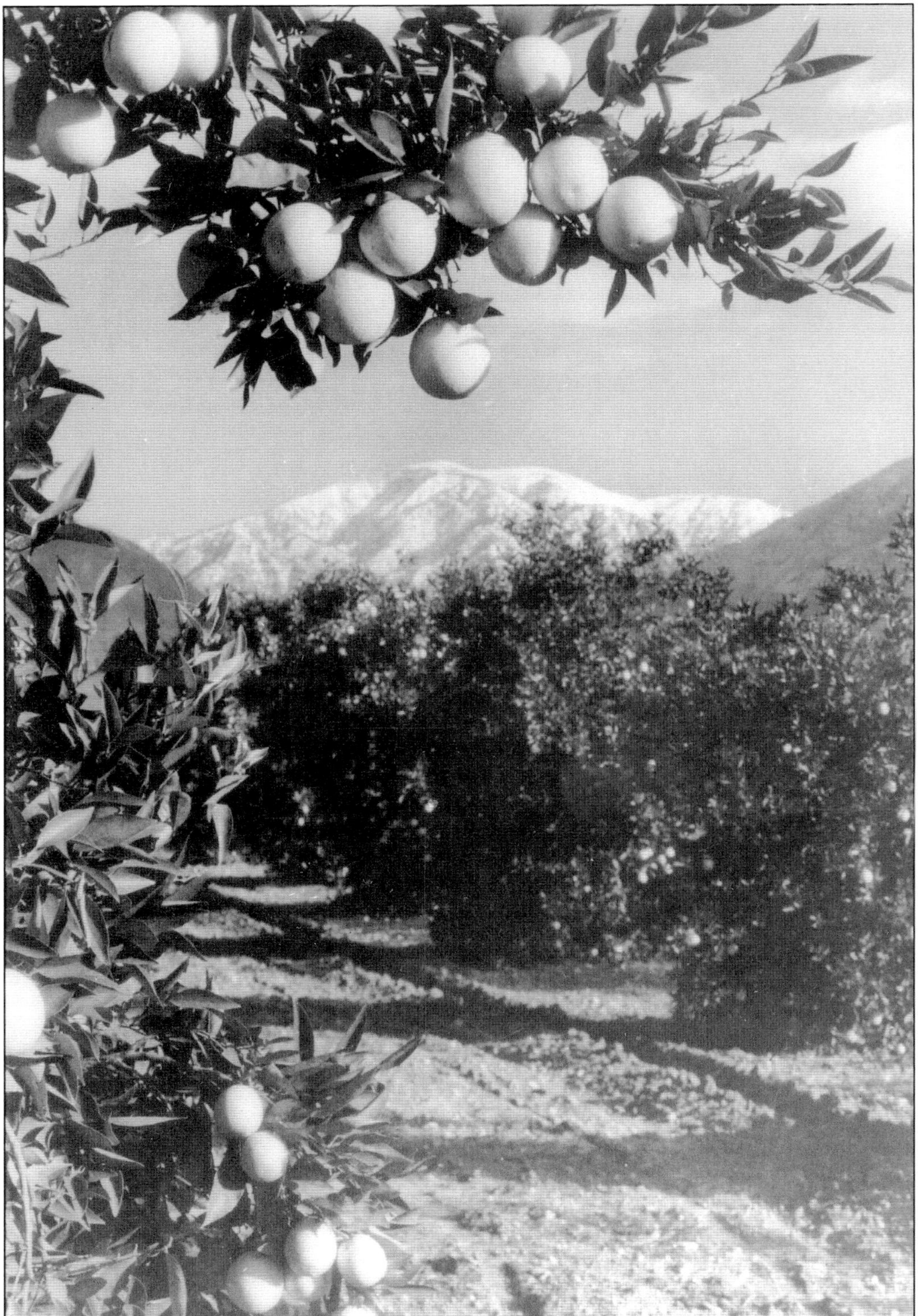

Mount San Antonio (Mount Baldy) rises majestically above the citrus groves of San Dimas. This type of picture was common of the many groves in Southern California.

Two

From Grasslands to Orange Trees
The Citrus Industry

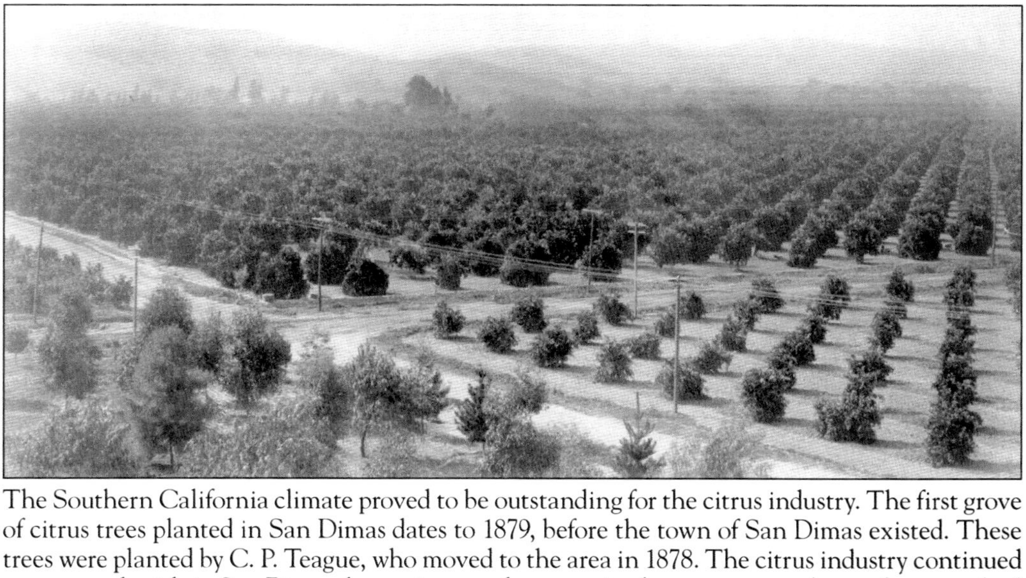

The Southern California climate proved to be outstanding for the citrus industry. The first grove of citrus trees planted in San Dimas dates to 1879, before the town of San Dimas existed. These trees were planted by C. P. Teague, who moved to the area in 1878. The citrus industry continued to grow and, with it, San Dimas, becoming another town in the vast groves of trees that stretched for 60 miles from Pasadena to San Bernardino.

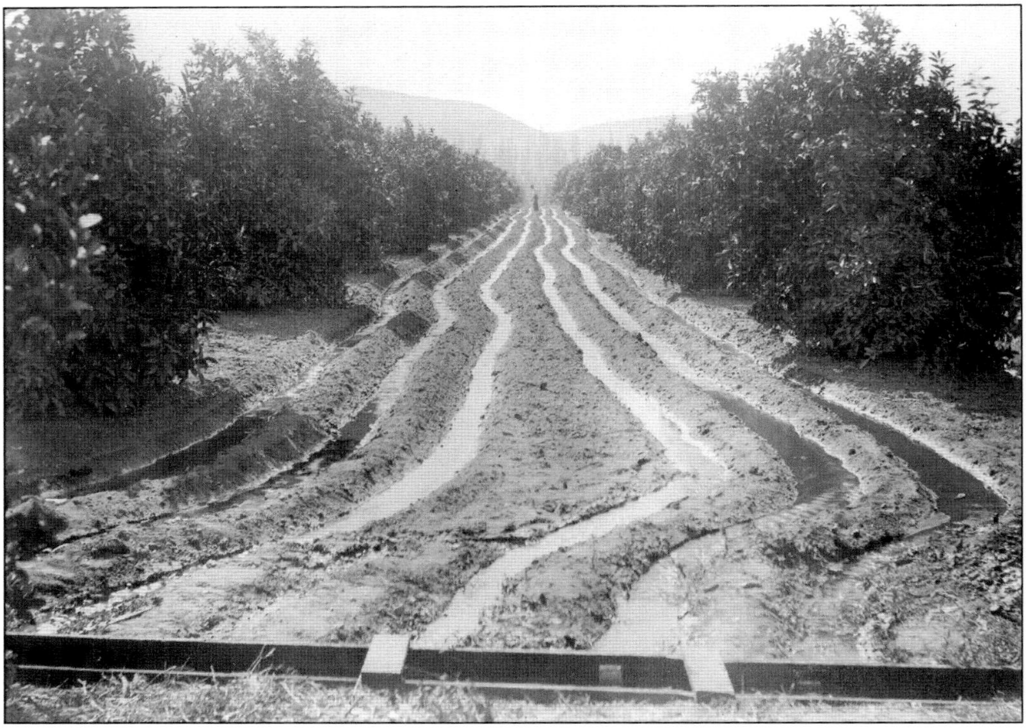

Water to irrigate the thirsty citrus groves proved to be a major problem for the early ranchers. Many wells were drilled in the area to provide the necessary water for the crops and water for the increase in population.

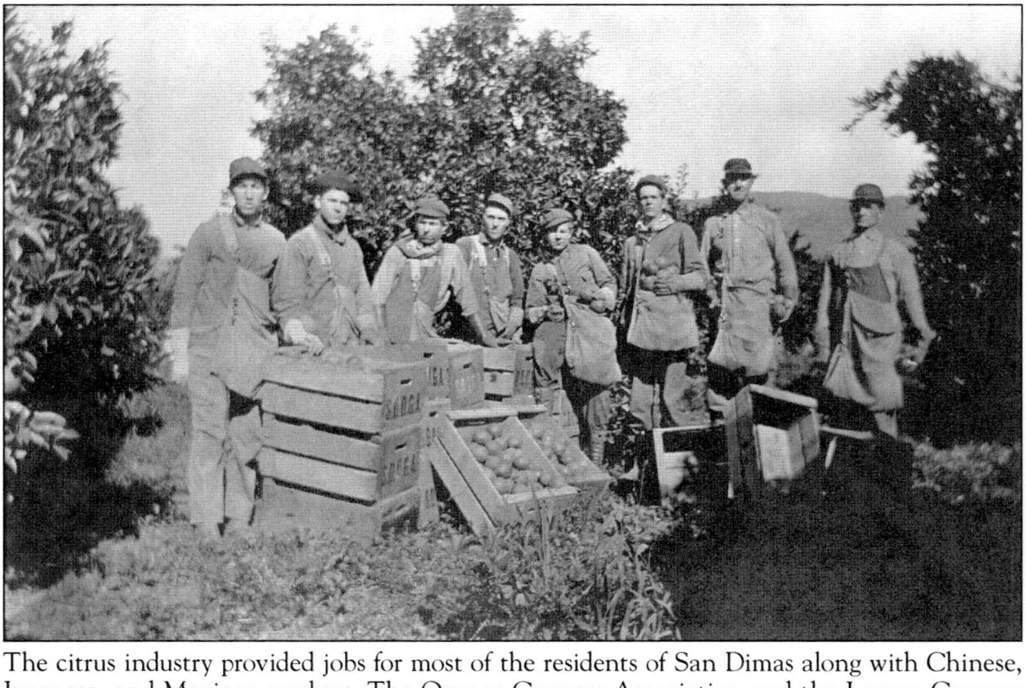

The citrus industry provided jobs for most of the residents of San Dimas along with Chinese, Japanese, and Mexican workers. The Orange Growers Association and the Lemon Growers Association provided homes for many of the Mexican workers.

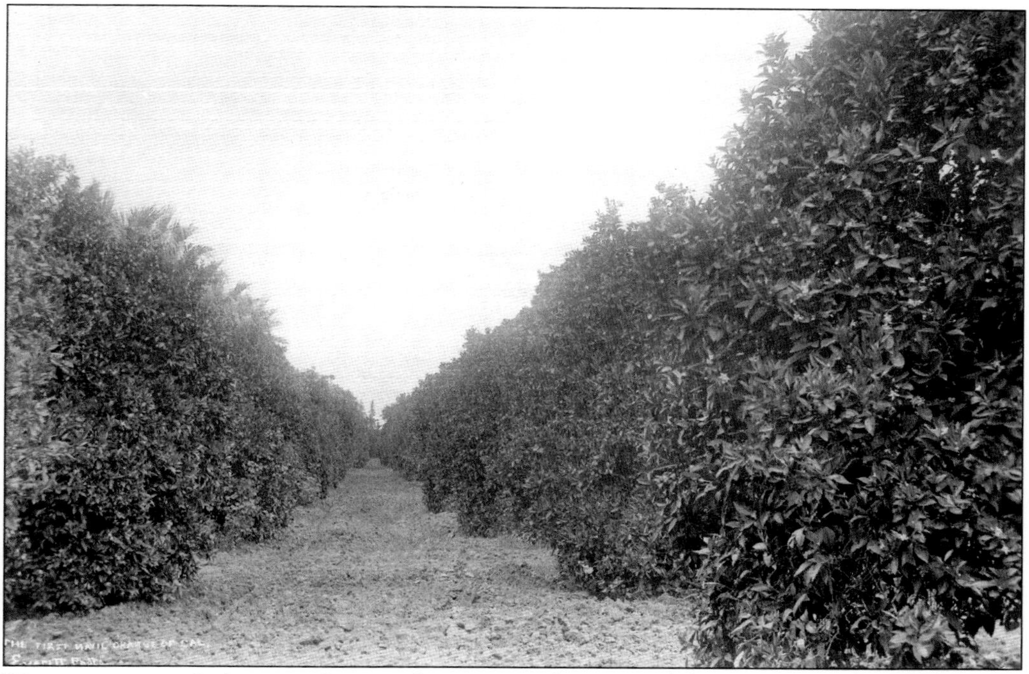

This picture reveals the typical grove of citrus trees that covered the area of San Dimas and many areas of Southern California.

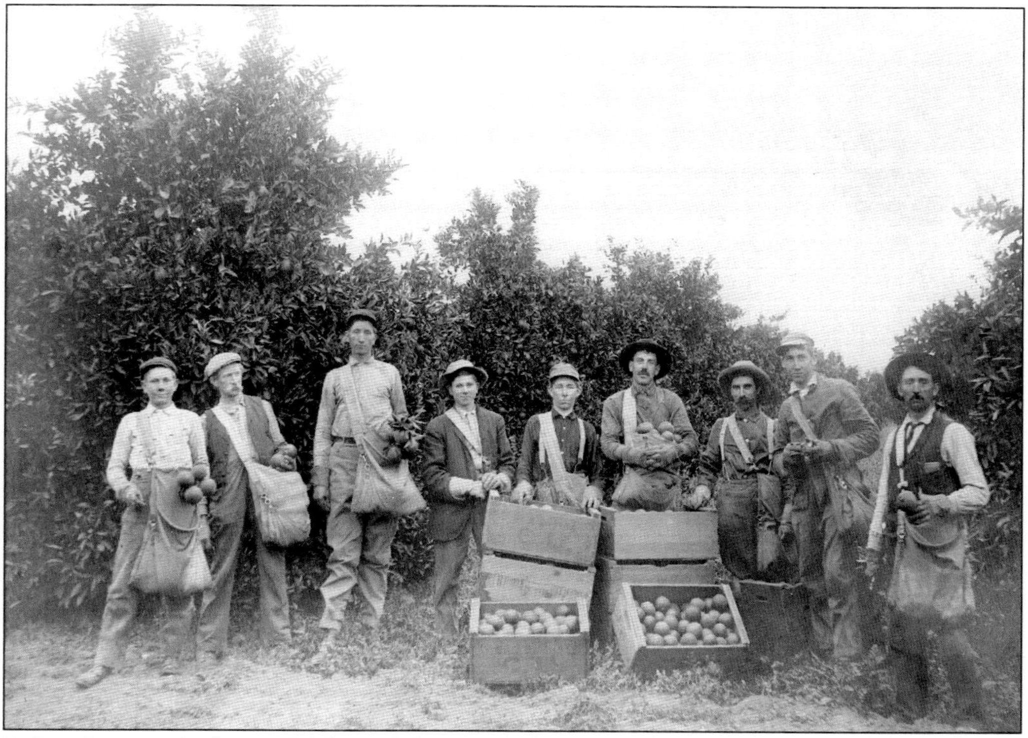

Pickers harvest the bountiful fruit of the many citrus trees in San Dimas. The pickers dropped the fruit into canvas bags slung over their shoulders, then when they were full, dumped them into wooden "grove boxes" that were transported to the packinghouse.

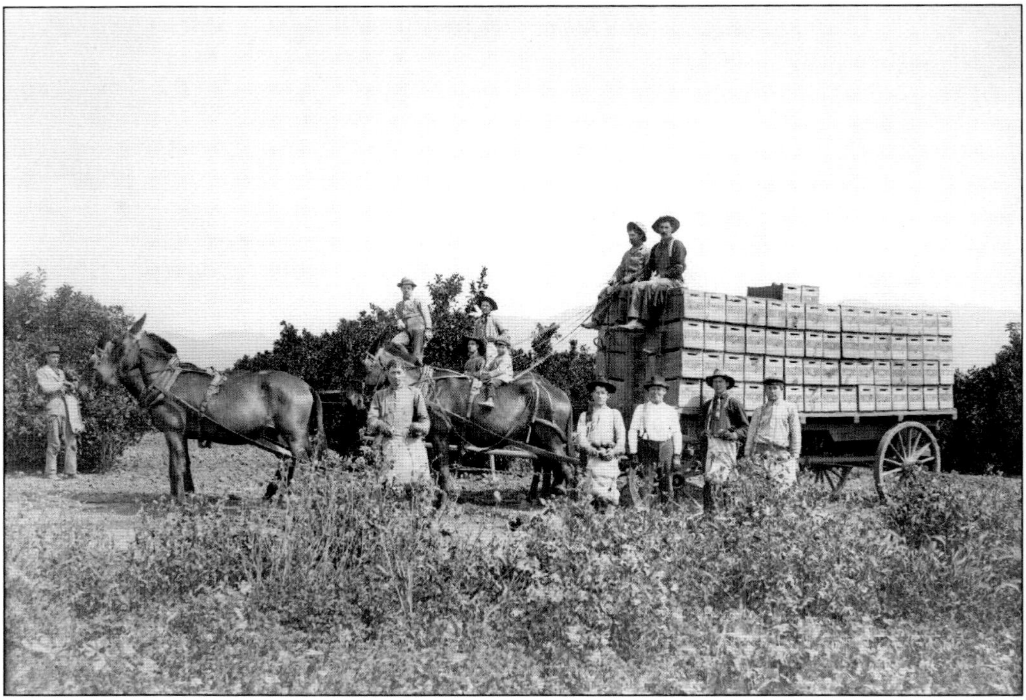

In the days prior to motorized vehicles, wagons were the way to transport the freshly picked fruit to the packinghouse for processing.

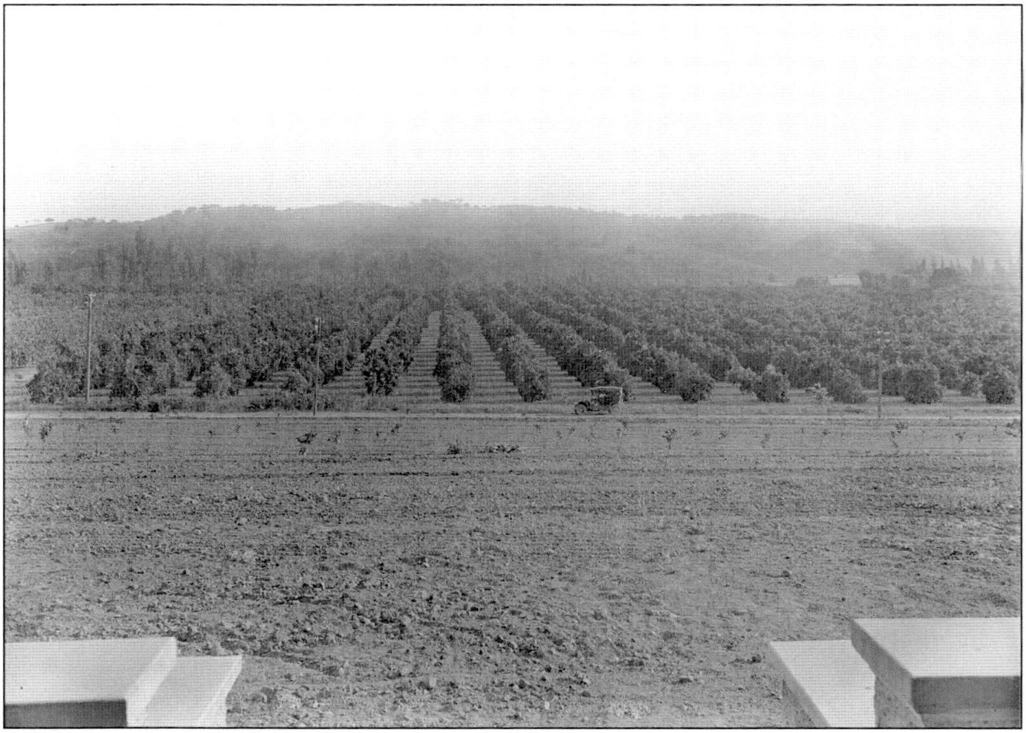

This picture shows the wonderful view from the front porch of a residence in San Dimas overlooking the groves of trees. This area is now the site of San Dimas High School.

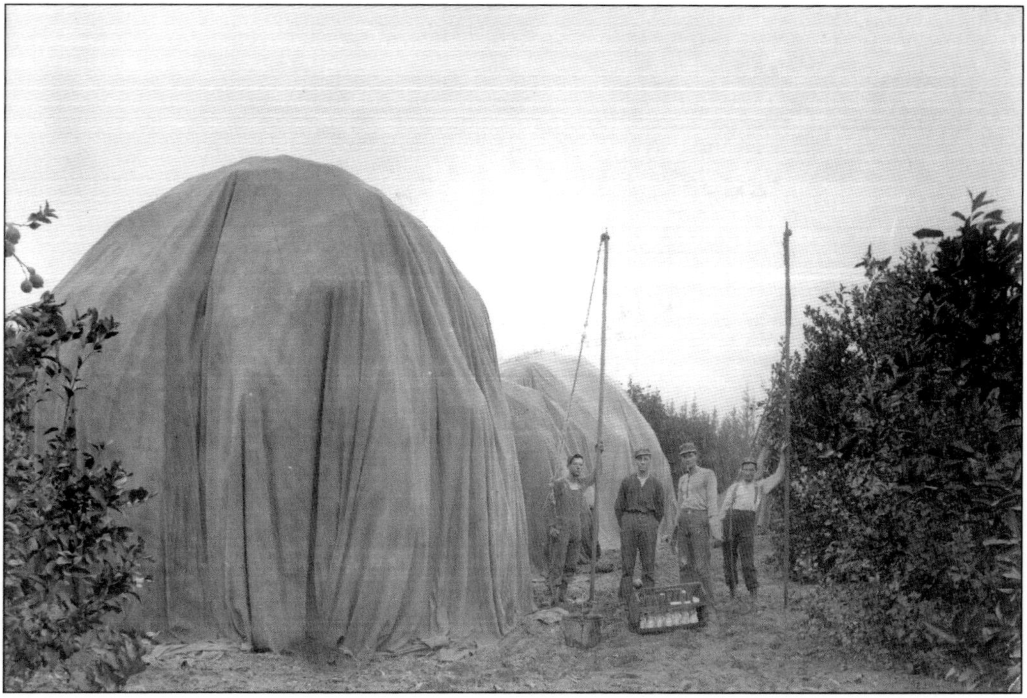

In the early days of the citrus industry, trees were fumigated using heavy tarps hoisted by hand over the trees. Chemicals were then released under the tarps in an effort to kill bugs and scale on the trees. This method was later replaced by the use of spraying equipment. These trees were part of the R. M. Teague orchard in 1909.

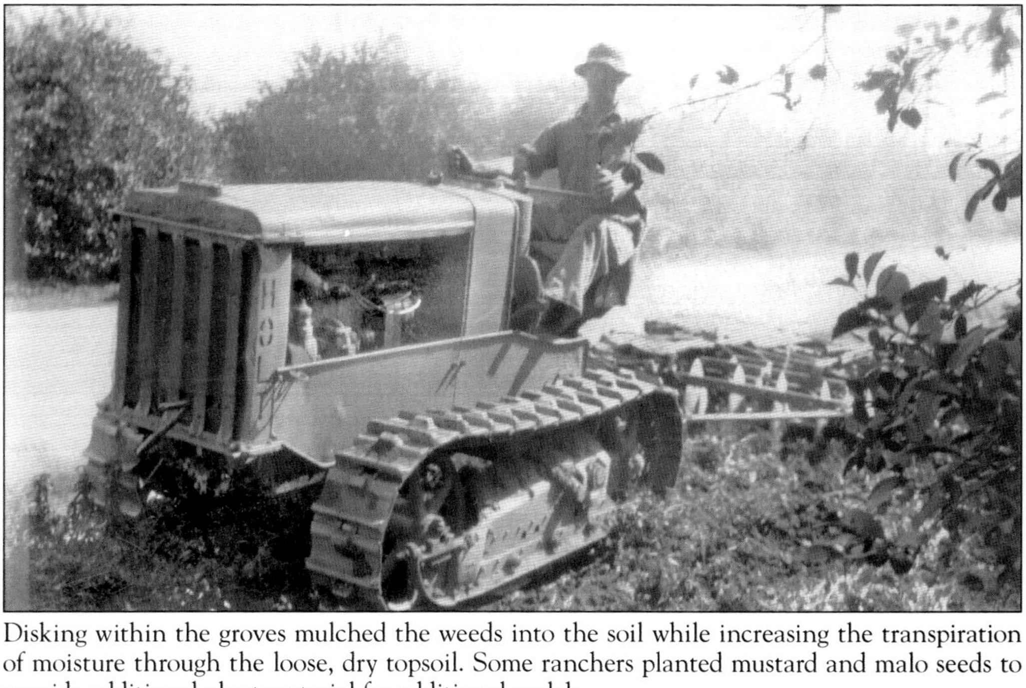

Disking within the groves mulched the weeds into the soil while increasing the transpiration of moisture through the loose, dry topsoil. Some ranchers planted mustard and malo seeds to provide additional plant material for additional mulch.

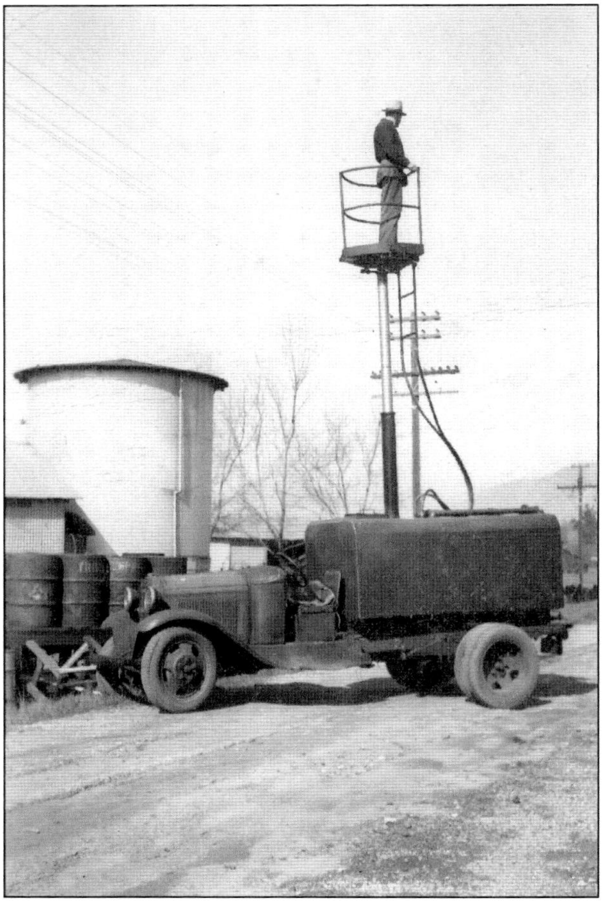

In the years 1928–1930, Harry Smead Sr. developed spray equipment for his citrus groves, thus eliminating the need to cover the trees with the heavy tarps. Although this had to be a much easier way to solve the insect problems in the groves, one has to wonder what the effect of spraying was on the workers.

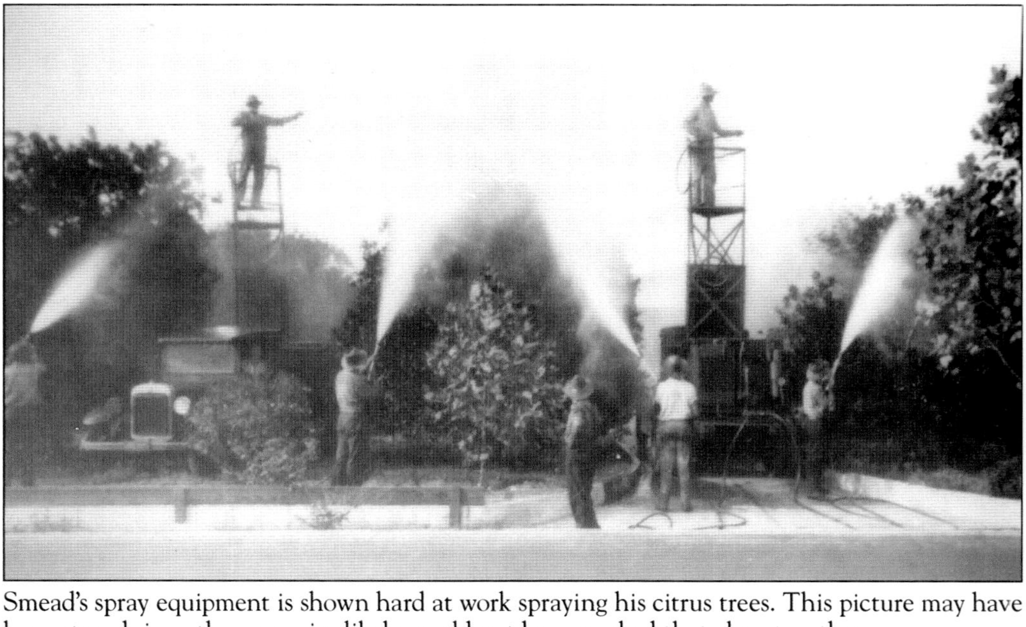

Smead's spray equipment is shown hard at work spraying his citrus trees. This picture may have been staged since the spray rigs likely would not have worked that close together.

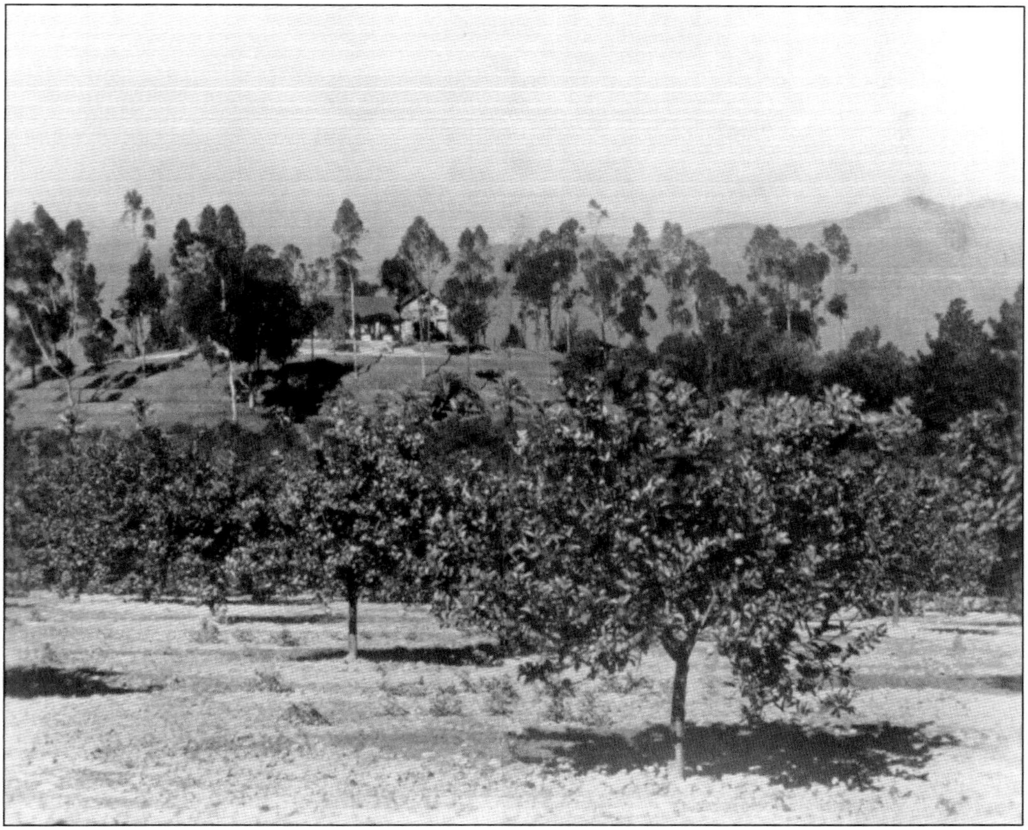

Located on the west side of San Dimas, the Dunning Ranch was one of the premier citrus ranches in the area. The ranch, known as Los Colinas, was the property of Alfred and Vera Dunning. Vera Dunning was of Russian royalty, and she was well known in the community. As the value of the land increased in later years, portions of the ranch were sold to become residential and commercial developments. Still later, the beautiful home overlooking the land burned, and the glorious days of Los Colinas were gone forever.

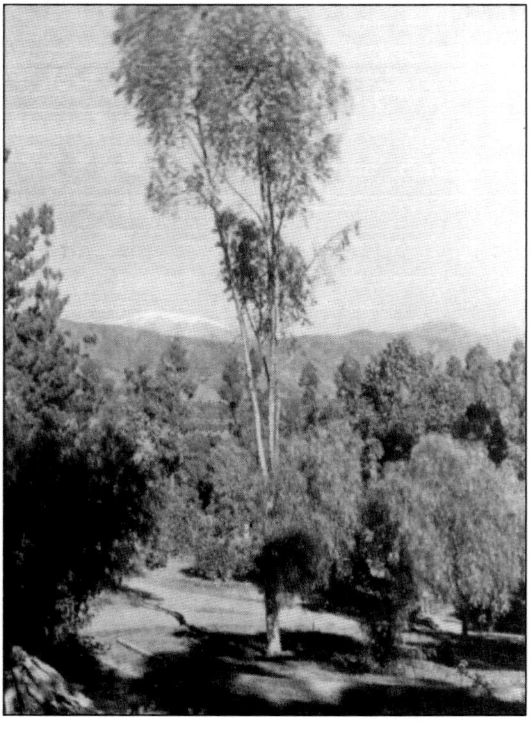

The views from Los Colinas had to be spectacular, as it overlooked the many groves in San Dimas looking west, east, and south and had views of the majestic San Gabriel Mountains to the north.

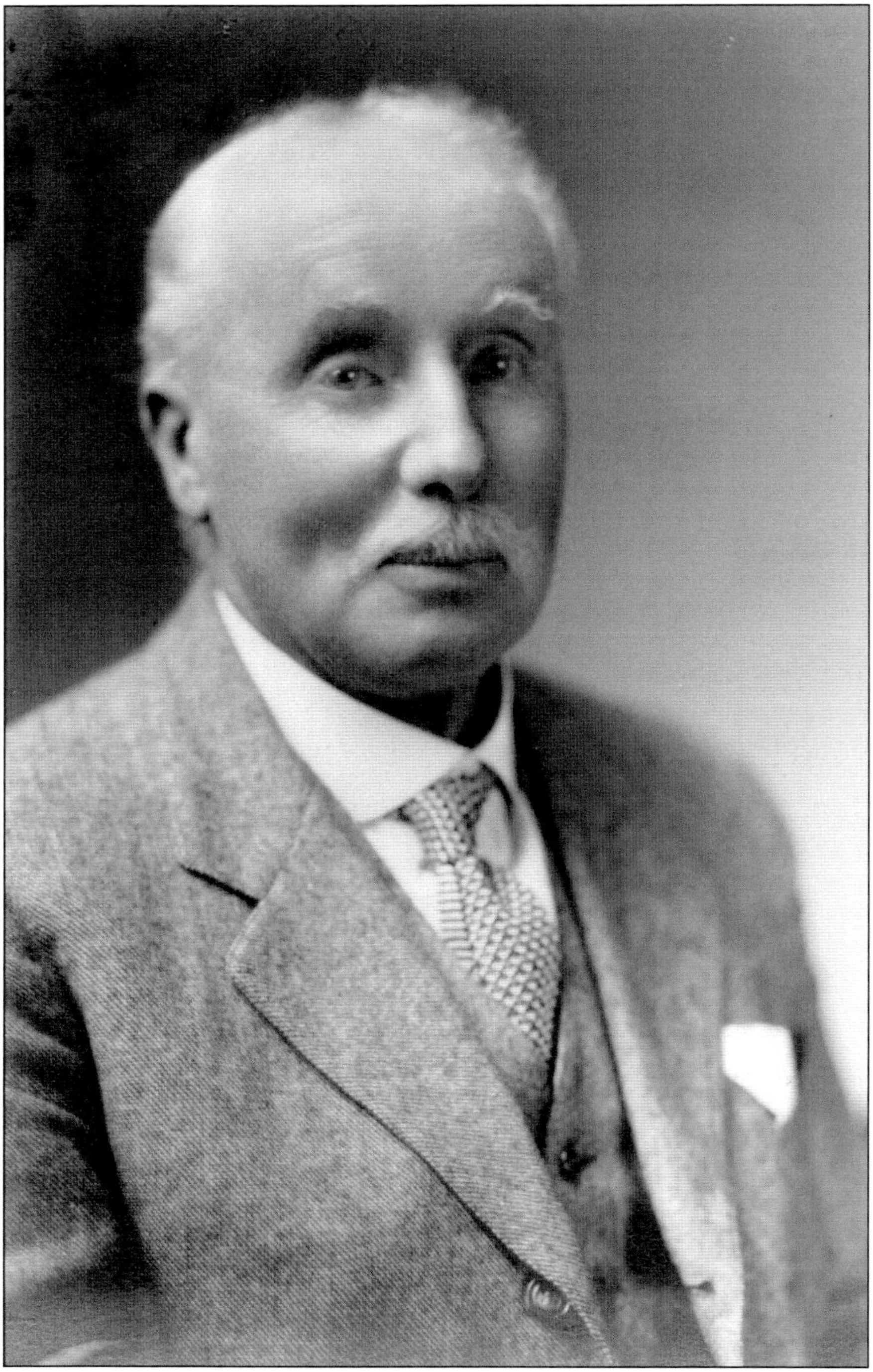

William Bowring was the "Granddaddy of the Water Company" in San Dimas and laid the foundation for a sound water system for the city. In 1888, while staying in Los Angeles, he purchased, sight unseen, 40 acres of the old San Jose Rancho. Because of his training as an engineer, Bowring became very active in the early development and handling of the main water system in the San Dimas region. William Mount later arrived in San Dimas and brought water from San Dimas Canyon north of the town to augment the water supply needed for the thirsty citrus crops.

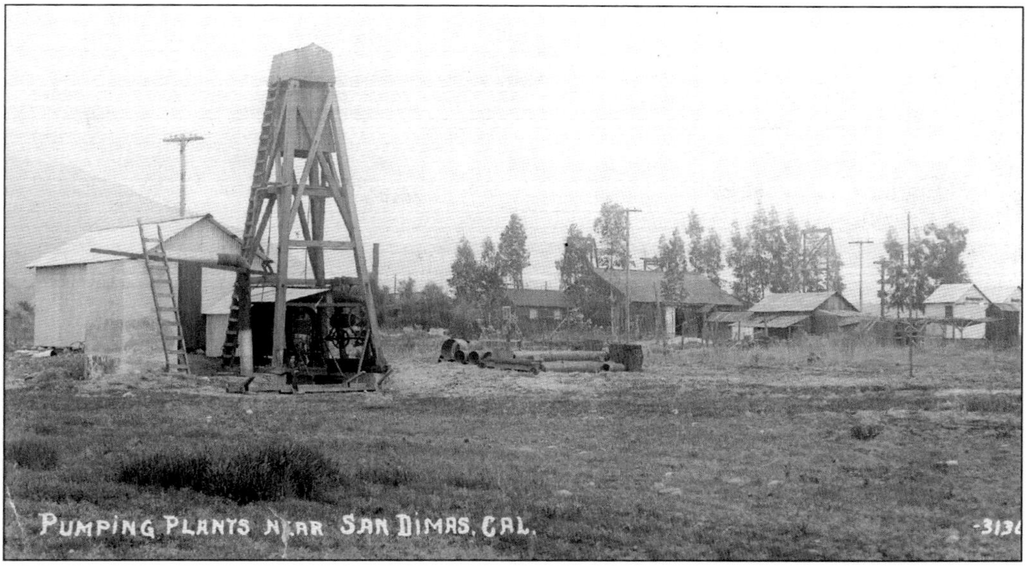

Pumping plants dotted the area around San Dimas in an effort to provide enough water for the thirsty citrus trees.

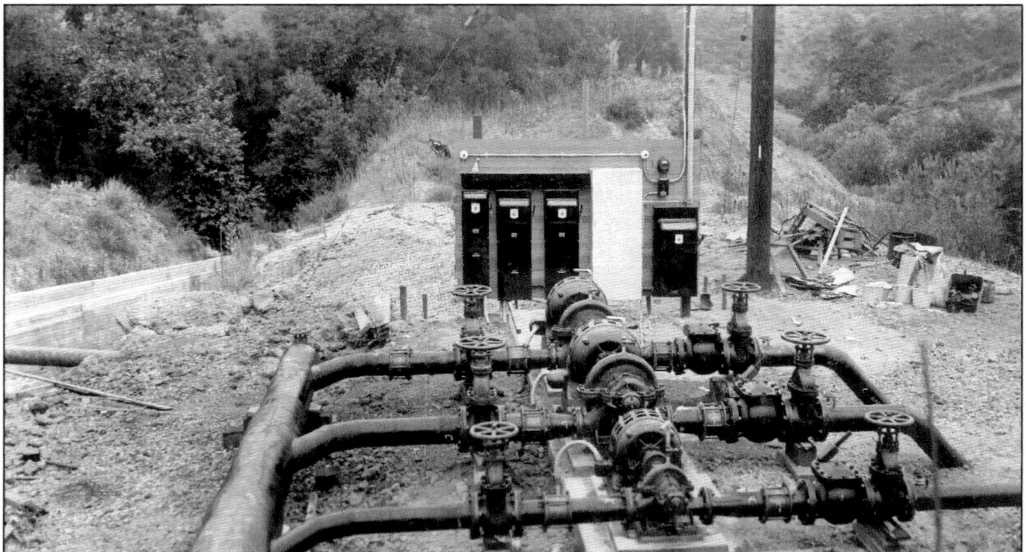

Three Fairbanks Morse pumps were used to pump water from the Puddingstone Reservoir to the San Dimas Water Company's reservoir located a few hundred feet northeast of the corner of Walnut Avenue and Cienega Avenue, today's Arrow Highway.

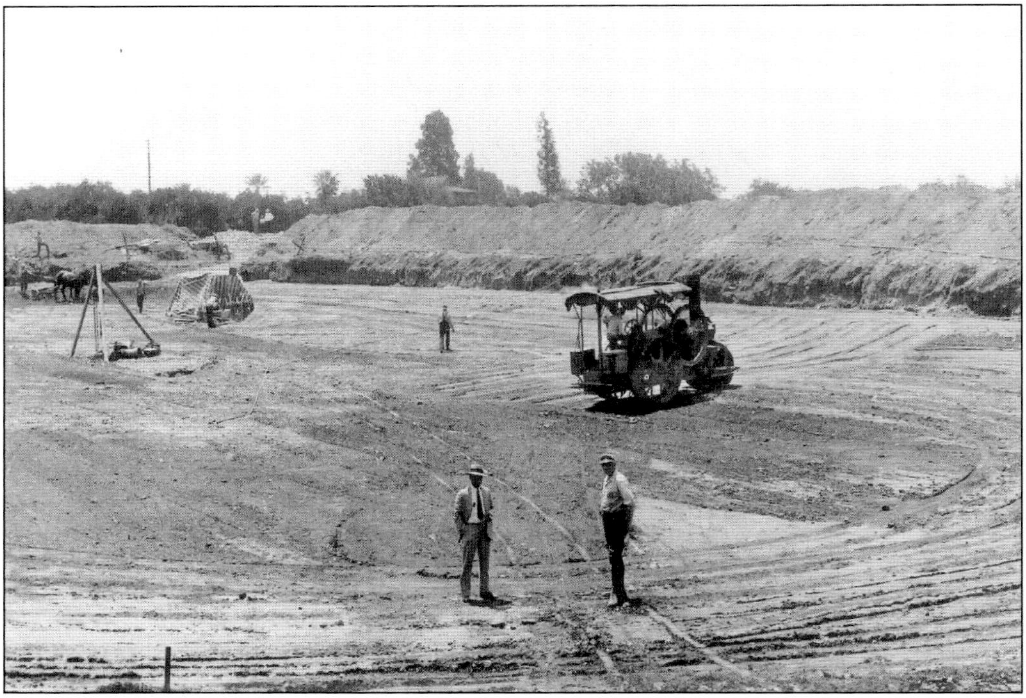

Water was always an issue for San Dimas to meet the demand of the many citrus groves. This reservoir was constructed to provide additional water for the area. Water was pumped over the hill from the Puddingstone Reservoir to supply this system.

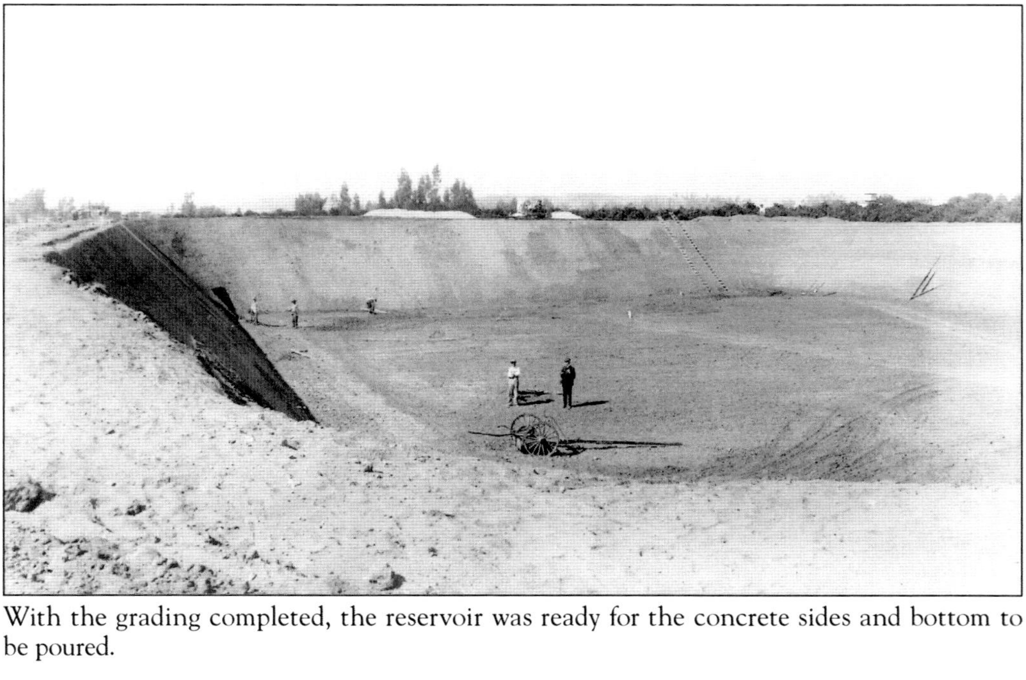

With the grading completed, the reservoir was ready for the concrete sides and bottom to be poured.

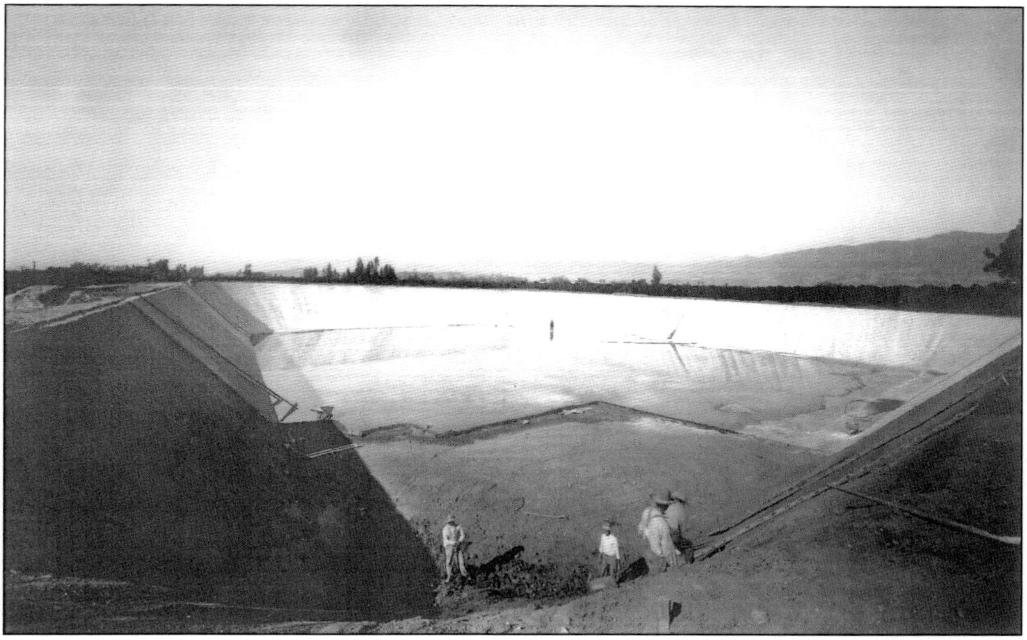

Cementing the reservoir was the final process toward the completion of the project. Although no longer used, the old reservoir still exists.

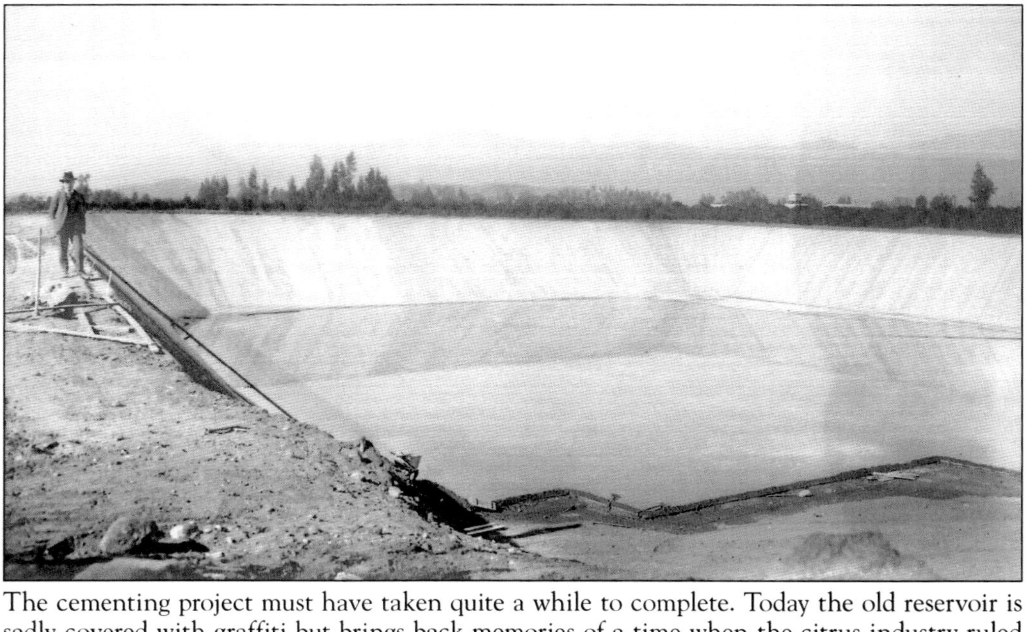

The cementing project must have taken quite a while to complete. Today the old reservoir is sadly covered with graffiti but brings back memories of a time when the citrus industry ruled the area.

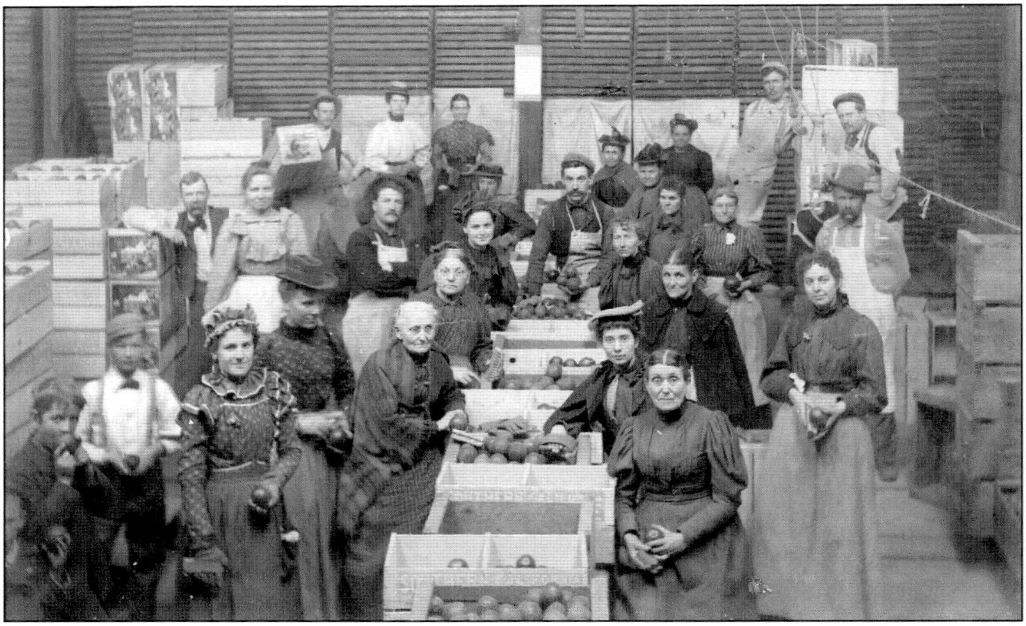

The first packinghouse in San Dimas was constructed in 1900. Located in the heart of the town, the building served both the orange and lemon packing needs. The building burned in 1910. By that time, other packinghouses had been constructed within the area, including the new Lemon Association Packinghouse.

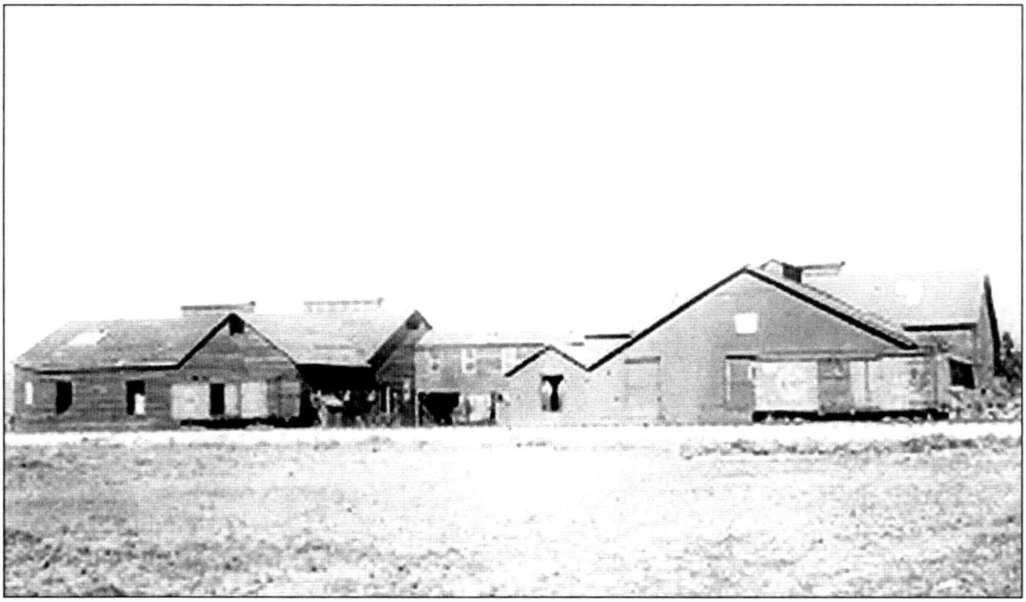

The old packinghouse was not much to look at and, with all the oil from the many citrus products that passed through the building, must have made a spectacular fire.

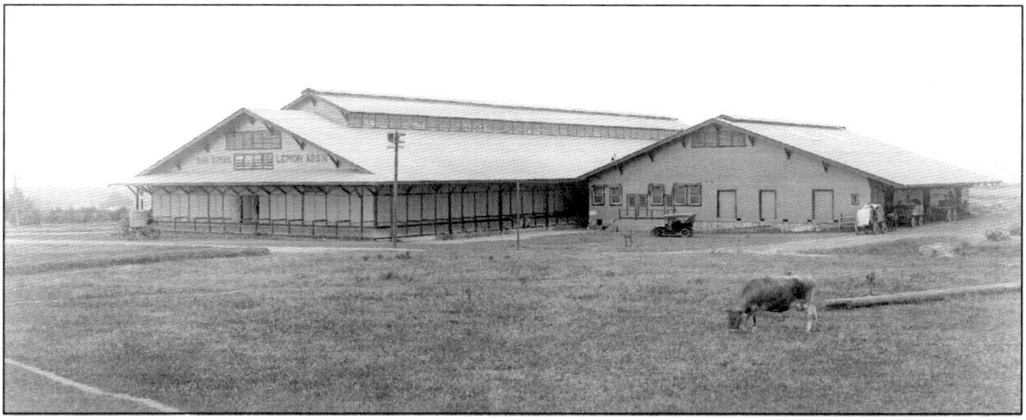

The San Dimas Lemon Association constructed their "new" packinghouse on the west side of town in 1908. It remained in operation until 1963 and became the last lemon packinghouse in Los Angeles County to close. At one time, this packinghouse was the largest lemon packinghouse in the world. A portion of the complex remains today.

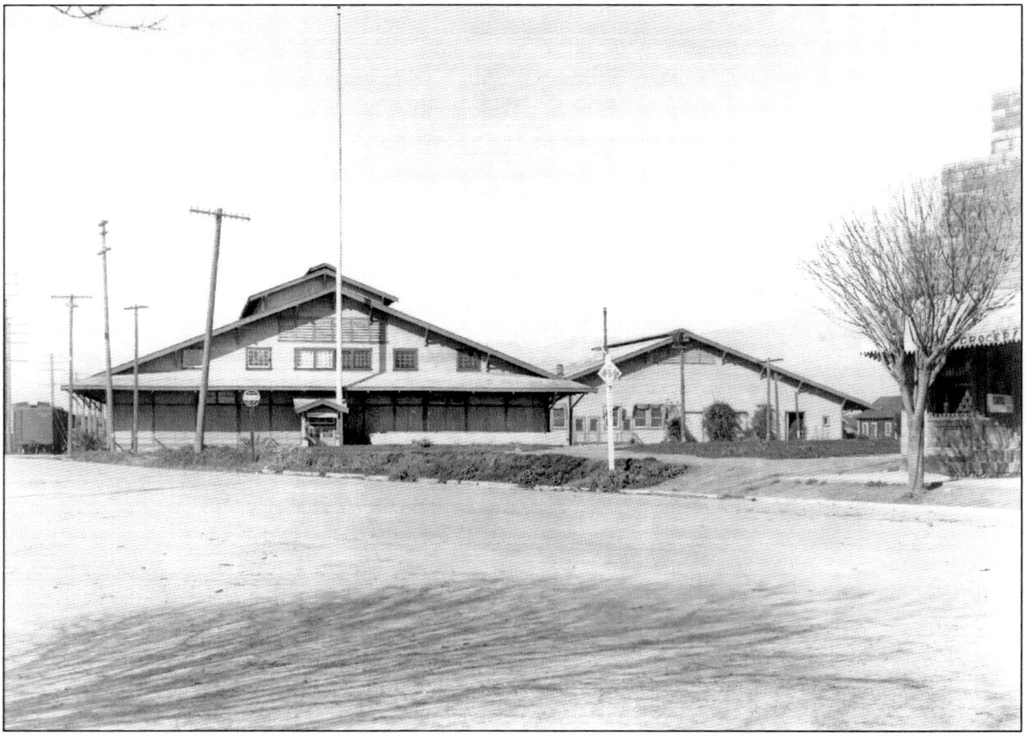

The imposing building made quite a statement for drivers leaving San Dimas to the west. The orange packinghouse was located just west of this building—to the left of this picture.

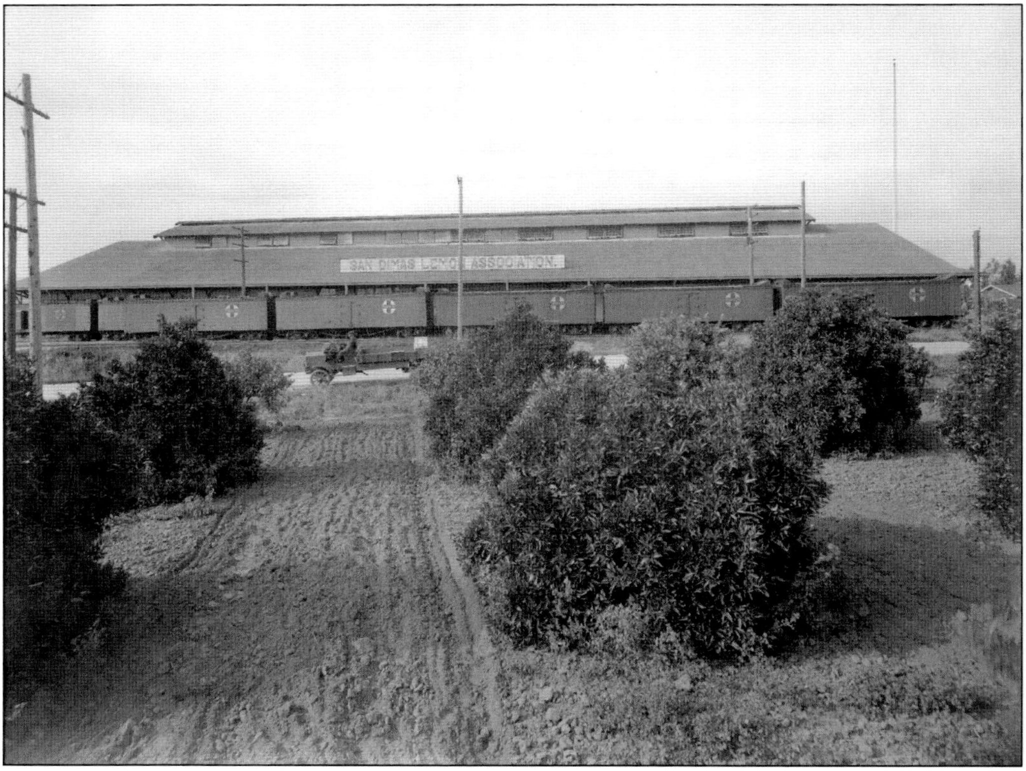

This picture shows the south side of the lemon packinghouse with railcars being loaded for shipment to the East Coast. The road in front of the building is Bonita Avenue, the main thoroughfare through town.

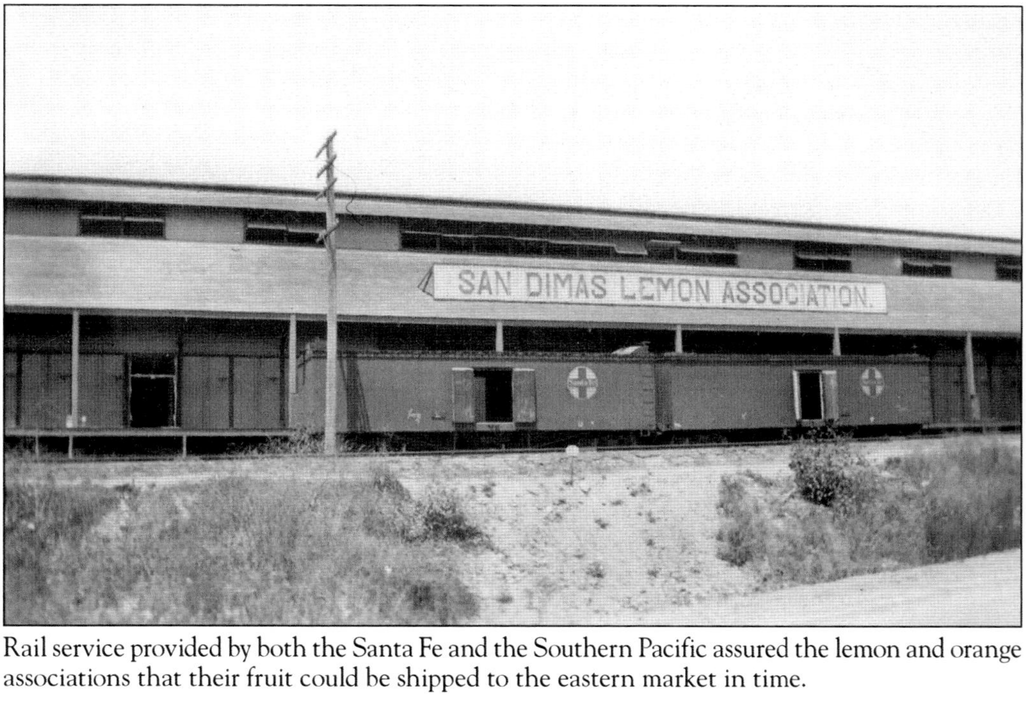

Rail service provided by both the Santa Fe and the Southern Pacific assured the lemon and orange associations that their fruit could be shipped to the eastern market in time.

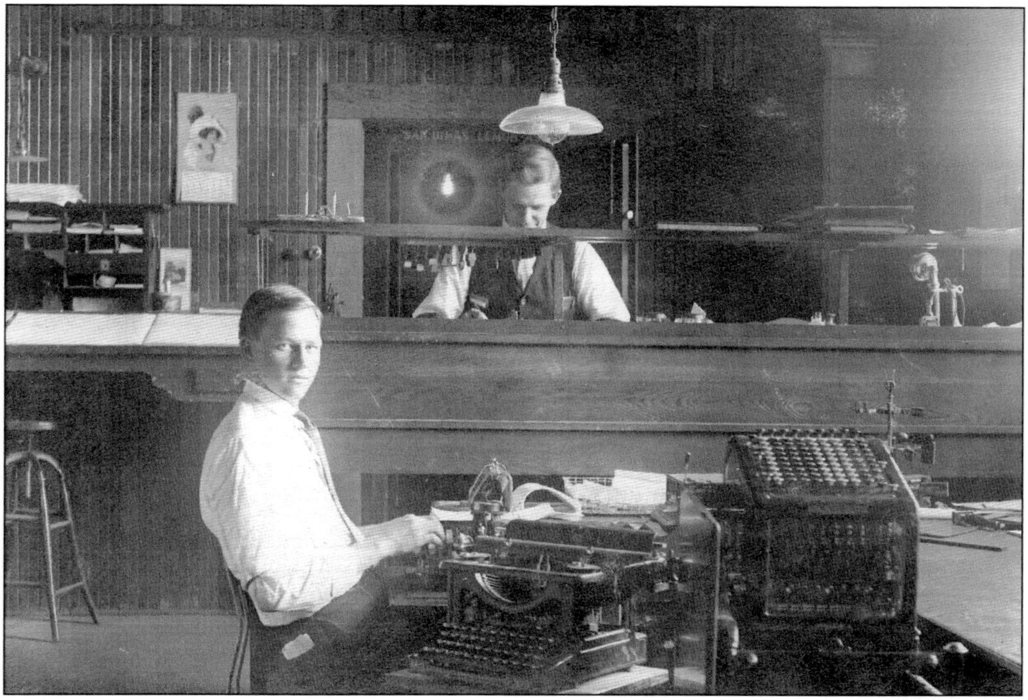

Seated at his desk, Clarence Dunbar keeps the paperwork straight in the office at the lemon packinghouse. Most of the residents in San Dimas were associated with the citrus industry—especially during harvest time.

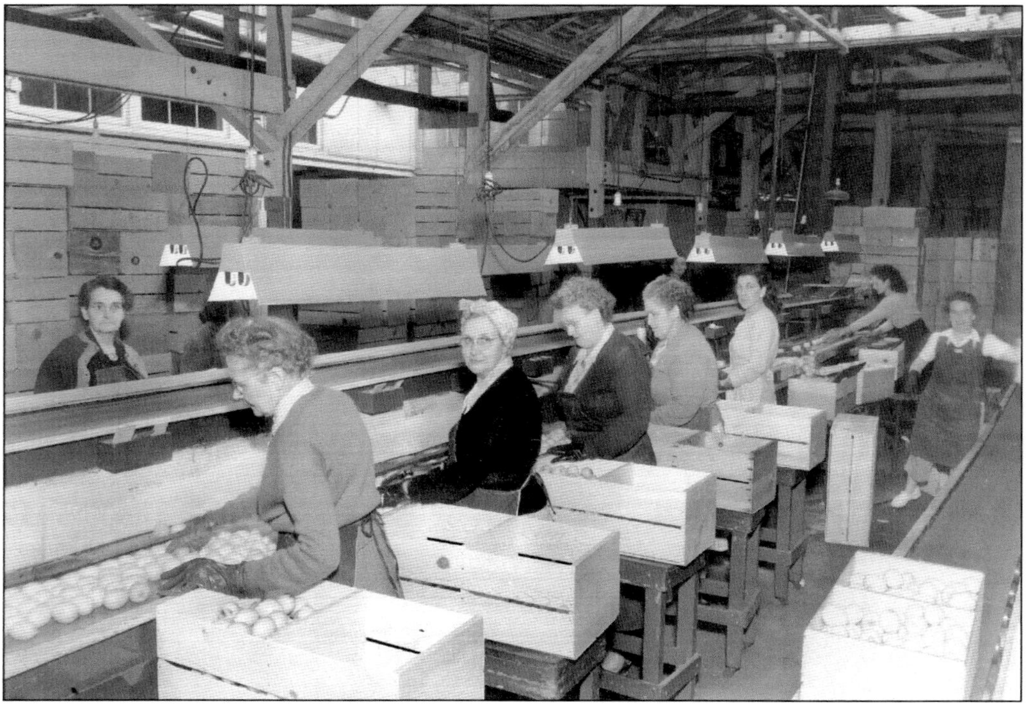

Most of the packing of the citrus fruit was done by women workers. In the 1930s, women packers earned between $3.25 and $3.50 a day.

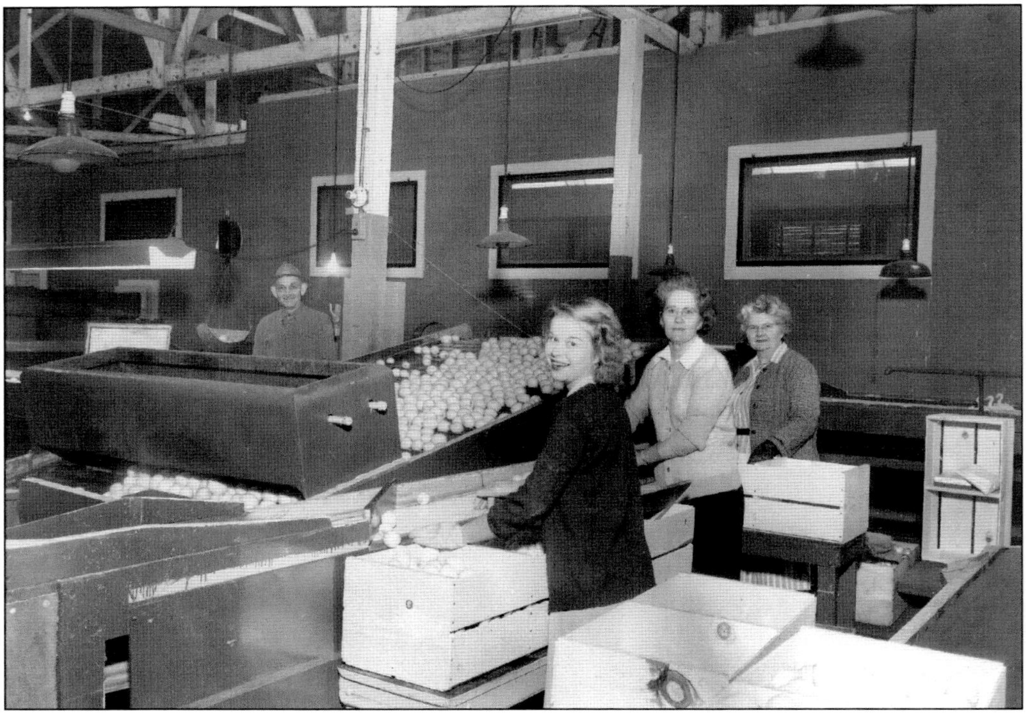

The fruit packing equipment became more modern in the late 1930s and into the 1940s. During the days of World War II, packers were making as much as $1.25 per hour.

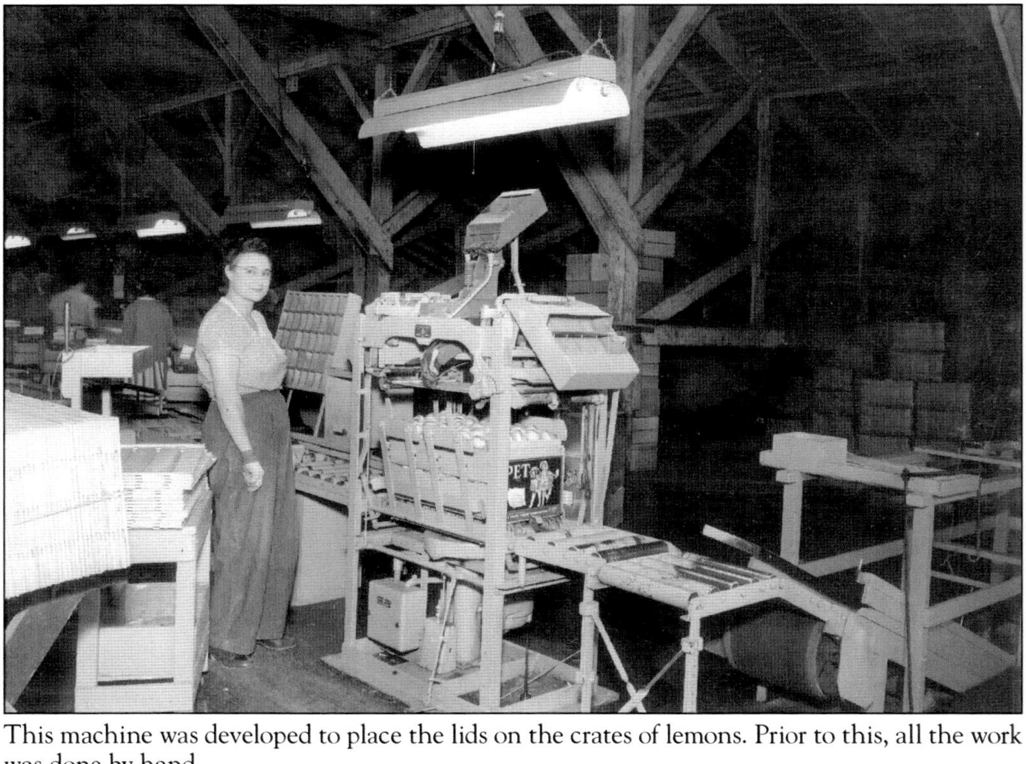

This machine was developed to place the lids on the crates of lemons. Prior to this, all the work was done by hand.

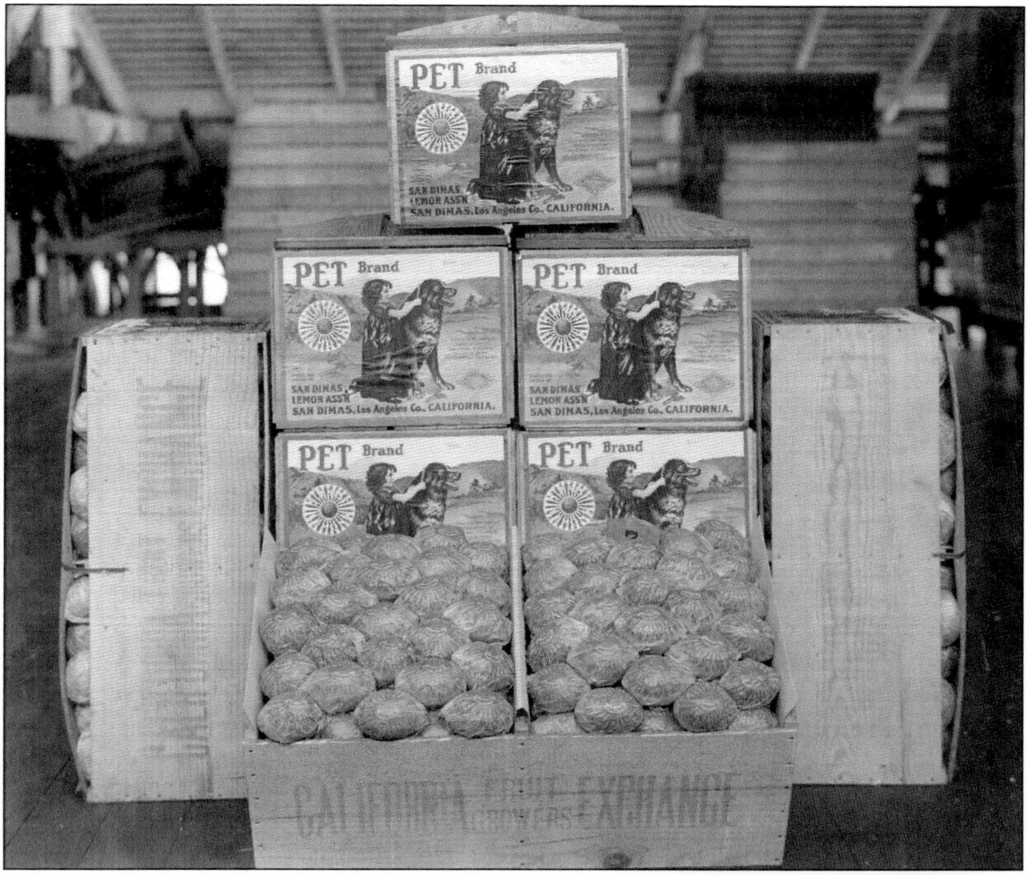

The finest San Dimas lemons are ready for shipping. All the fruit had to be wrapped with the names on the wrappers showing just right, a tedious job. The Pet label was a popular brand for many years with both the lemon packinghouse and the orange packinghouse. Note the "California Fruit Growers Exchange" on the boxes.

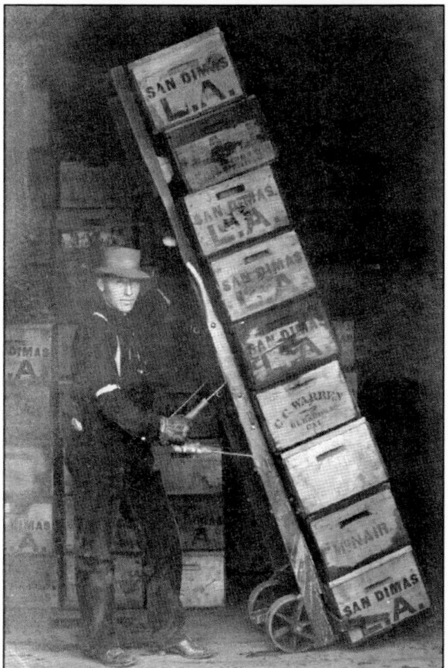

Hubert "Scubie" Mills of La Verne moves the grove boxes in the San Dimas Lemon Association's packinghouse. The grove boxes were of heavier material and were used to bring the lemons from the groves to the packinghouse.

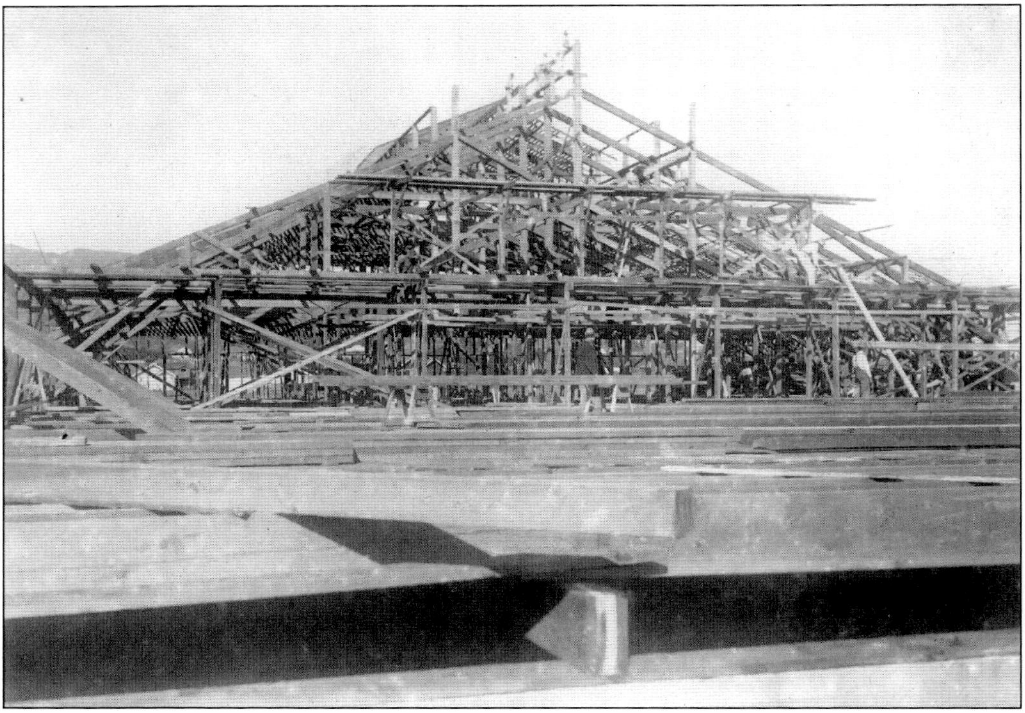

The San Dimas Orange Growers Association constructed their new packinghouse in 1911 following the loss of their old building to fire in 1910.

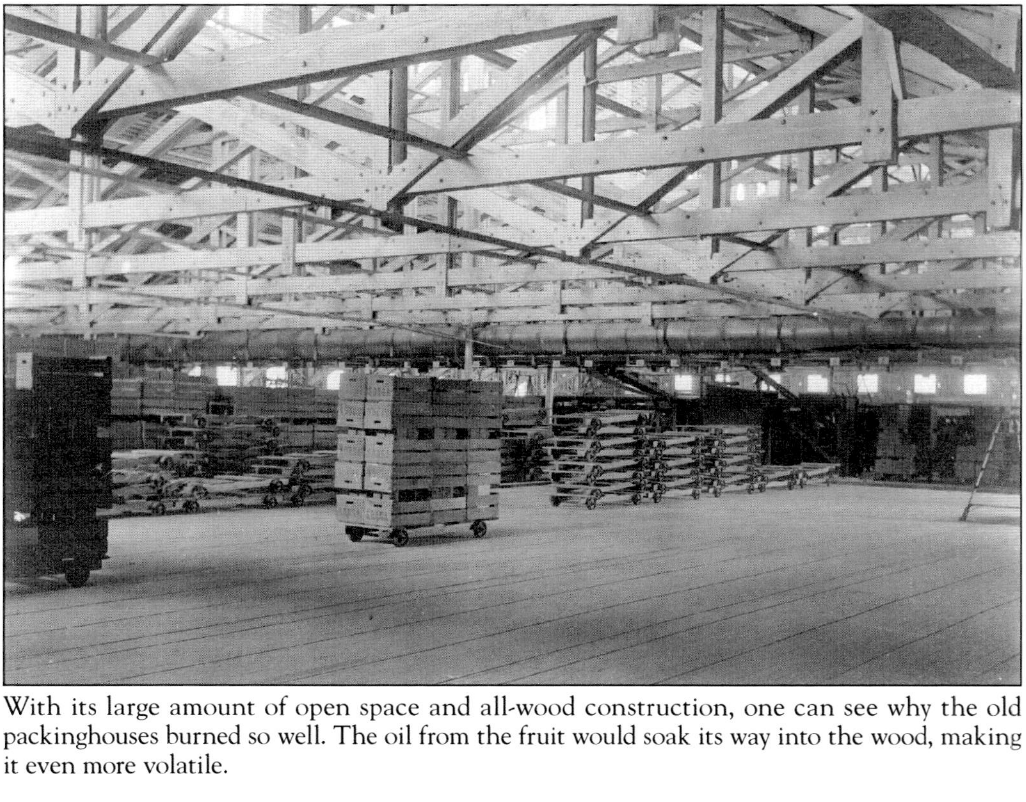

With its large amount of open space and all-wood construction, one can see why the old packinghouses burned so well. The oil from the fruit would soak its way into the wood, making it even more volatile.

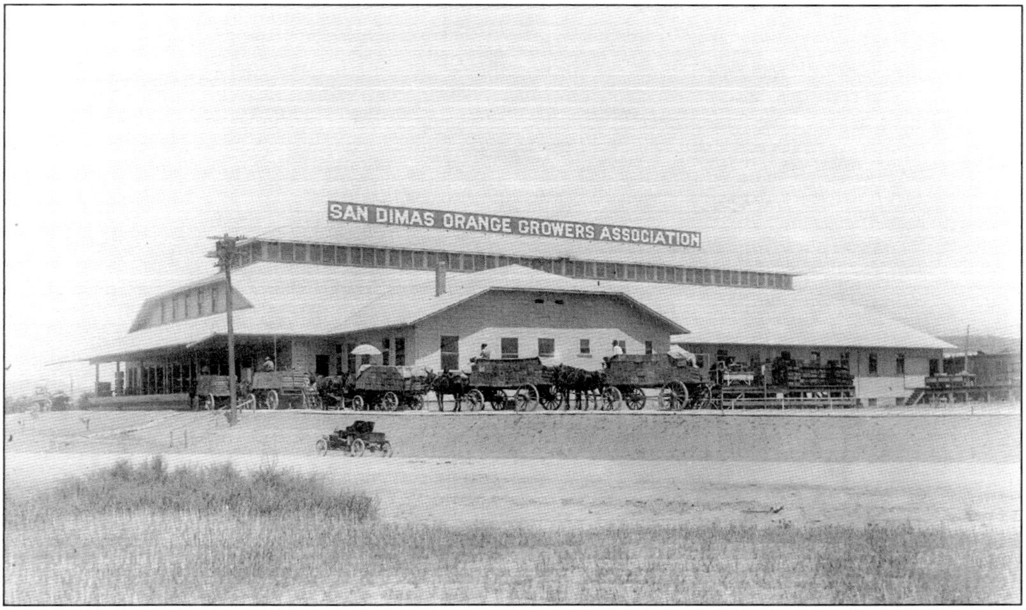

The orange packinghouse served San Dimas and the surrounding communities for 42 years before it closed in 1953. It was used for other businesses until it burned to the ground in 1966.

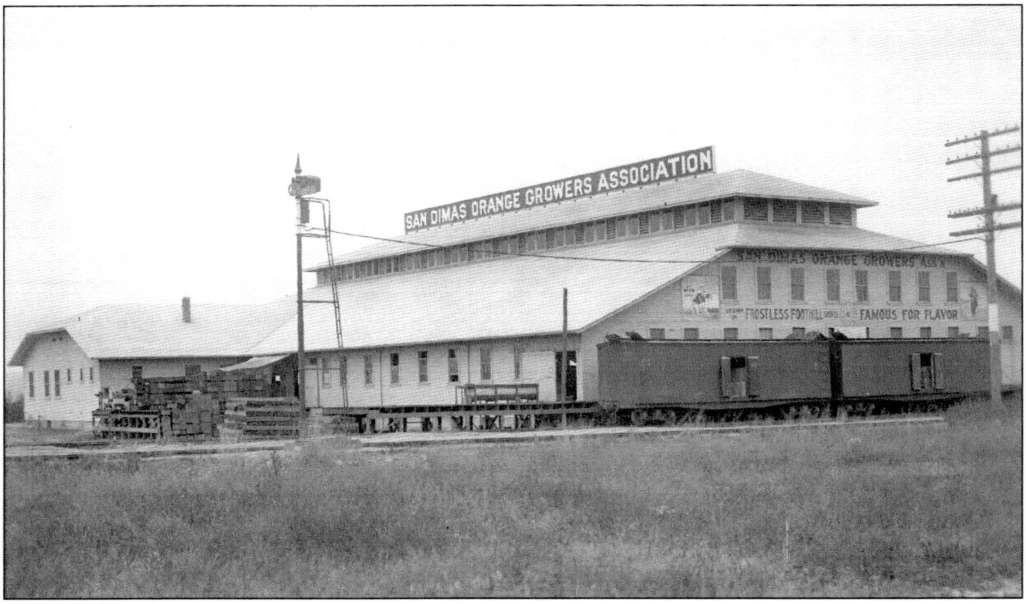

As time went on, the San Dimas Orange Growers Association constructed a large cooling tower just to the left of this picture and produced their own ice to keep the fruit cool in the railcars.

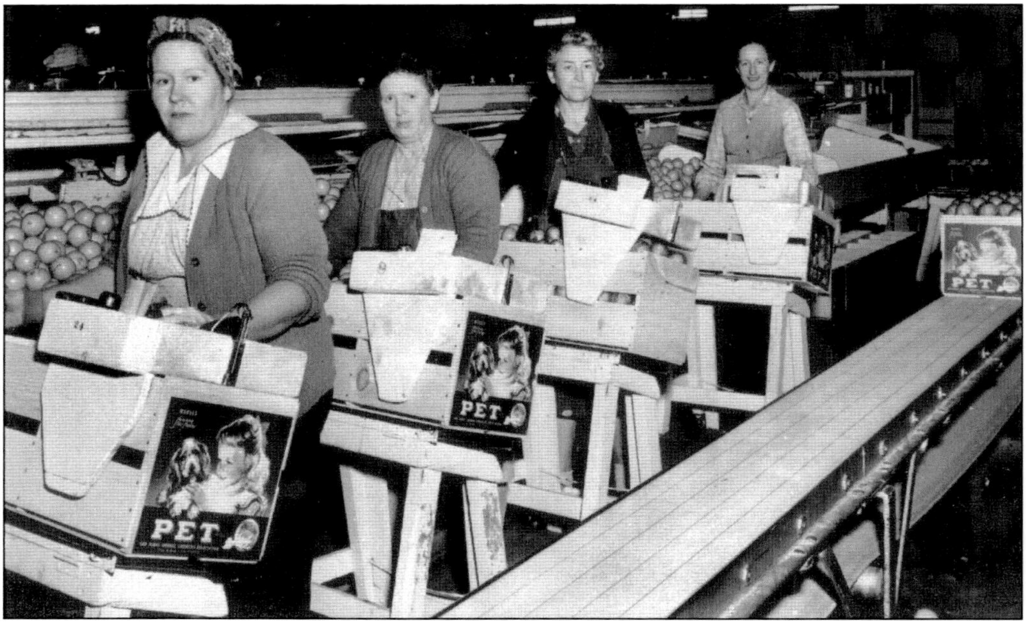

As in packinghouses throughout Southern California, the packing of oranges in preparation for shipping was a tedious job mainly performed by women.

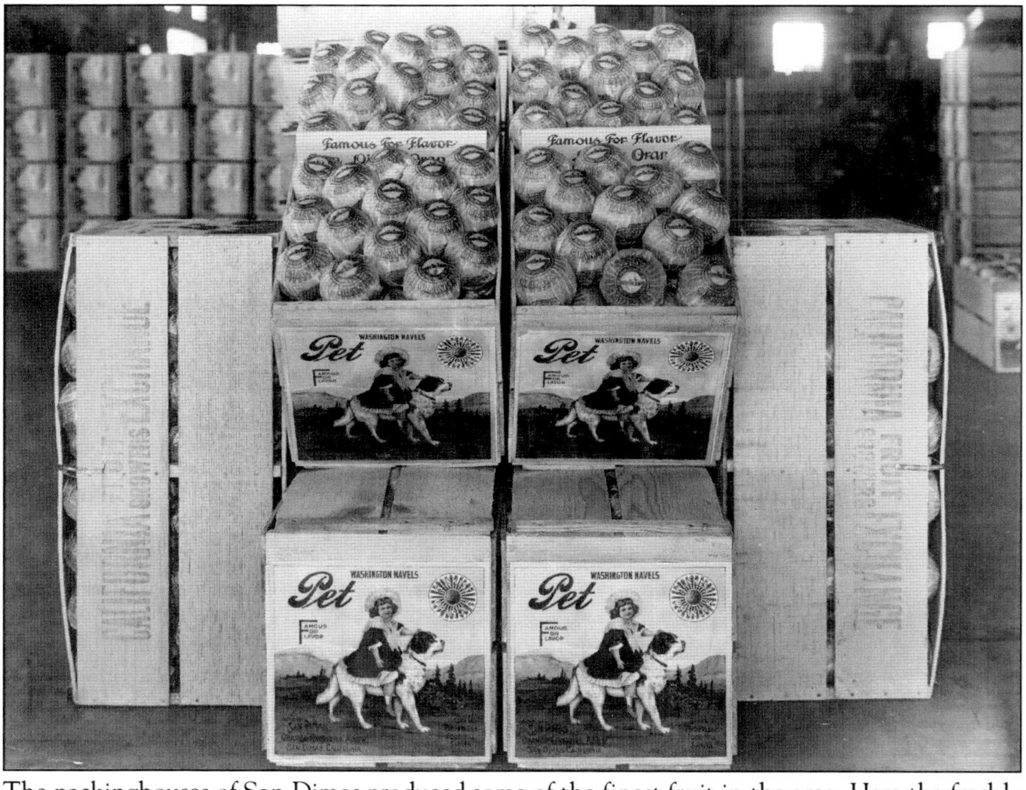

The packinghouses of San Dimas produced some of the finest fruit in the area. Here the freshly wrapped and packed oranges stand ready for shipment to the East Coast. It is still possible to find the California Fruit Growers Exchange boxes used for many years.

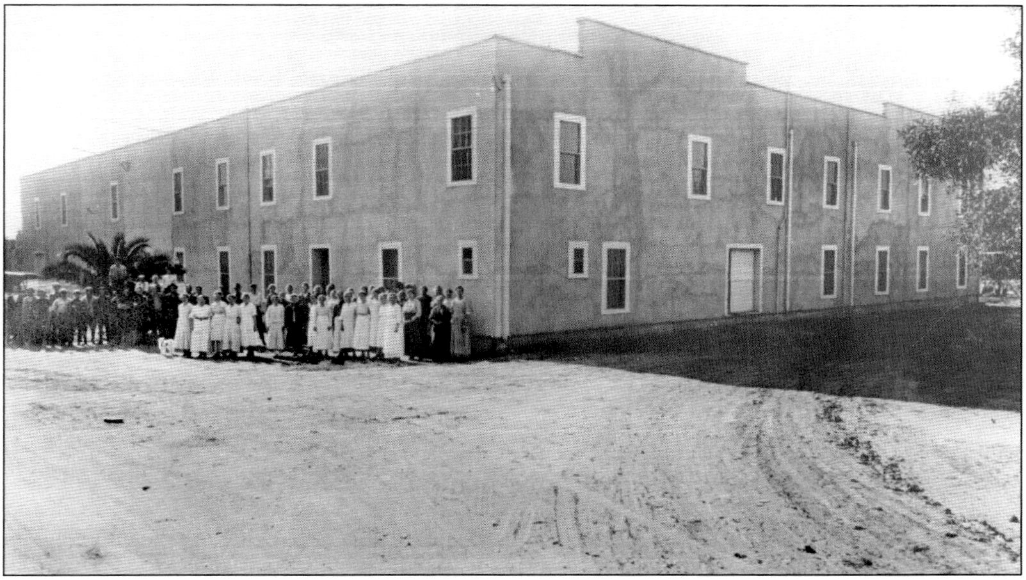

A by-product of the citrus industry was the marmalade factory in San Dimas. The business was opened in 1919 and lasted until 1926, when it moved east to Ontario, California. Residents of San Dimas were happy to see the factory move because of the smell of the rotting rinds that were dumped into the canyon south of the building.

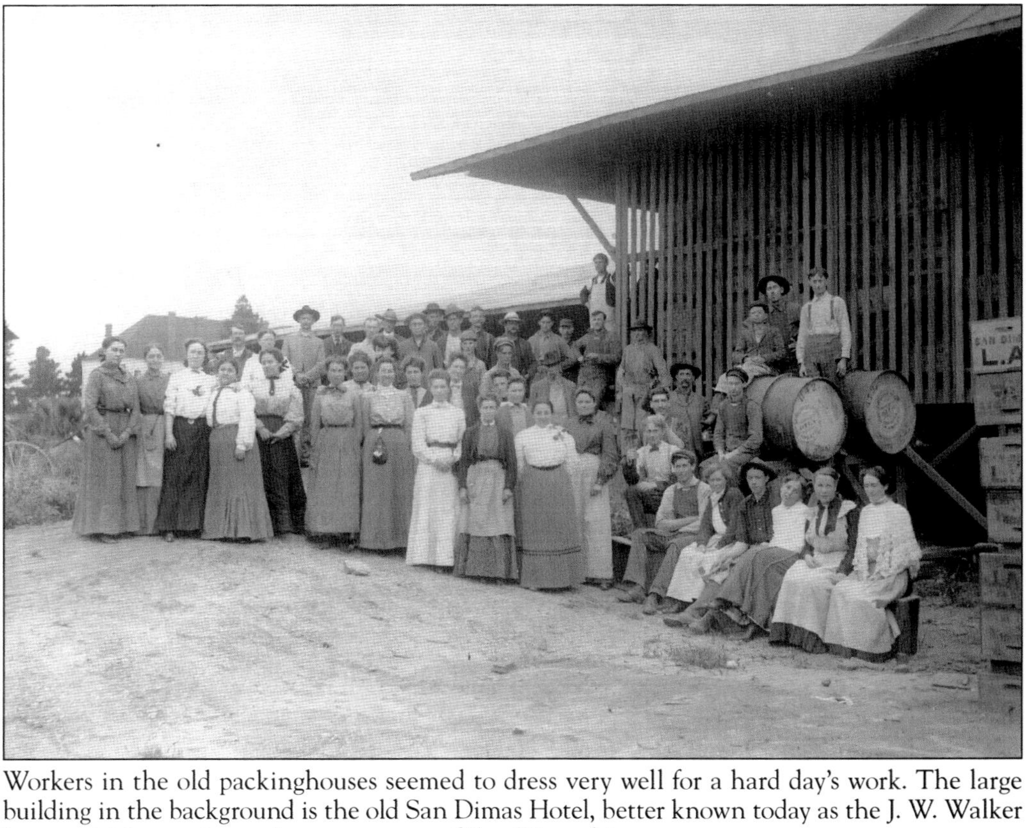

Workers in the old packinghouses seemed to dress very well for a hard day's work. The large building in the background is the old San Dimas Hotel, better known today as the J. W. Walker home, which remains an important part of San Dimas history.

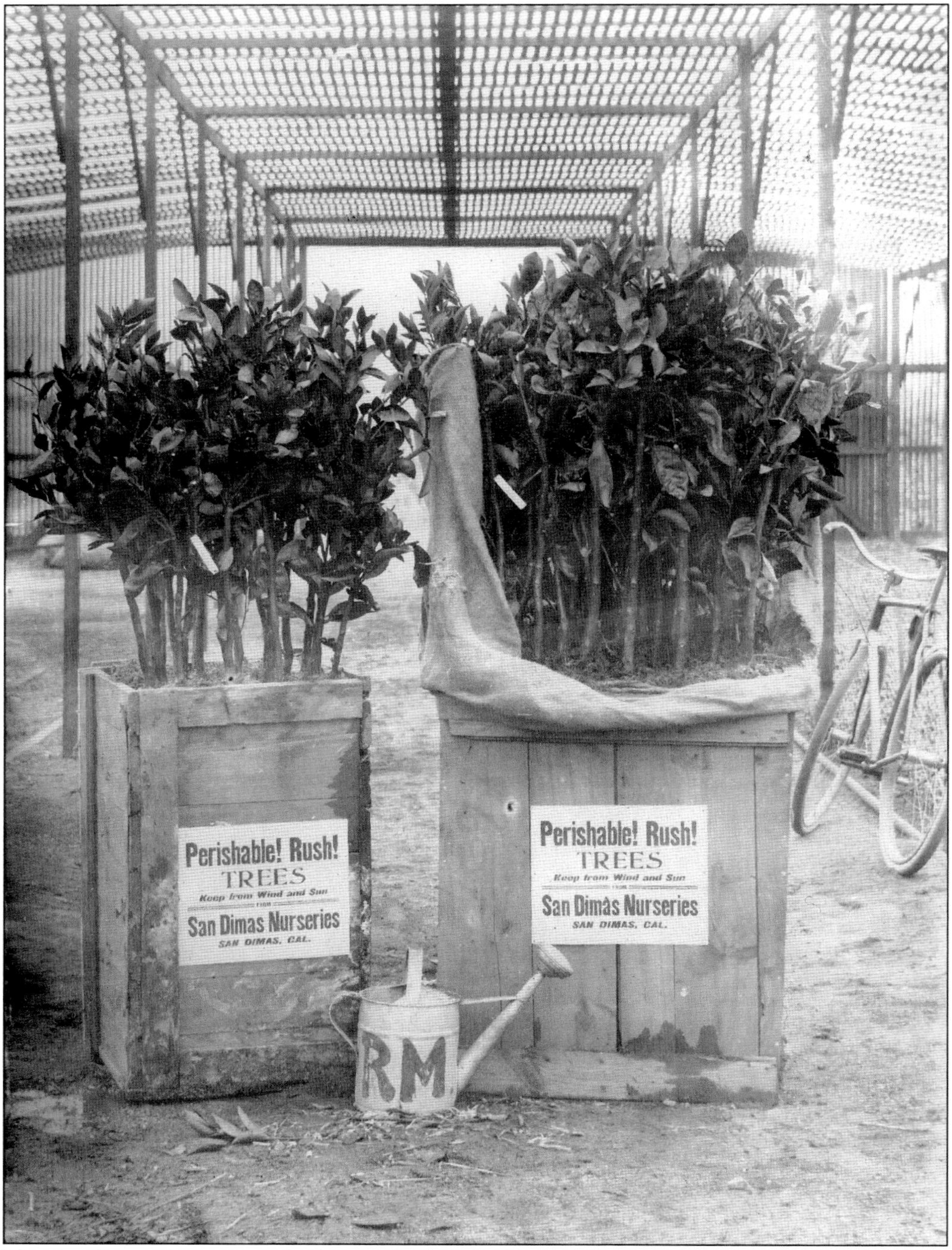

The San Dimas Nurseries, also known as the Teague Nurseries, was the largest grower of citrus trees in the world and shipped trees to all parts of the globe.

Three

THE TEAGUE CITRUS NURSERIES

"HERE'S TO THE TEAGUES"

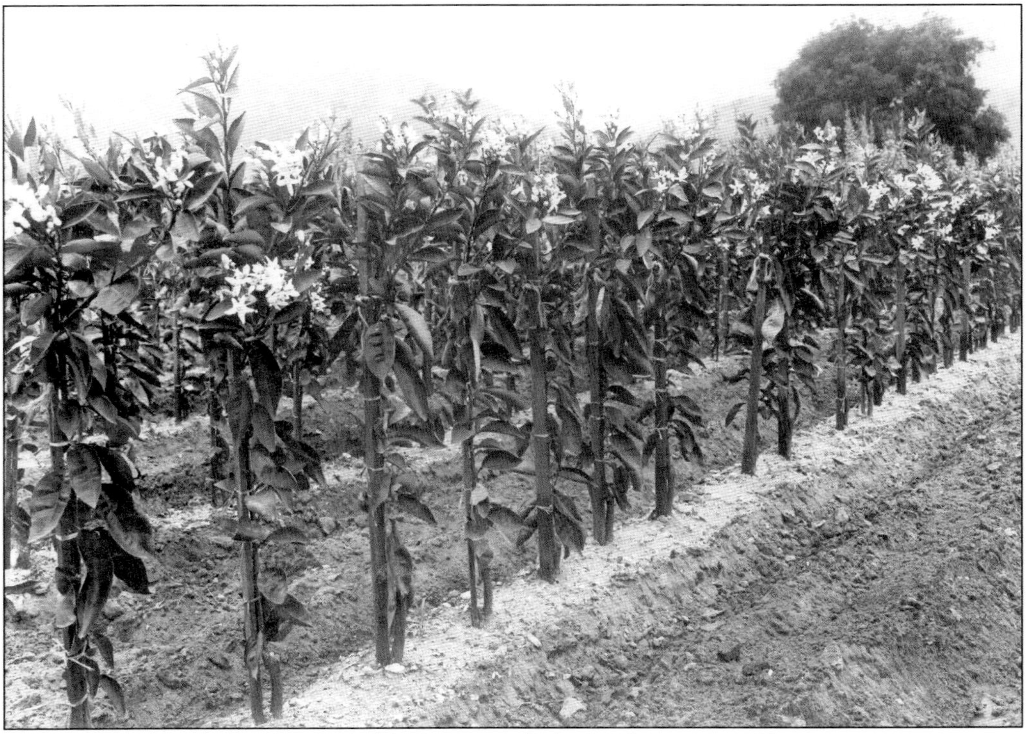

"Here's to the Teagues, who farmed by leagues, all the land now owned between us—
And mowed their hay where the Santa Fe, laid tracks into San Dimas.
To old Mud Springs, whose story rings, of the efforts of men to try
To save their land with its water—and—drained the cienega dry.
To Bowring and Mount and others who count, when times were not a snap—
We owe it to these, and the orange trees, for putting us on the map."

—J. Howard Hoover
from *The Saga of Rancho San Jose*, c. 1929

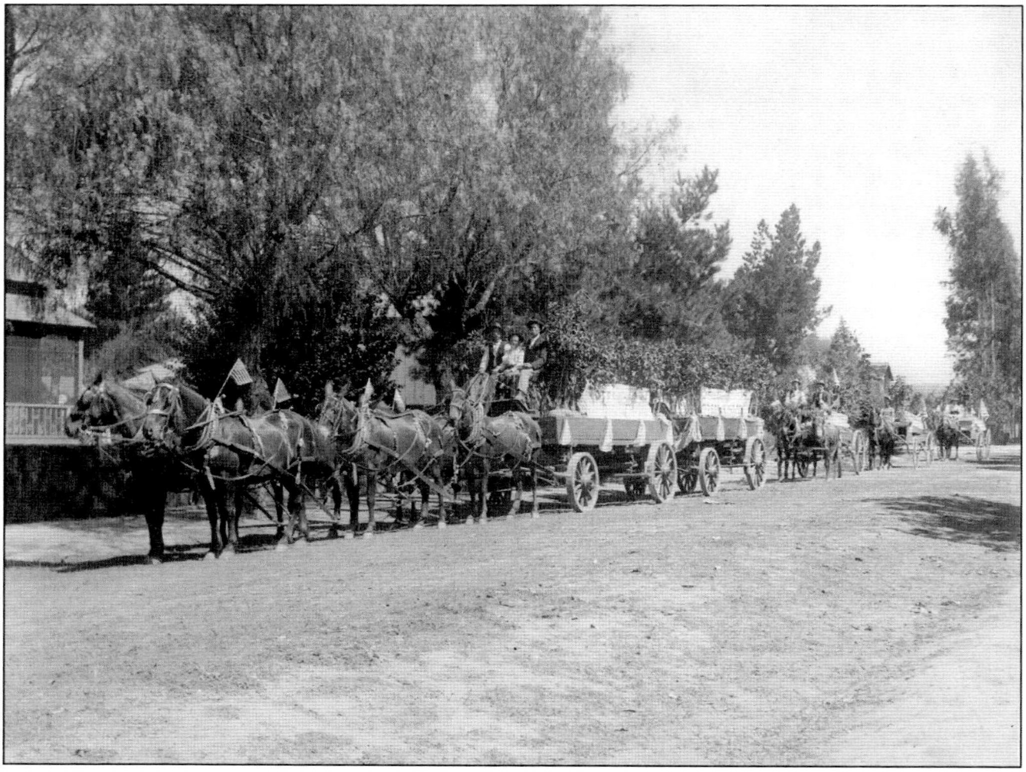

The Teague wagons loaded with young citrus trees prepare for a parade in Claremont to honor the arrival of Pres. Teddy Roosevelt around 1903.

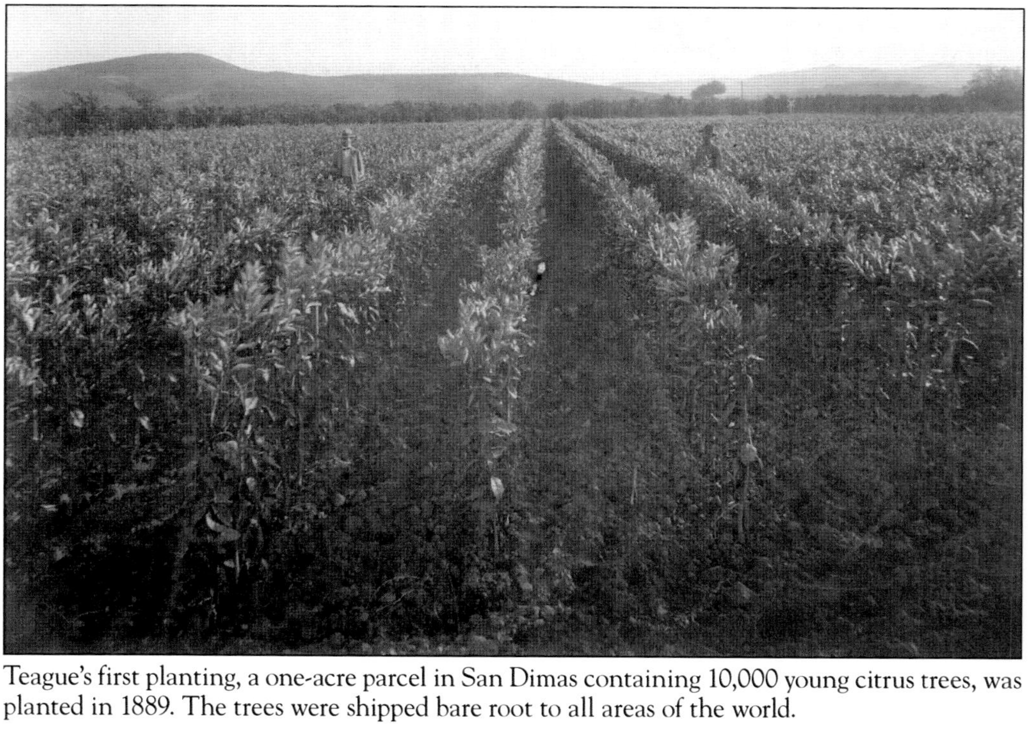

Teague's first planting, a one-acre parcel in San Dimas containing 10,000 young citrus trees, was planted in 1889. The trees were shipped bare root to all areas of the world.

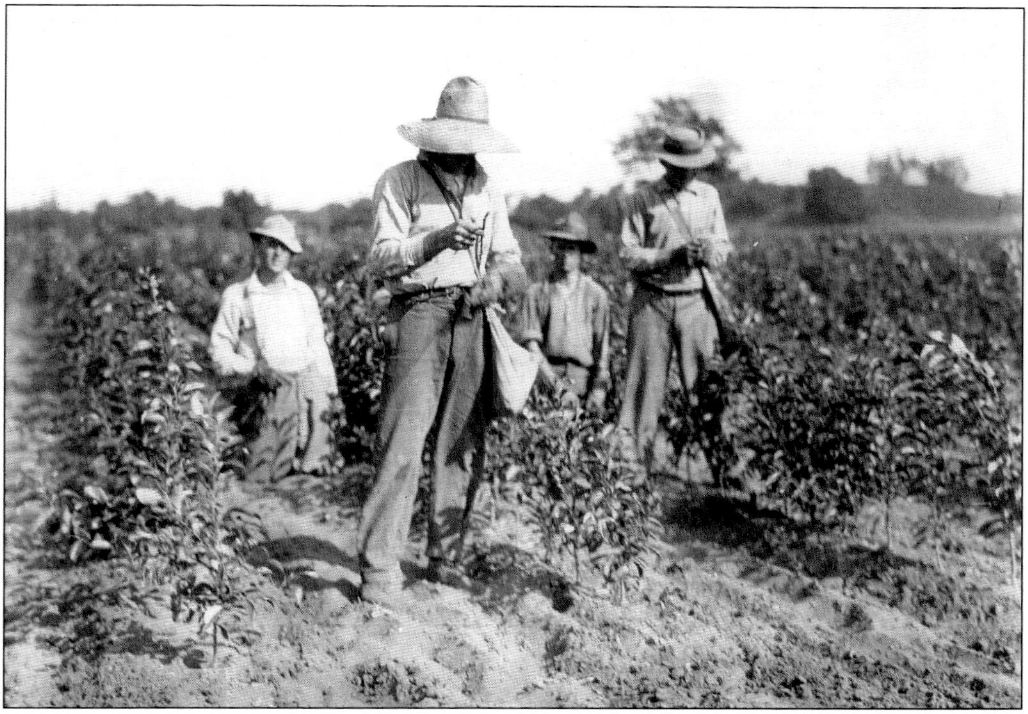

Workers are seen in one of the many fields of young citrus trees located in San Dimas. Work like this had to be backbreaking but provided work for the town's residents.

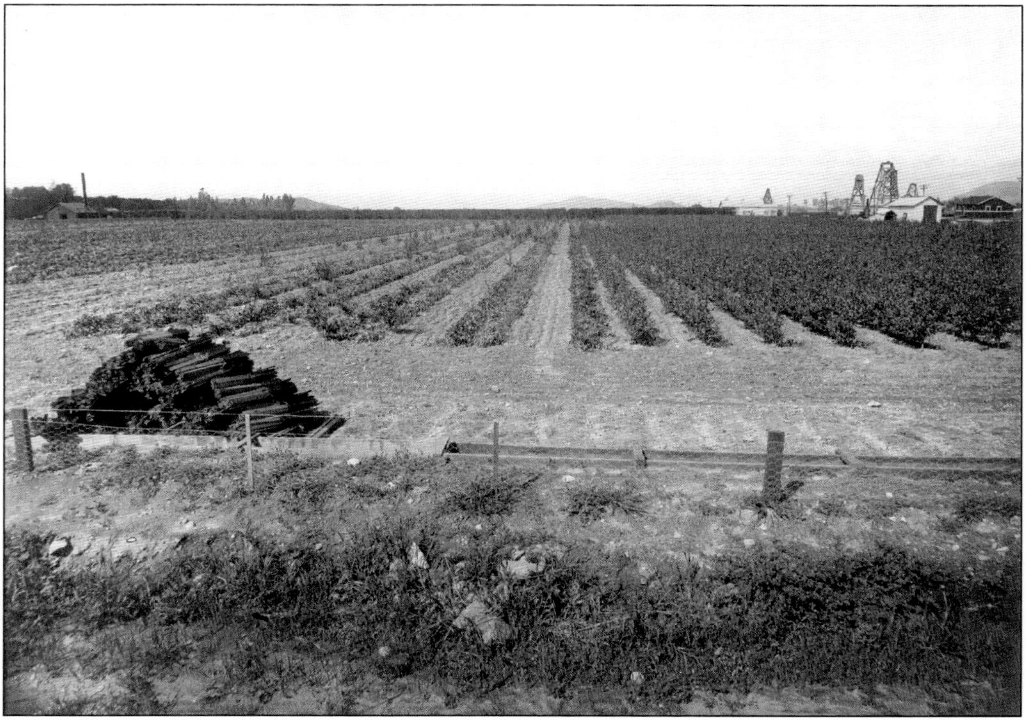

The Teague Nurseries used every available space in town to grow their seedlings. This site in the upper part of town is now homes and a freeway.

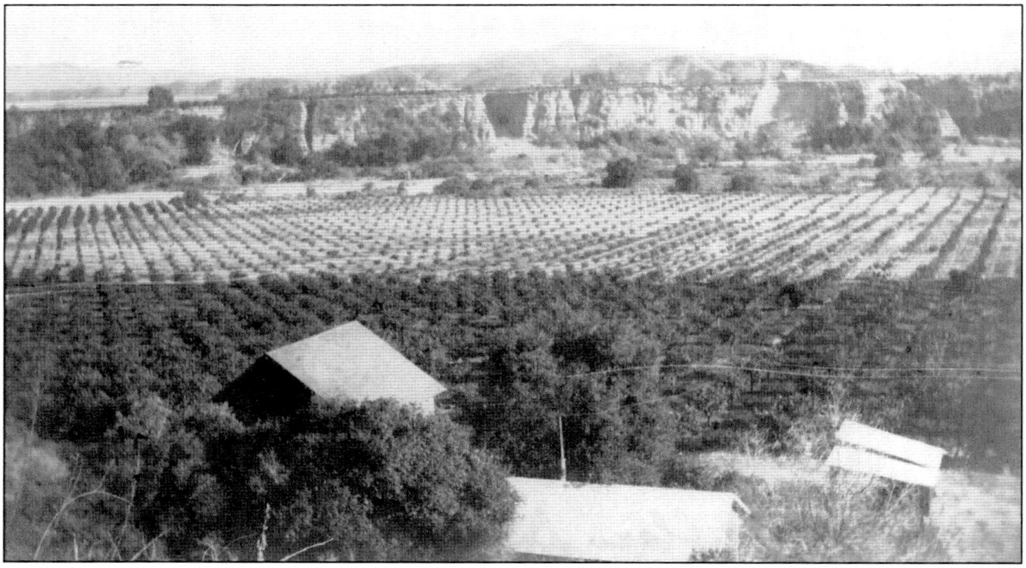

This area is located at the mouth of San Dimas Canyon. Although most of the areas were used to raise small seedlings, some of the site was planted as permanent groves. The grove site in the upper photograph lasted into the 1960s, when it was removed in favor of more homes. Most of this area is now in the city of La Verne.

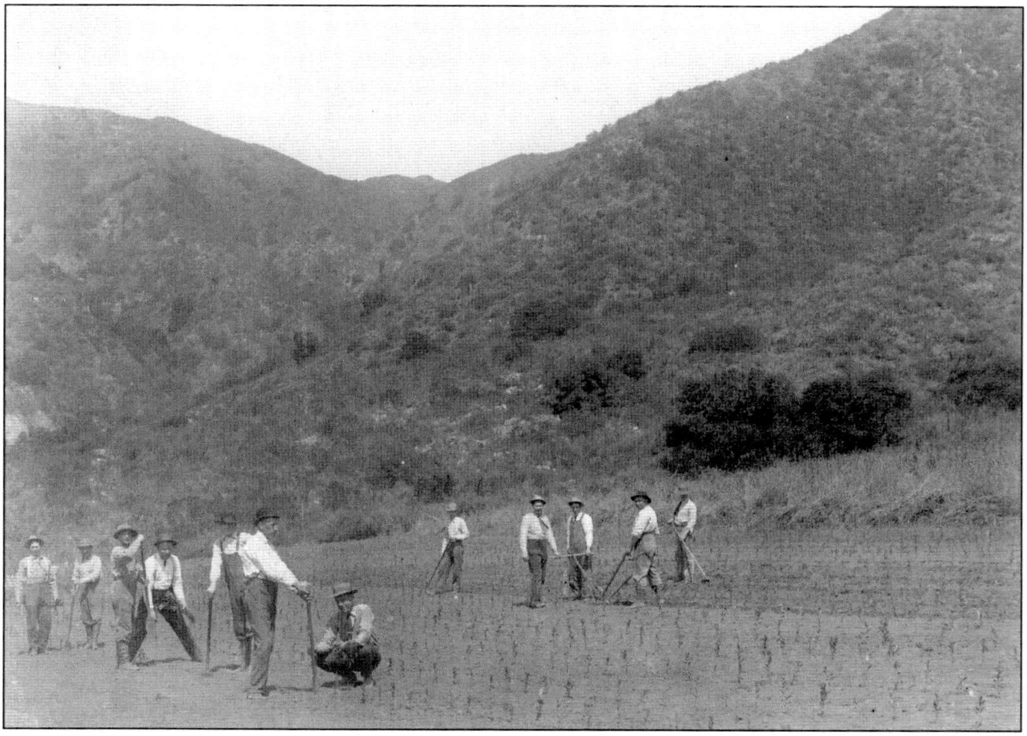

A crew of workers sets out new seedlings to begin their growing process. After one to two years, the trees were dug up and shipped to Teague customers.

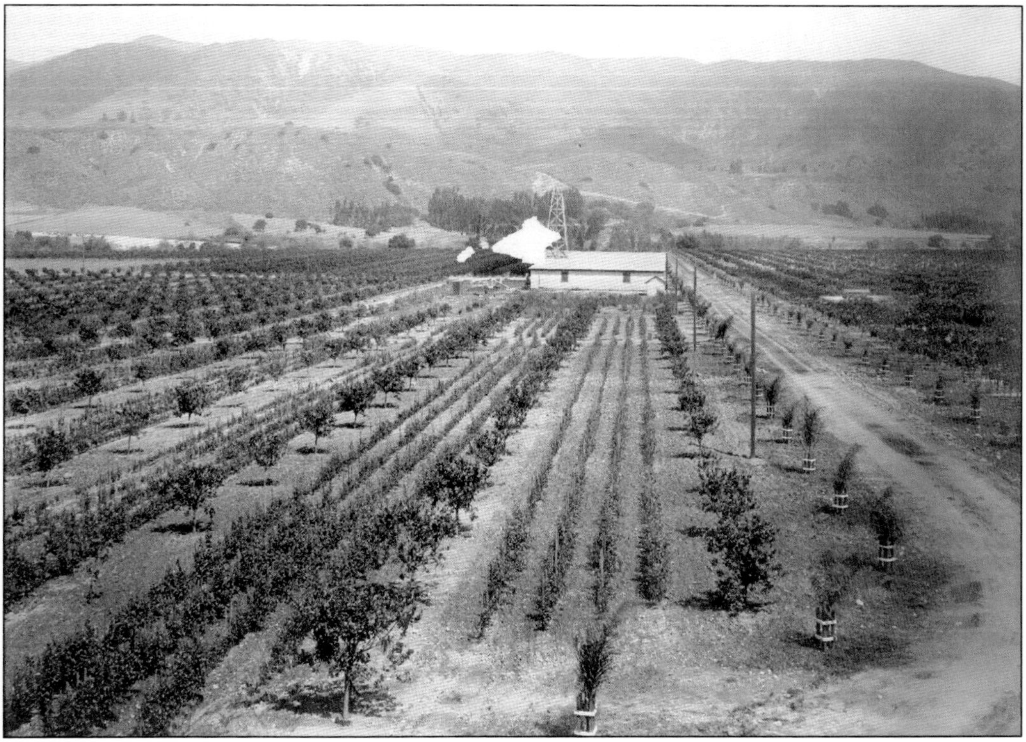

This photograph shows the young trees extending to the foothills. The road is today's San Dimas Canyon Road, and development has reached into the foothills.

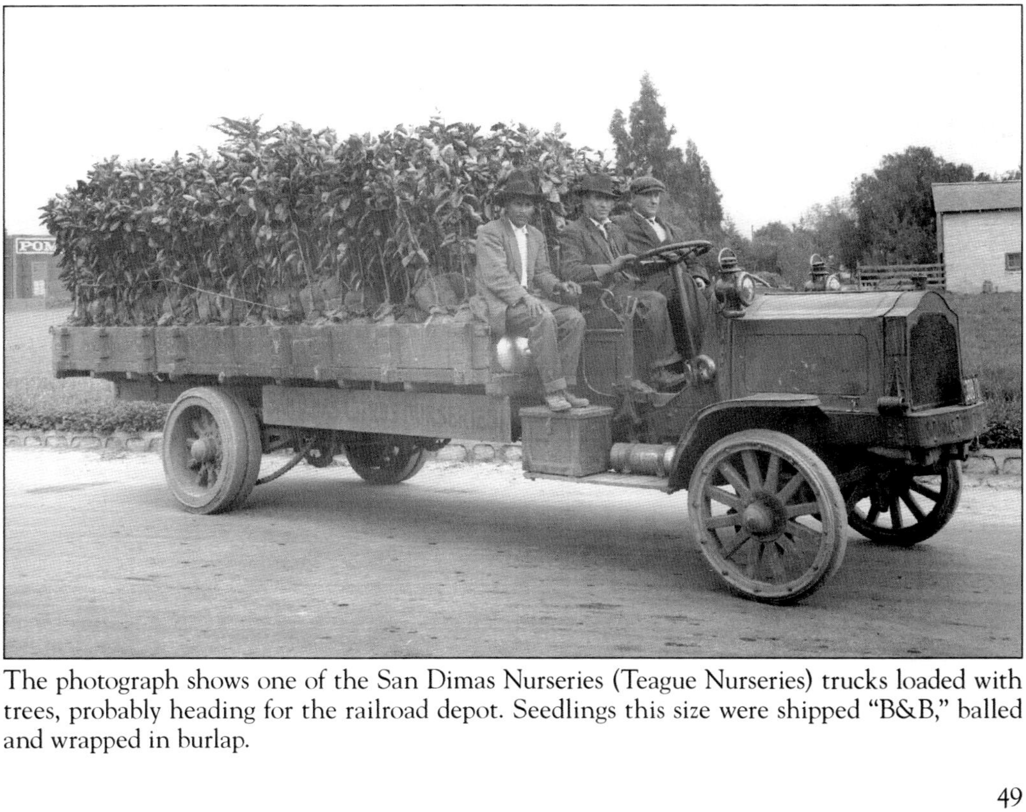

The photograph shows one of the San Dimas Nurseries (Teague Nurseries) trucks loaded with trees, probably heading for the railroad depot. Seedlings this size were shipped "B&B," balled and wrapped in burlap.

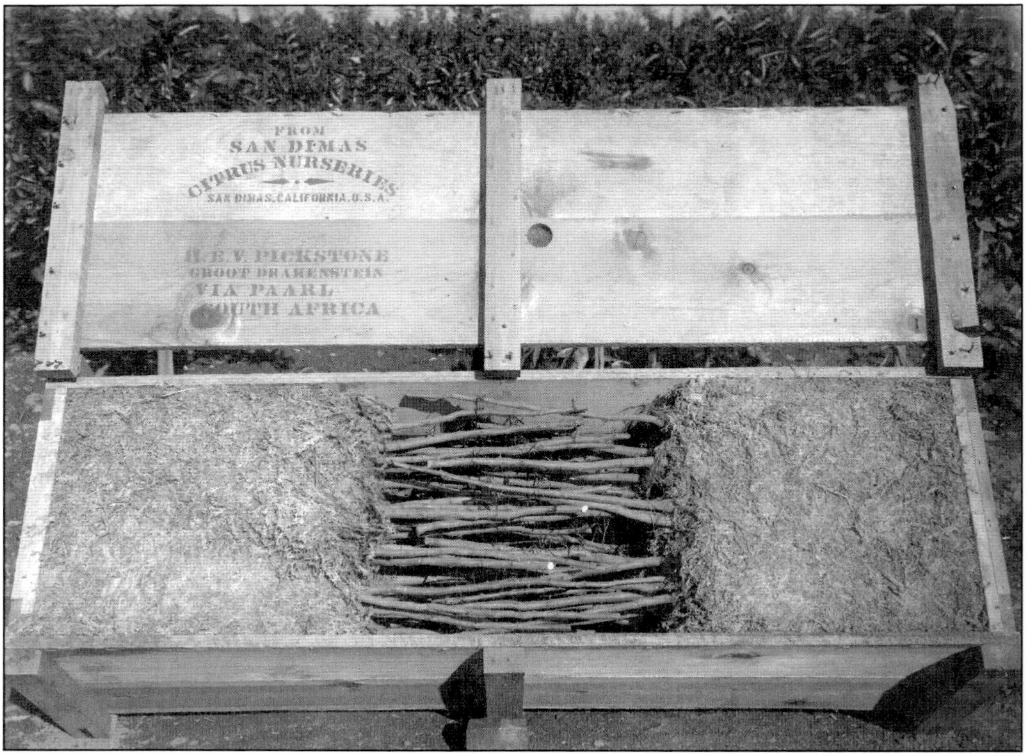

The Teague Nurseries shipped their seedlings all over the world. These trees were packed for export to South Africa and were received 65 days after shipment. One may be able to notice that the trees are already starting to leaf out *c.* 1911.

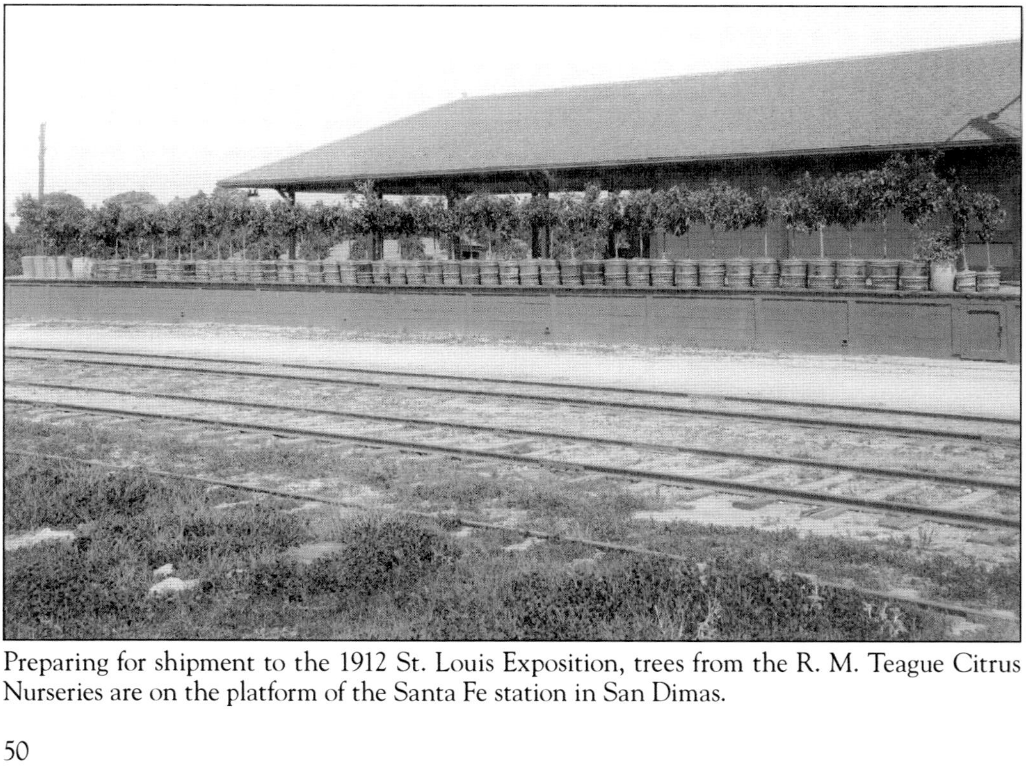

Preparing for shipment to the 1912 St. Louis Exposition, trees from the R. M. Teague Citrus Nurseries are on the platform of the Santa Fe station in San Dimas.

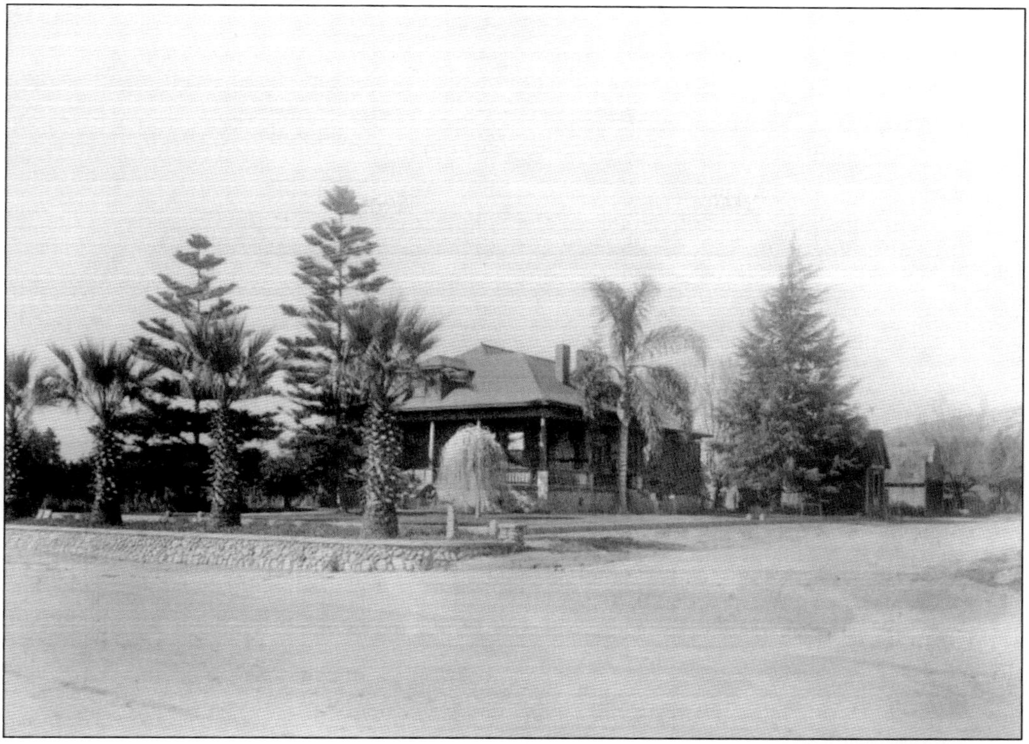

The R. M. Teague home and office located at the corner of Bonita and Iglesia Avenues included their office, the middle building on the right side of the picture, and their garage, the building on the far right. Both the office and garage survive today, although the home was destroyed.

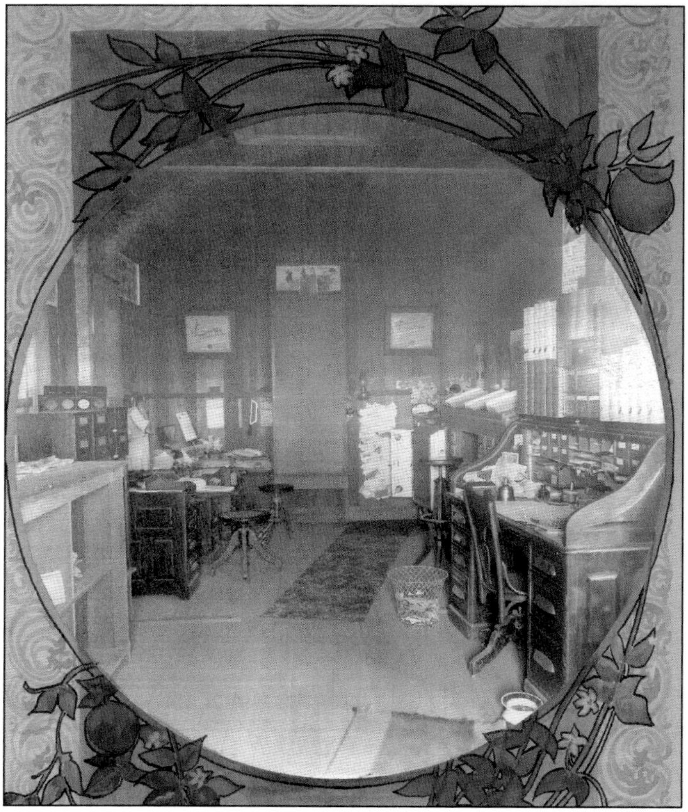

This unusual picture of the Teague Nurseries office shows the cramped quarters in the old building. Today this building has been moved a few hundred feet away, now faces onto First Street, and is used as a single-family dwelling.

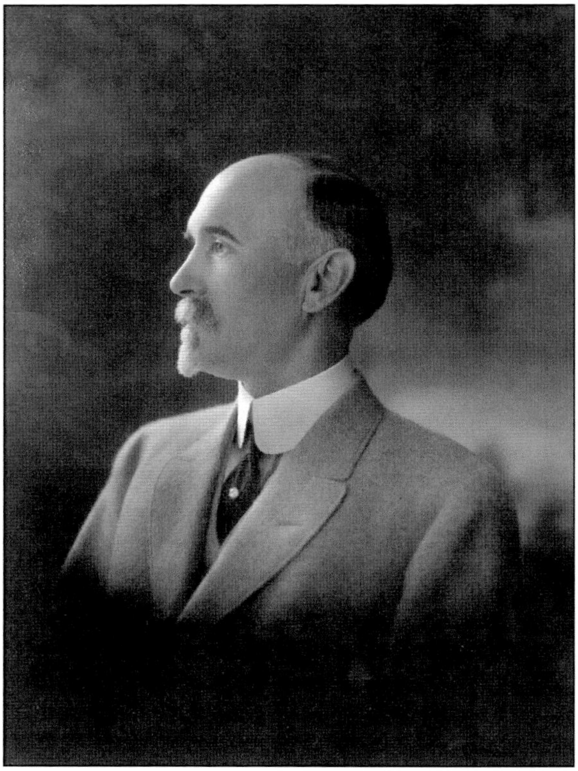

Robert M. Teague founded the Teague Citrus Nurseries in 1904. He was a very prominent member of the community for many years. In 1907, Teague had 700,000 seed bed stock—grown in the open at San Dimas, without a heater of any kind. In those days, the area was advertised as "Frostless San Dimas."

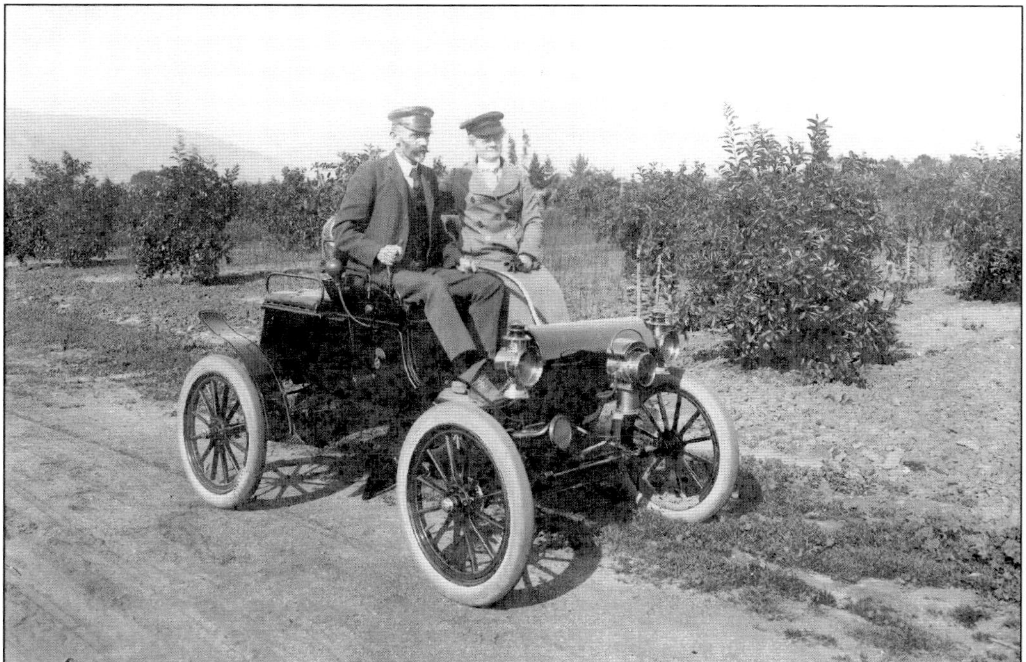

This picture shows Robert M. and Minnie Teague and their first automobile, a 1903 Oldsmobile. This was the first auto in San Dimas and one of the first, if not the very first, in the eastern part of Los Angeles County.

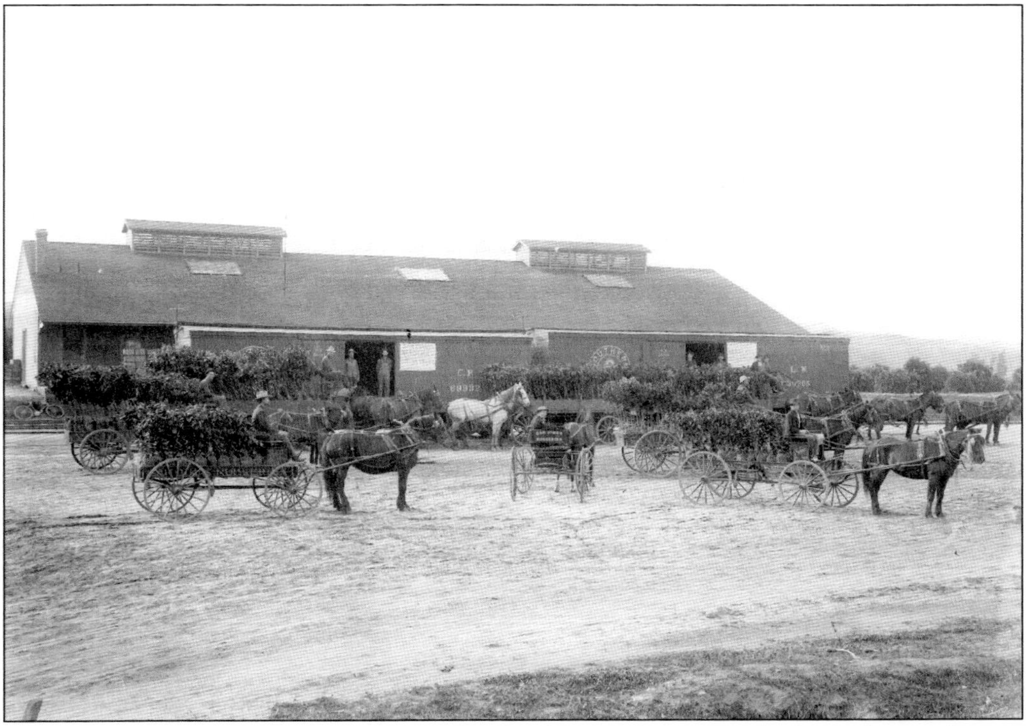

Wagonloads of small citrus trees are readied for loading into box cars to be shipped somewhere in the world. These trees have been "balled and burlapped," which means they were dug out with the soil still attached to the roots, then wrapped in burlap and tied to hold the soil in place. Obviously they were not going to be shipped out of the country but used somewhere in the United States.

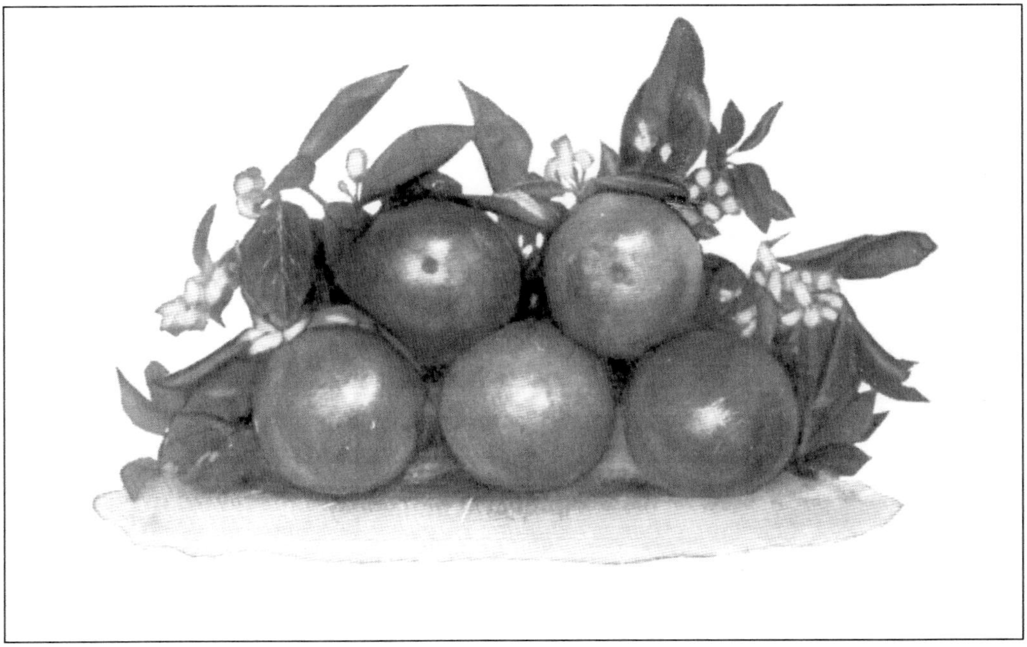

One of the many drawings of citrus fruit used in advertisements for the Teague Nurseries is seen here.

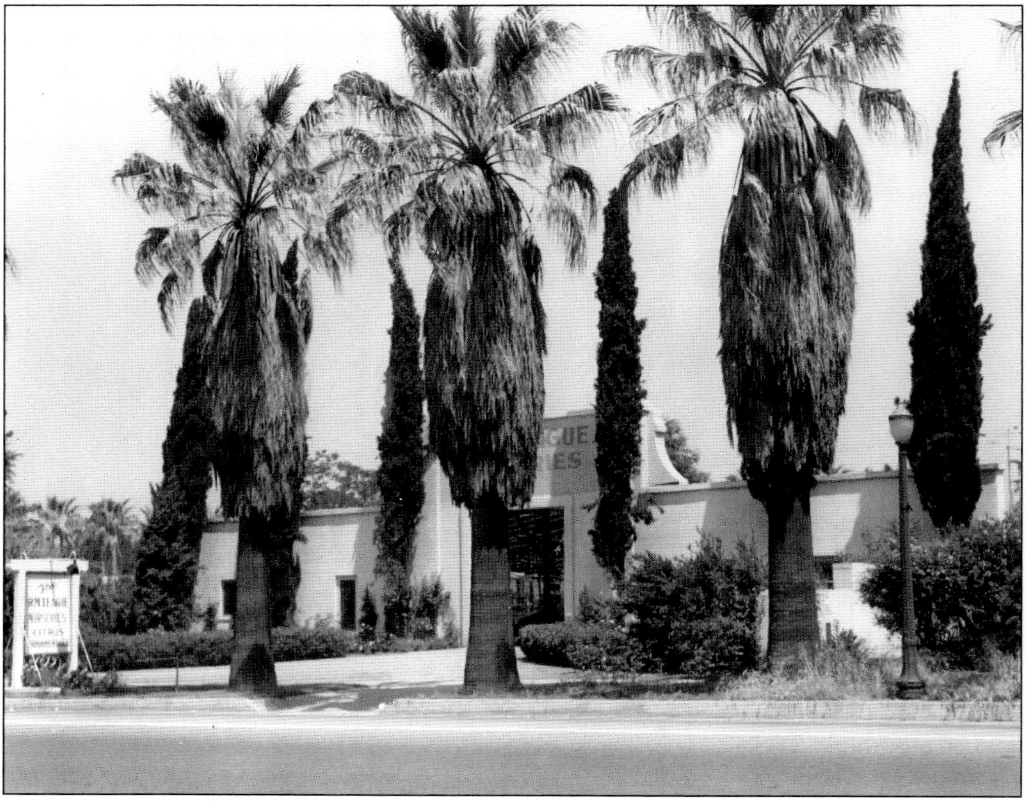

Teague Nurseries, also know as the San Dimas Nurseries, established their showroom on Bonita Avenue to display their trees when they took over the Hobbs-Gregg Nurseries building. In the peak years of 1910–1912, sales ran as high as $100,000 a year; however, there were years when the demand for trees went down and the Teague Nurseries suffered large losses.

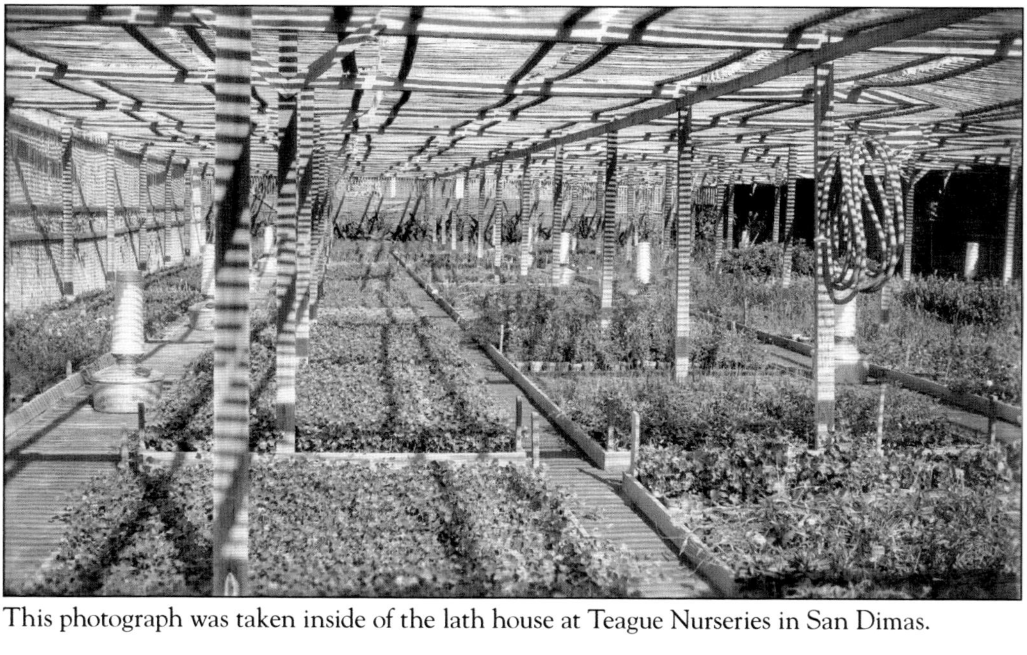

This photograph was taken inside of the lath house at Teague Nurseries in San Dimas.

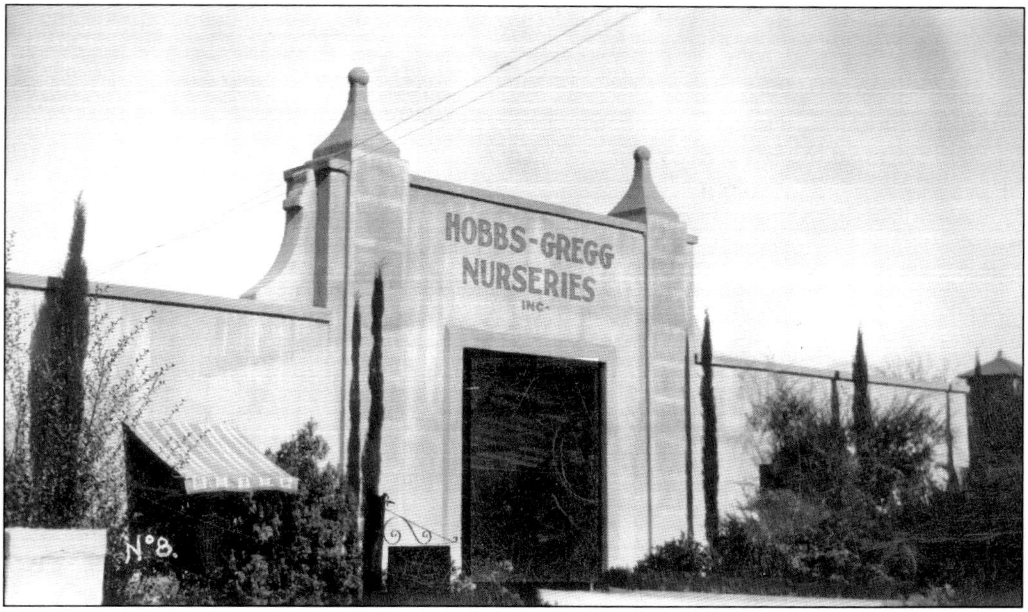

This is the facade of the Hobbs-Gregg Nurseries building in San Dimas. The name was changed to the R. M. Teague Nurseries and the structure stood until 1997, when it was removed to construct a new building. Another piece of history was lost in San Dimas.

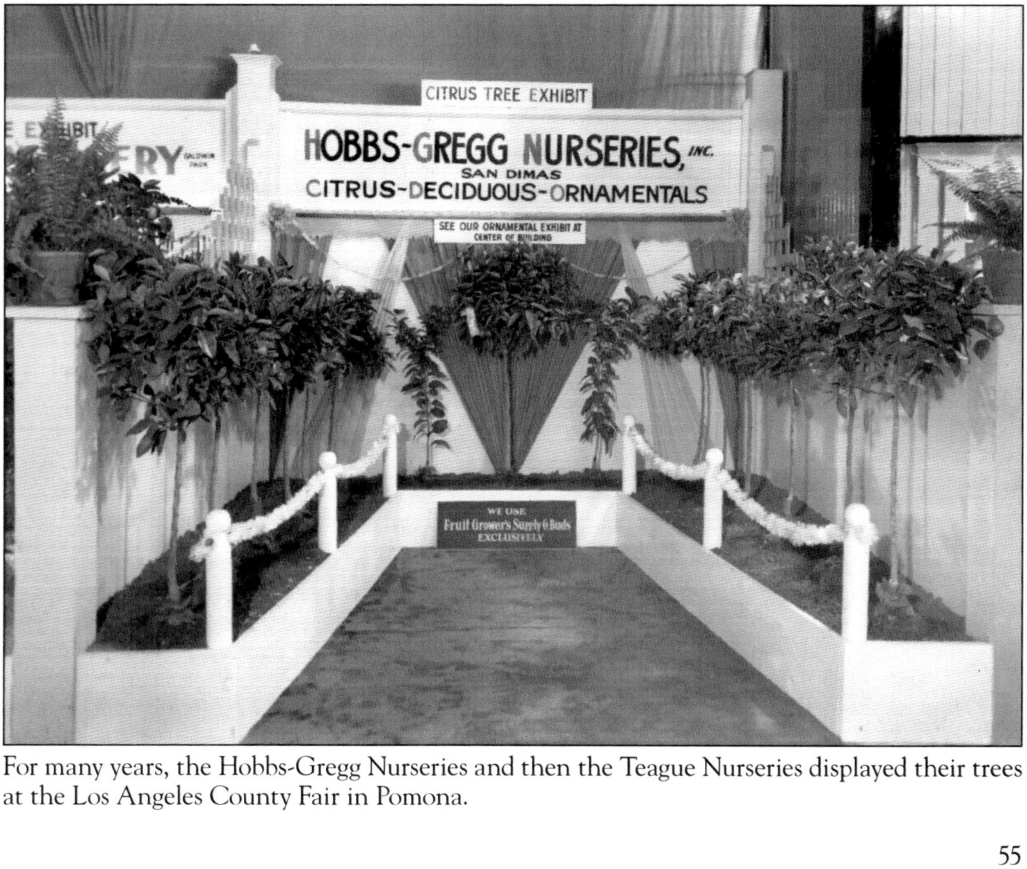

For many years, the Hobbs-Gregg Nurseries and then the Teague Nurseries displayed their trees at the Los Angeles County Fair in Pomona.

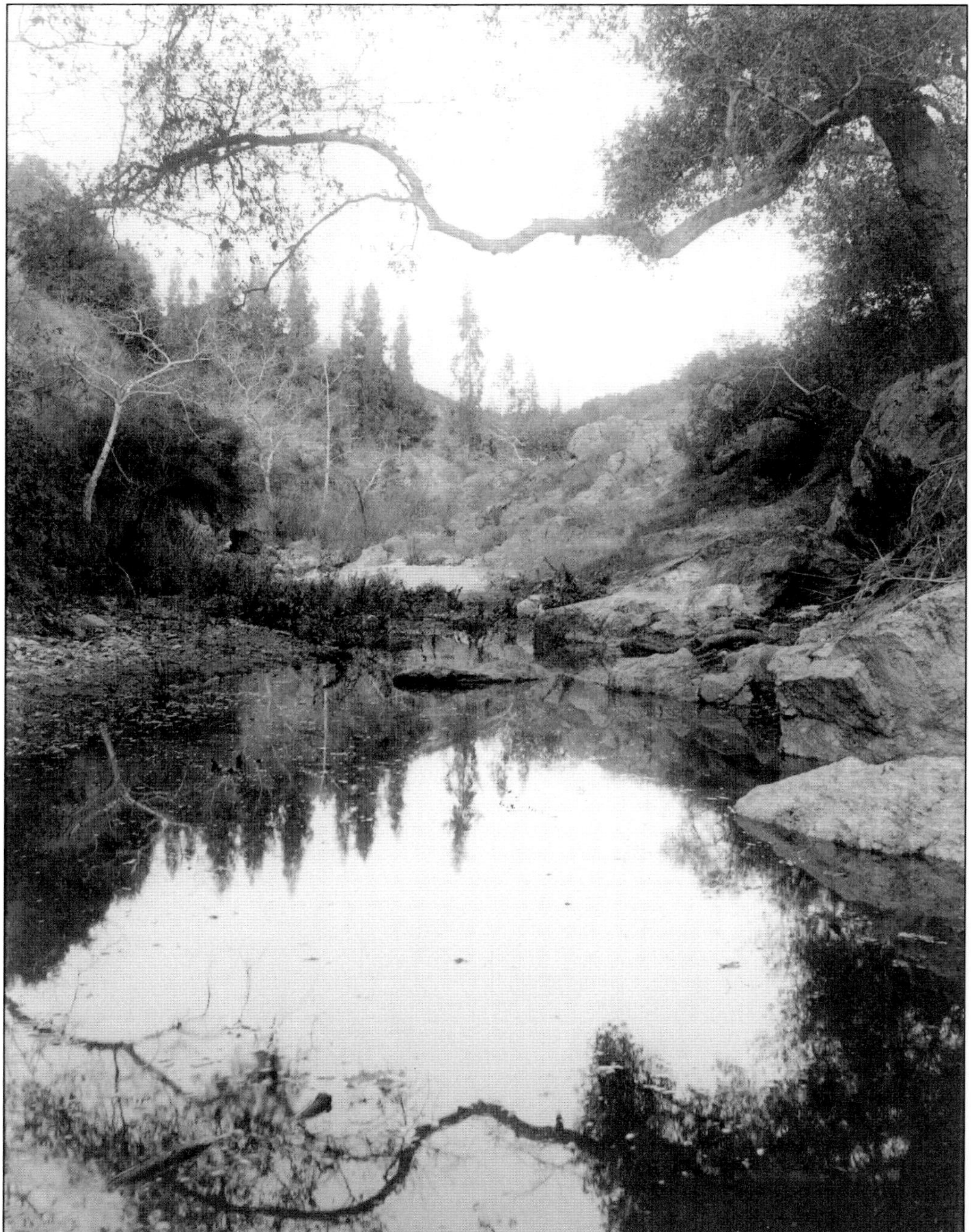

Rancho Sierra Vista encompassed 1,200 acres of the southern part of today's San Dimas. The land was purchased by I. N. Walker (father of Harry Walker), who moved to San Dimas to manage the property. Today most of the rancho is developed except for Walnut Creek, pictured above.

Four

Rancho Sierra Vista
The South Side of San Dimas

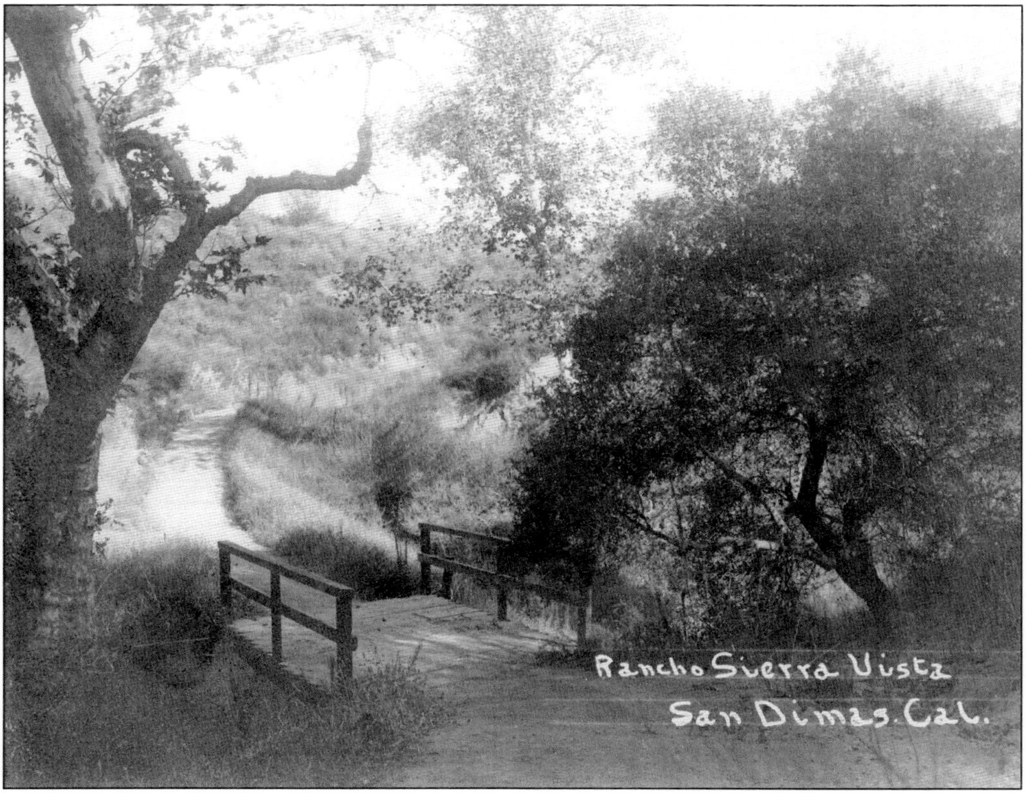

This pastoral view of Rancho Sierra Vista is an example of the tranquil settings that once were part of San Dimas. Like other communities throughout the area, much of this type of open space has given way to developments.

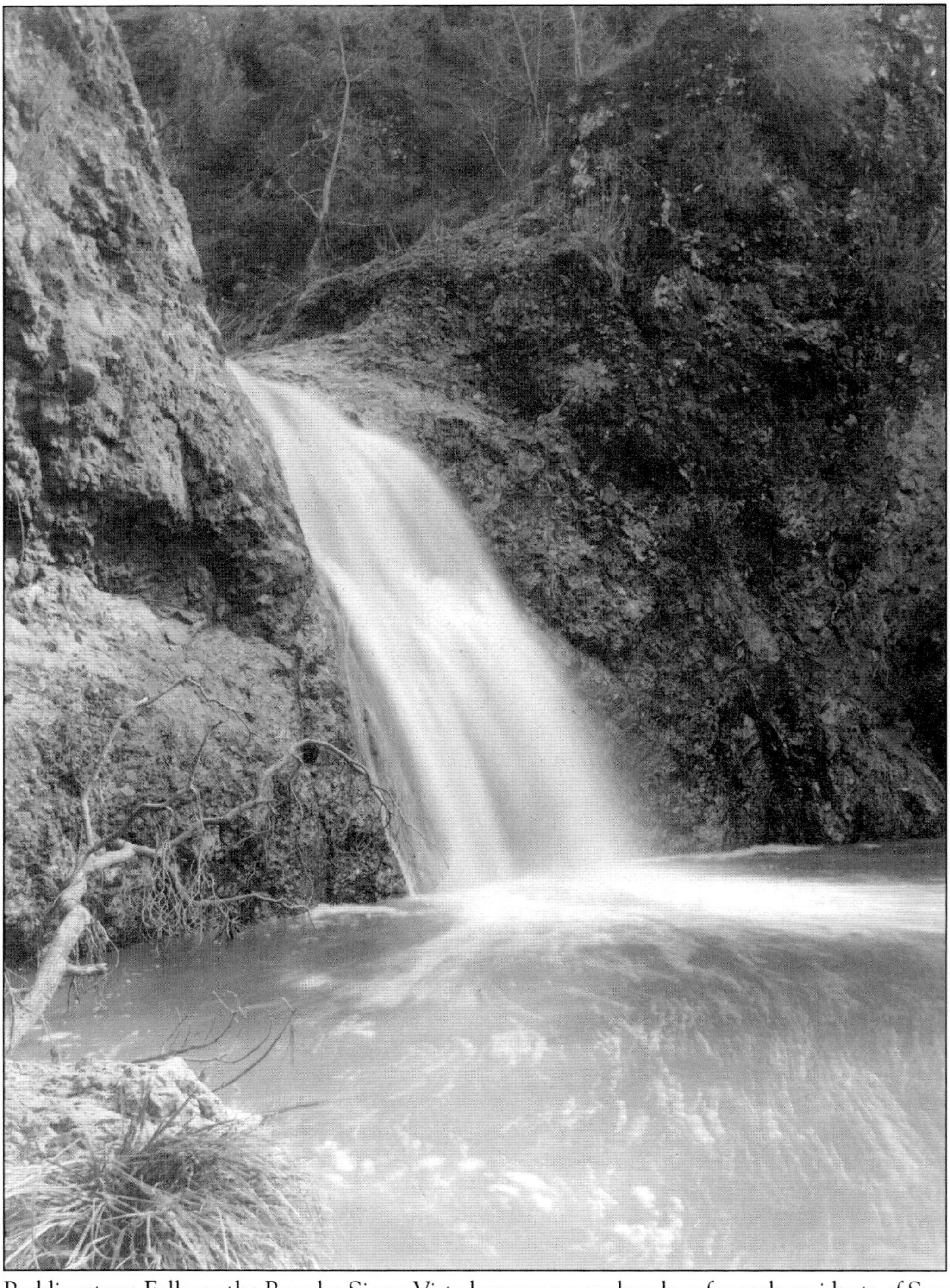

Puddingstone Falls on the Rancho Sierra Vista became a popular place for early residents of San Dimas to visit and picnic. The falls were fed by the natural springs, once called Mud Springs.

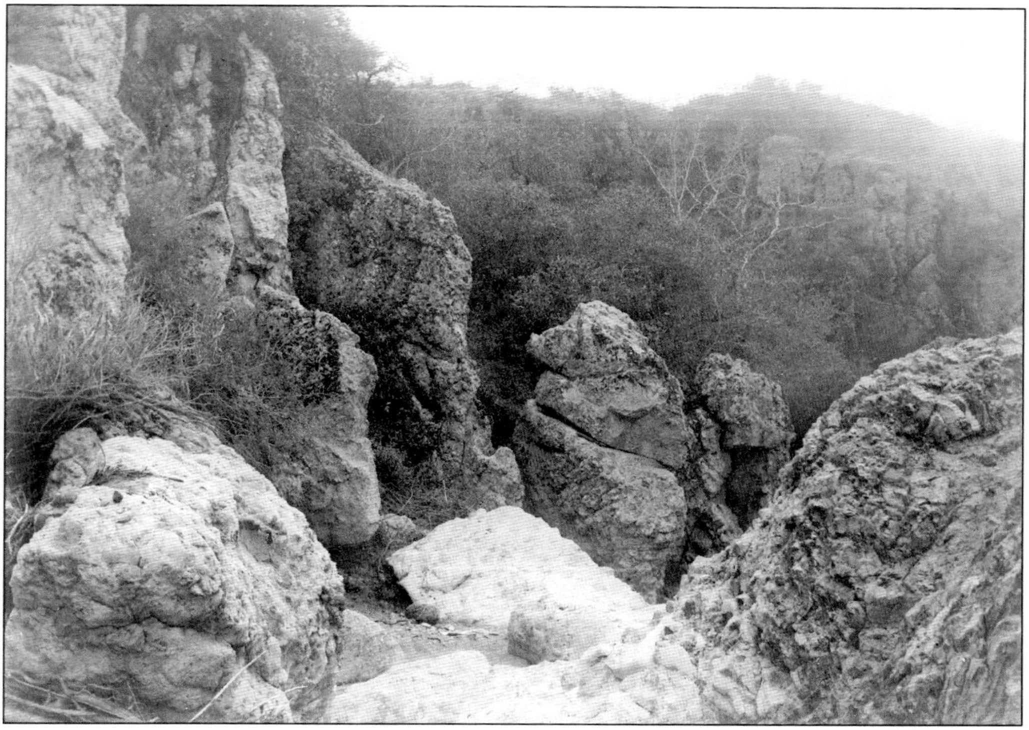

While visiting the canyon below Puddingstone Falls, one visitor stated that the rock formations looked like pudding, thus the name Puddingstone was established. Today the name is still used for the large reservoir and recreation area just south of the canyon.

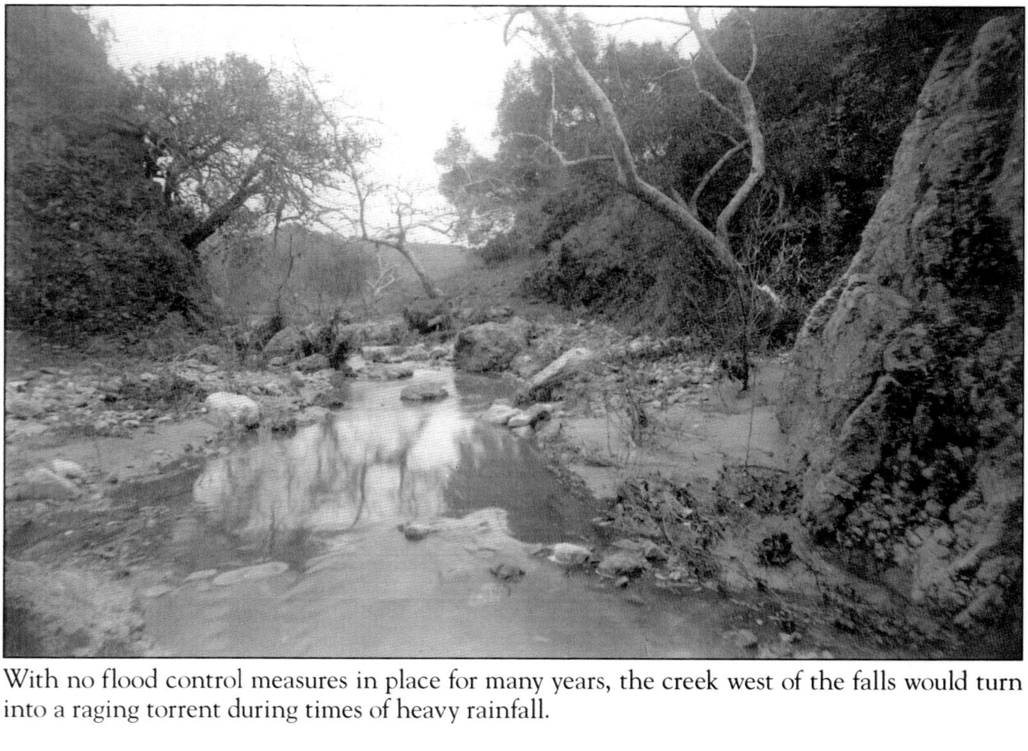

With no flood control measures in place for many years, the creek west of the falls would turn into a raging torrent during times of heavy rainfall.

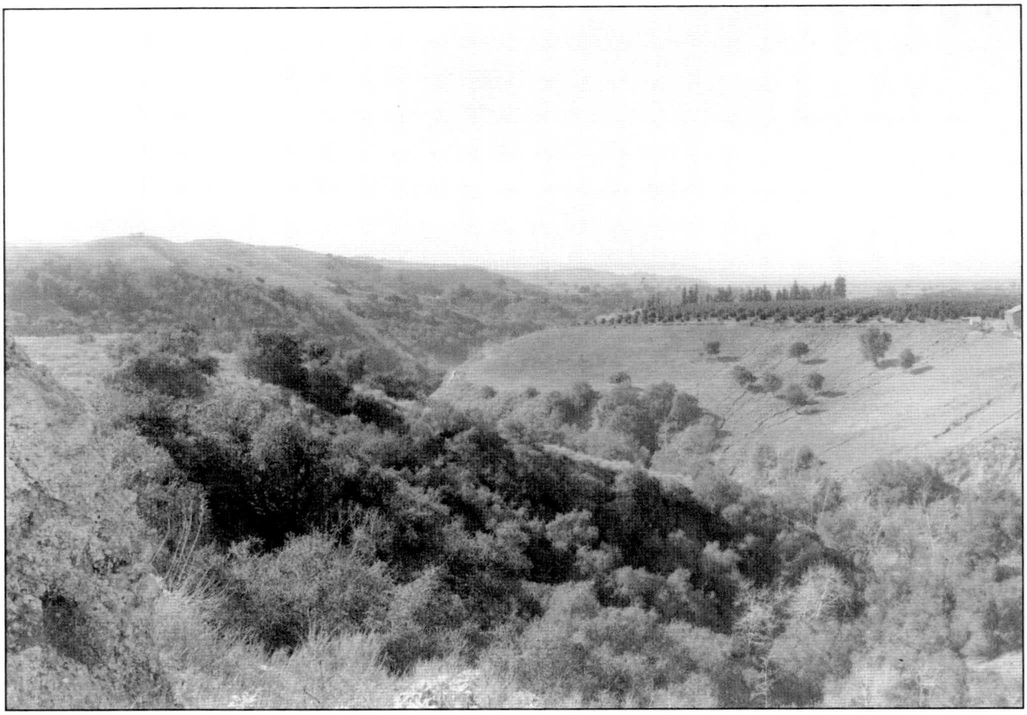

The vistas from Rancho Sierra Vista were something to behold. This westward-looking view shows part of the orchards of the William Johnstone property.

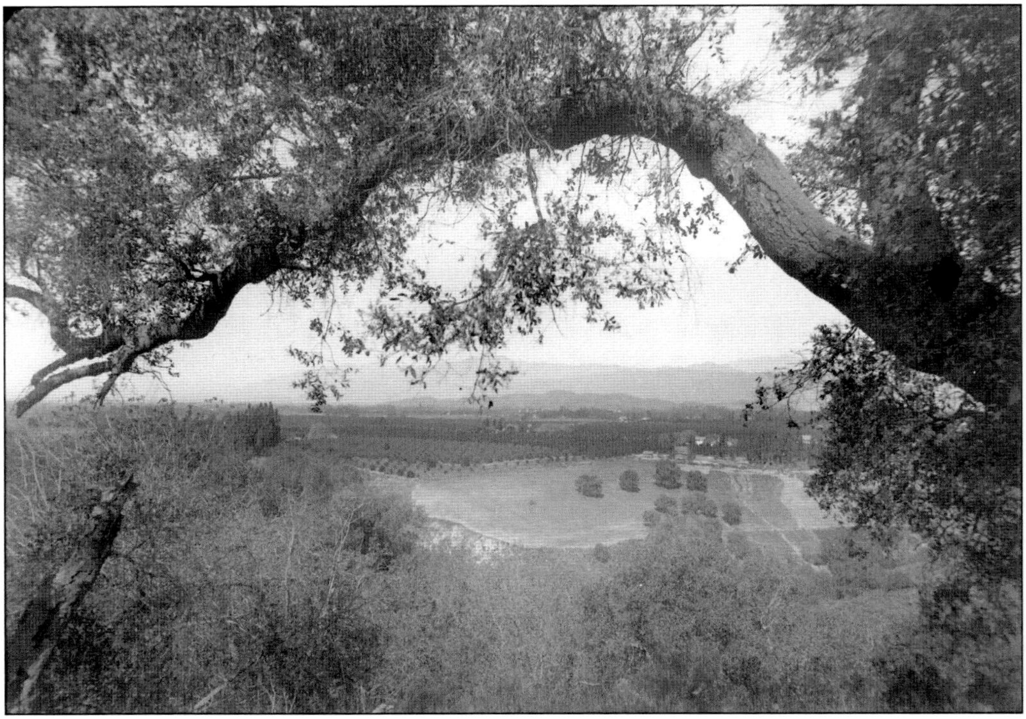

A very early *c.* 1908 view of the town of San Dimas peeks through the trees as the citrus groves continue to spread across the landscape.

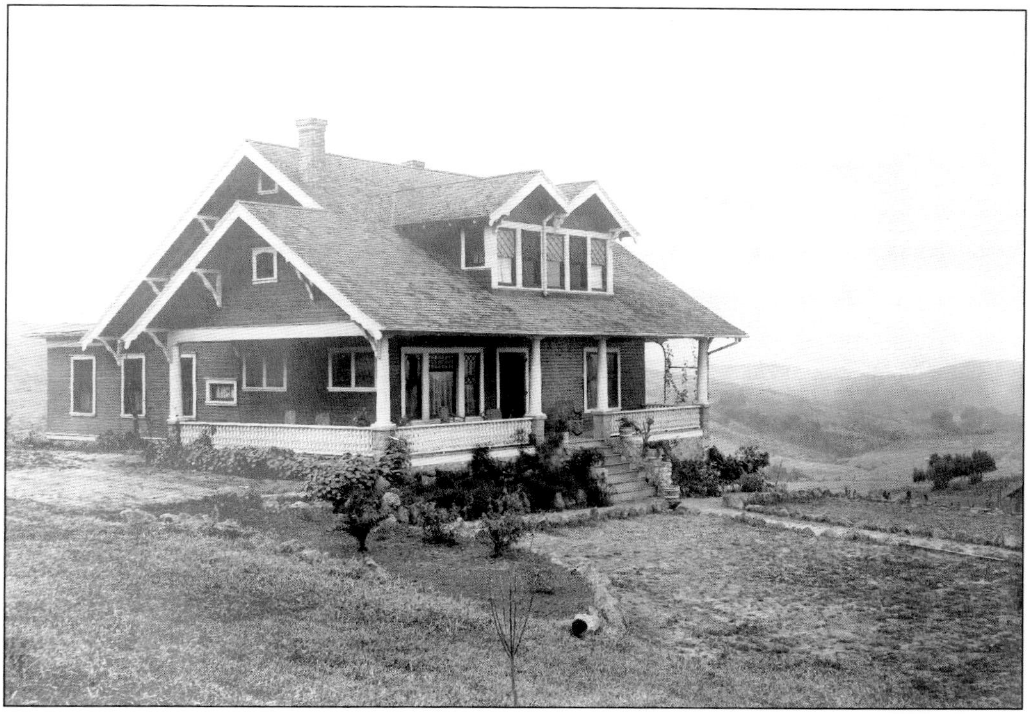

Harry and Genevieve Walker built their first home on a bluff overlooking the town of San Dimas in 1908. They lived in the home until 1930, when they tore it down and constructed a new Monterey Colonial home that still stands on the site.

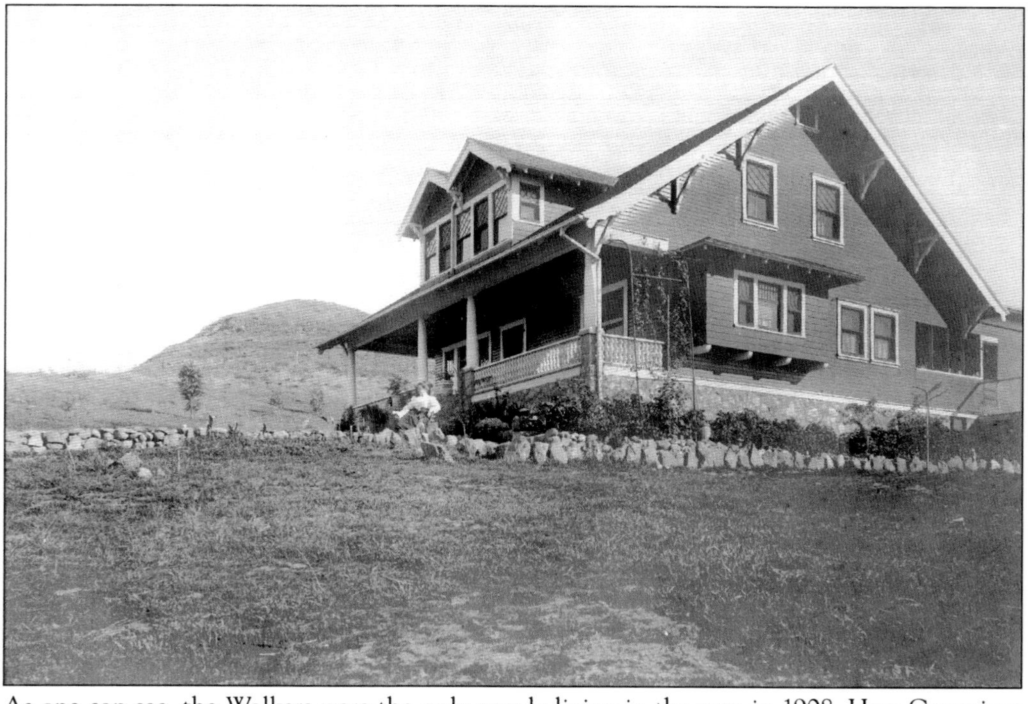

As one can see, the Walkers were the only people living in the area in 1908. Here Genevieve Walker tends to her flower gardens in front of the home.

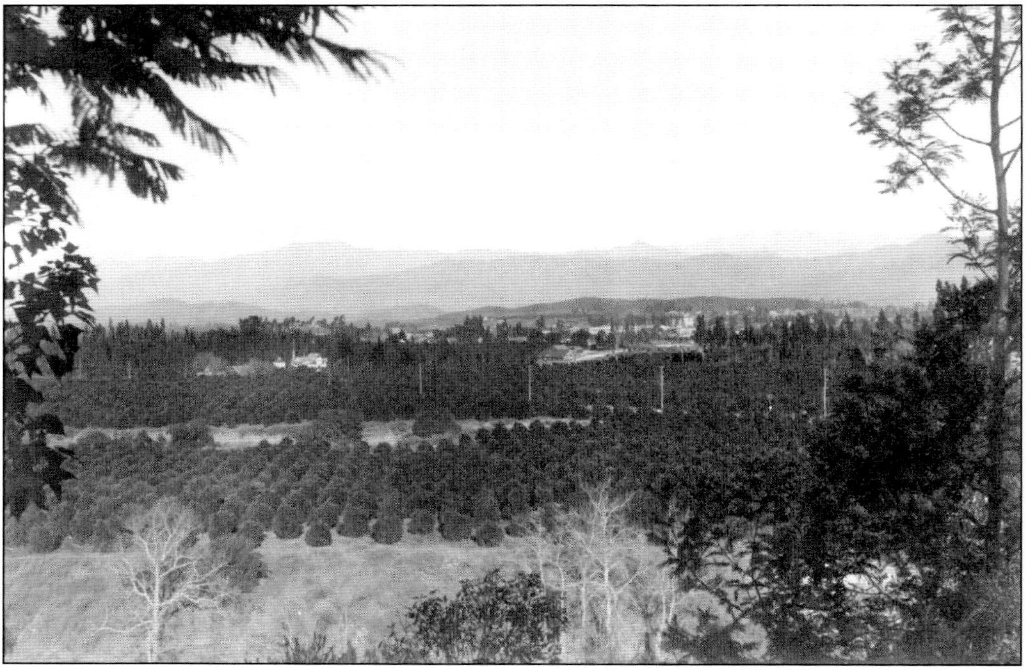

This photograph is yet another view of early San Dimas with the majestic San Gabriel Mountains in the background. These were the days when the citrus industry ruled the area, leading to an idyllic life for the residents.

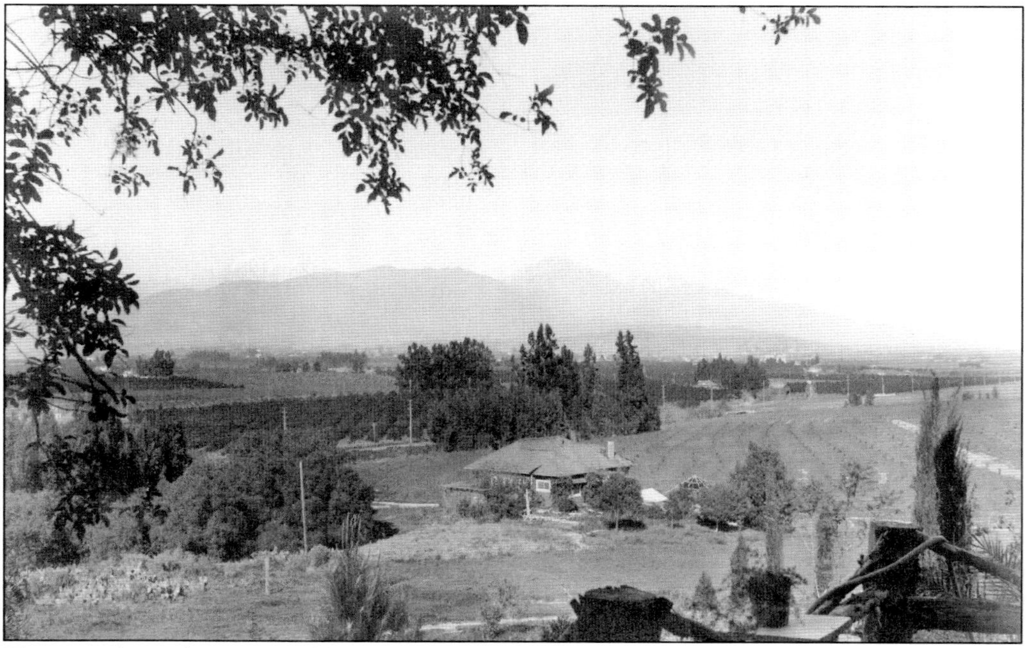

The view from the Harwood home near the Walkers' place shows San Antonio Peak (Mount Baldy) in the background (left) with Ontario and Cucamonga Peaks to the right.

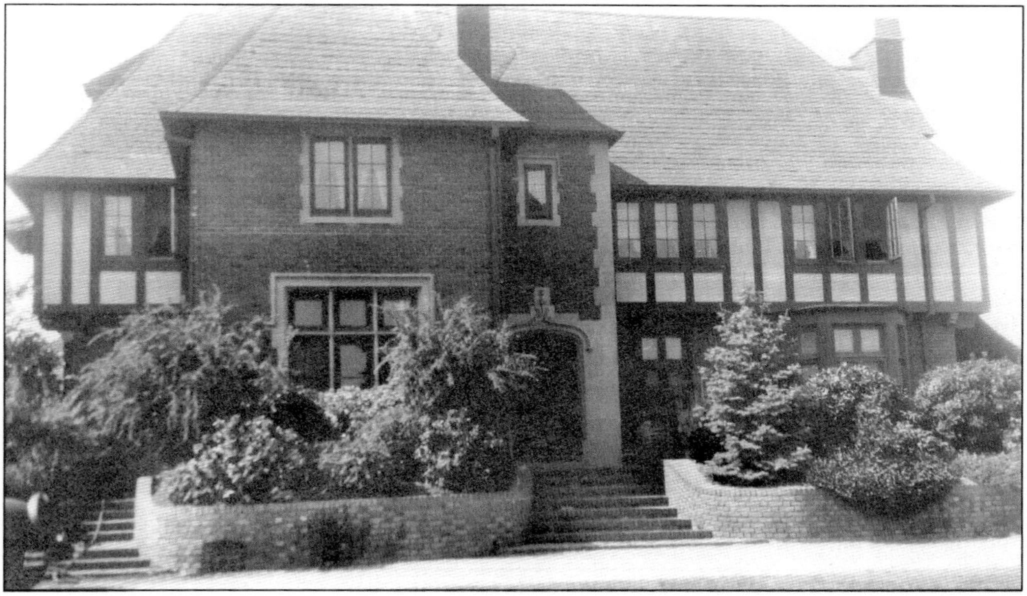

On property sold by the Walkers, Frank Harwood constructed this magnificent home on a hill overlooking the entire valley. The home, with its expansive views of the San Gabriel Mountains, offered the Harwoods the lifestyle that many in San Dimas admired and provided a venue for many civic activities.

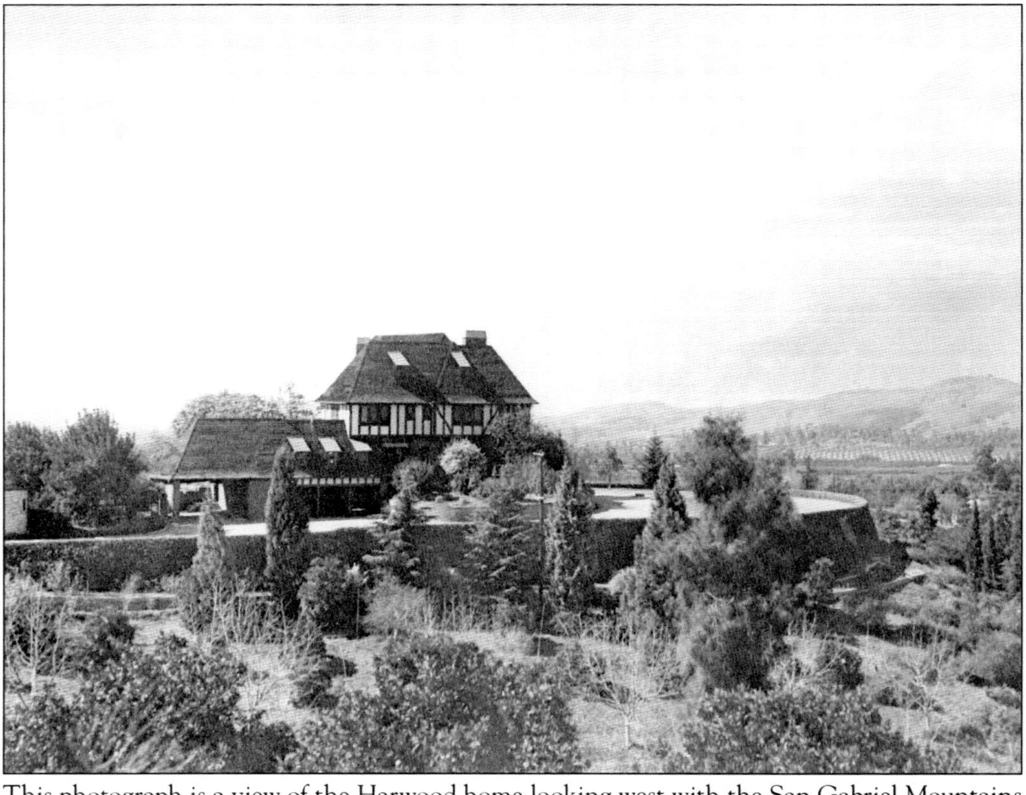

This photograph is a view of the Harwood home looking west with the San Gabriel Mountains in the background. The beautiful home burned in the devastating fire of September 1, 1955.

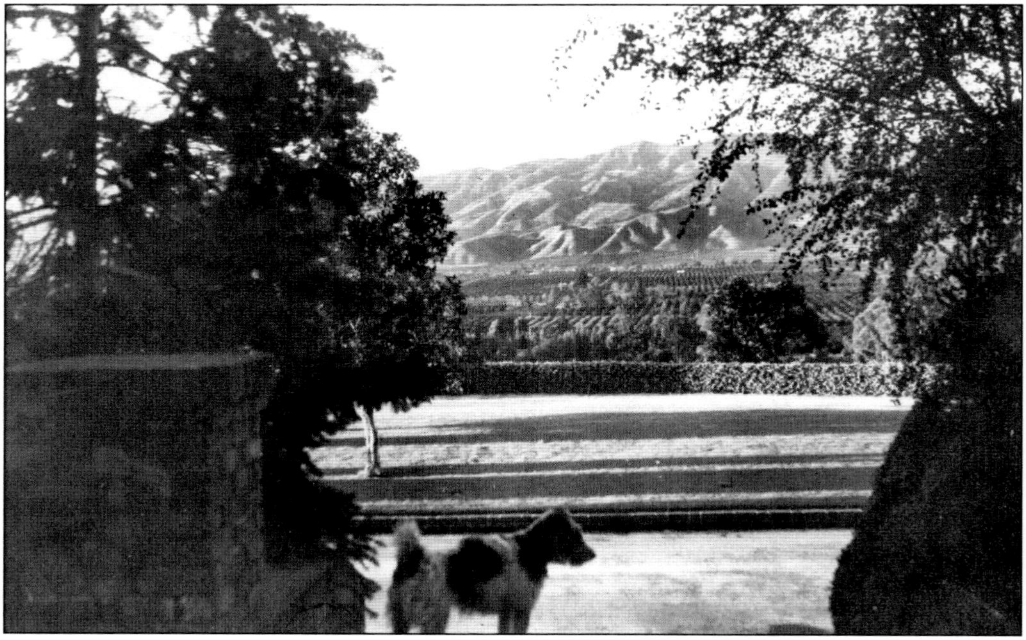

This picture shows the early area of San Dimas as seen from the Frank Harwood property, with the family dog in the foreground. The Harwood home was one of the finest residences in the town of San Dimas.

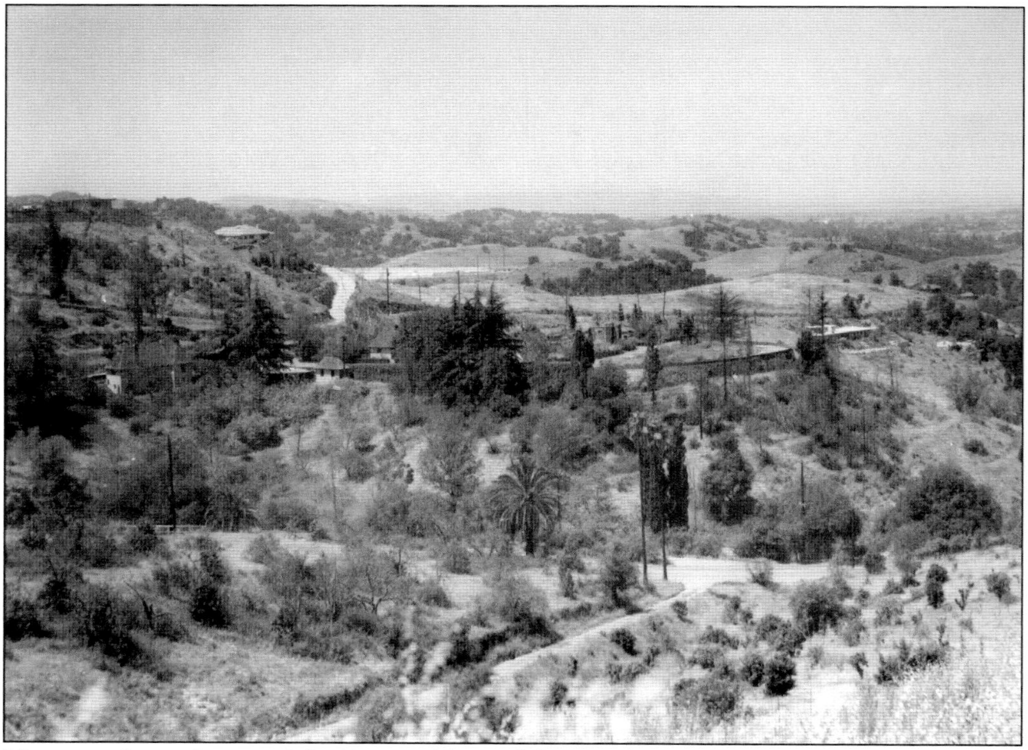

This view shows the site of the Harwood home following the fire of September 1, 1955. Today a new home has been constructed on the site that looks very much like the original home.

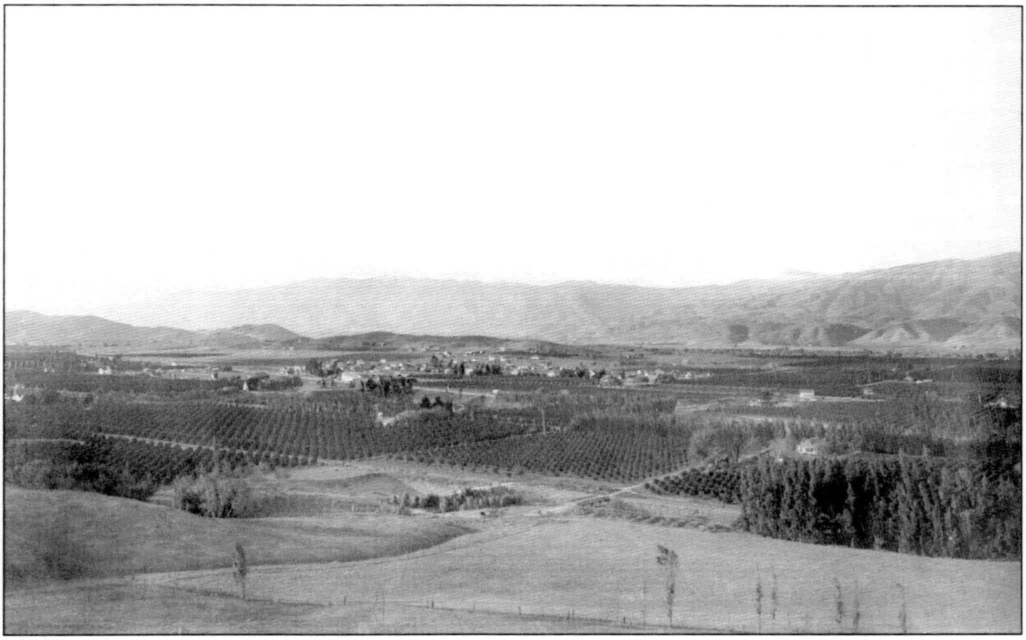

This is a wonderful c. 1908 view of the town of San Dimas with its ubiquitous citrus groves spreading toward the foothills and west to the town of Glendora.

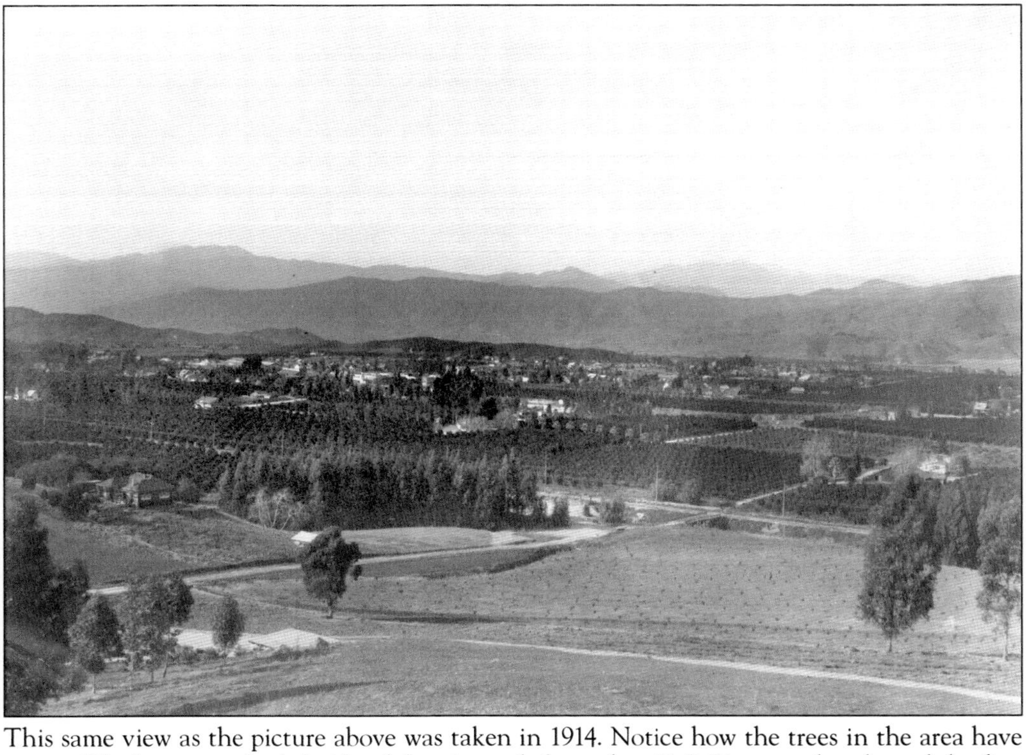

This same view as the picture above was taken in 1914. Notice how the trees in the area have grown. The home on the left side of the picture belonged to C. P. Teague, who planted the first citrus trees in San Dimas in 1879.

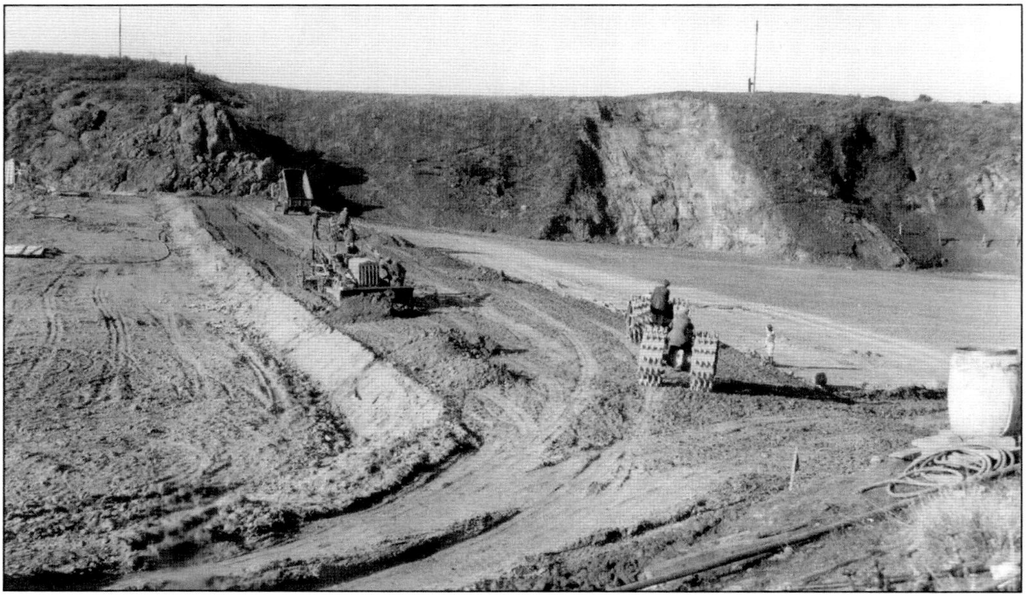

In 1923, the County of Los Angeles Flood Control purchased a large piece of Rancho Sierra Vista to construct a dam to hold back floodwaters from an area covering 303 square miles. Work on the dam started in 1925 and was completed in 1928. Its maximum height is 182 feet above the foundation.

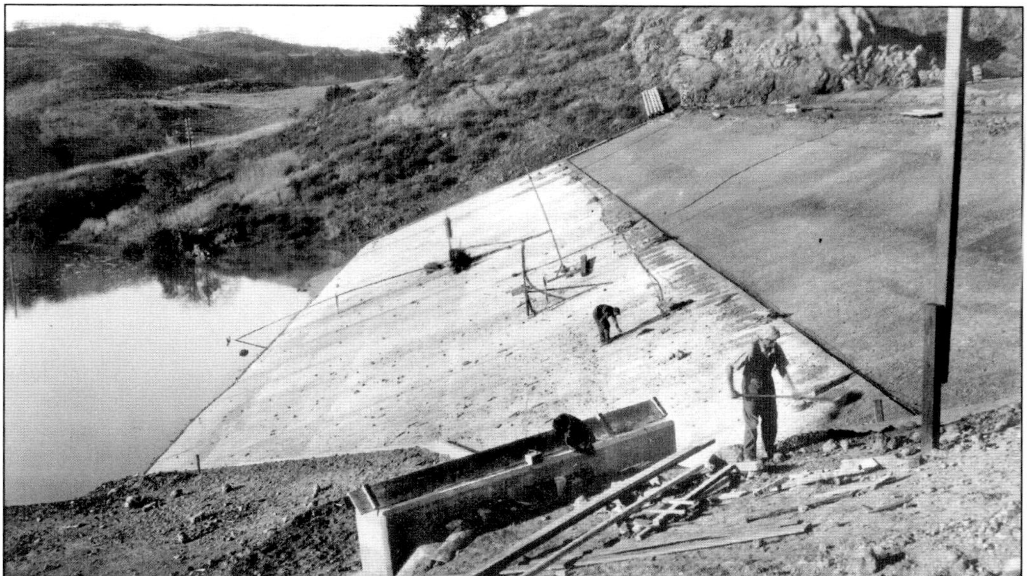

As the earth-filled dam was nearing completion, the face of the dam was covered with concrete. Later this became a popular place for people to swim and sun themselves while lying on the concrete.

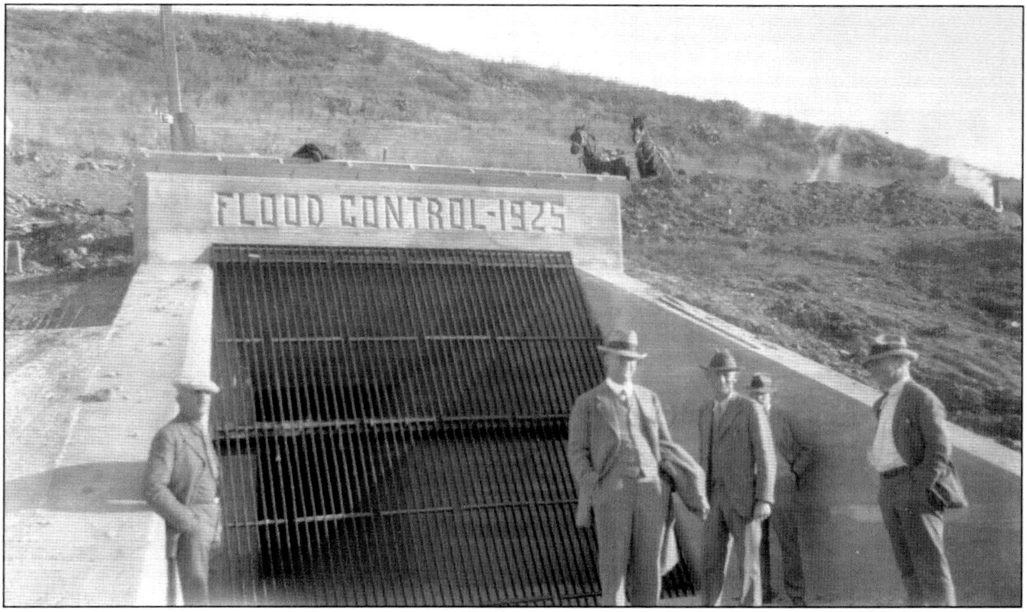

This photograph shows the water release gate of the Puddingstone Dam with Harry Walker, the third man from the right, who was then the president of the San Dimas Water Company.

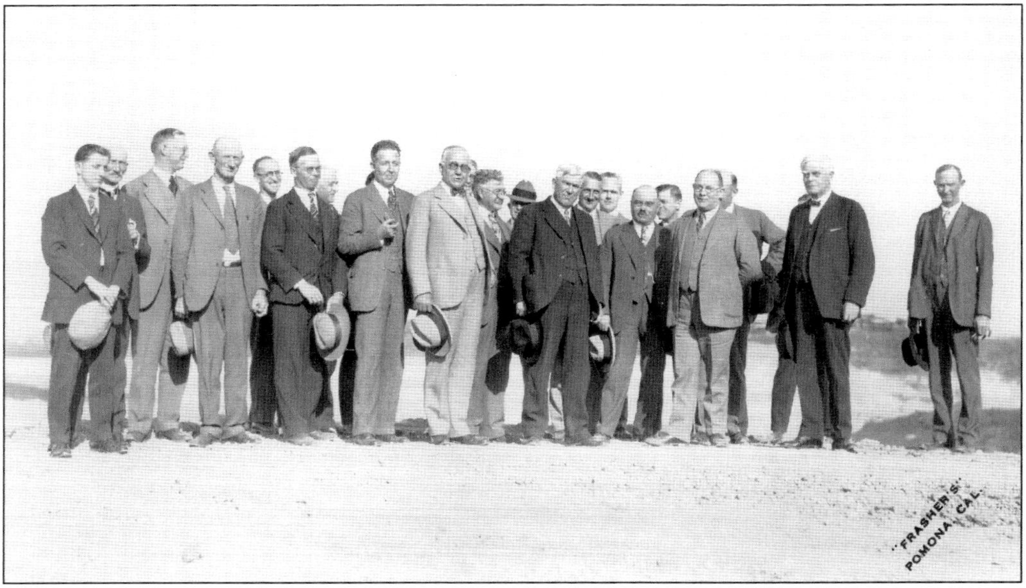

The dedication of the Puddingstone Reservoir and dam was held on January 5, 1928. Many of the early movers and shakers who made this project happen are pictured here, including Harry Walker, fourth from the left.

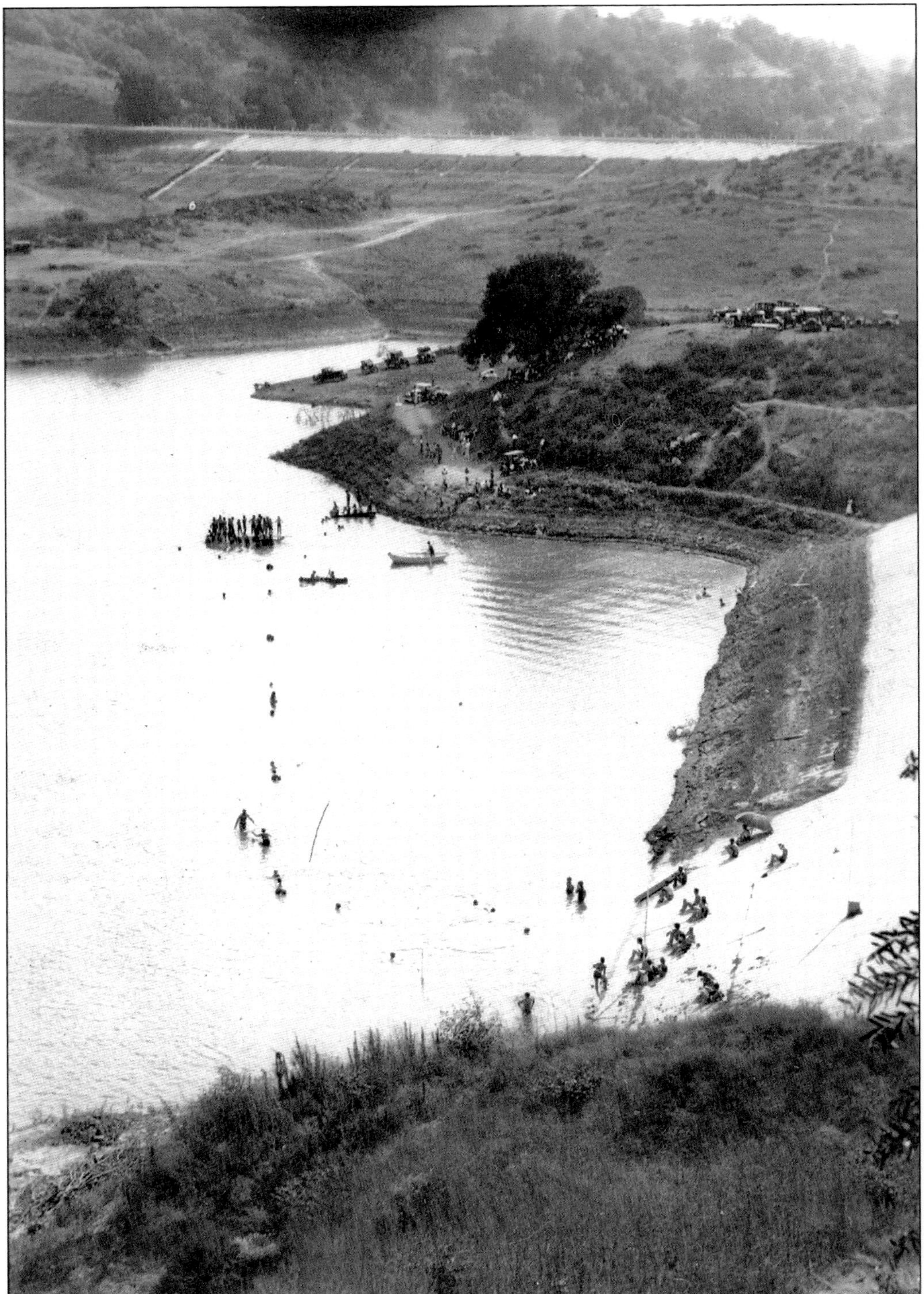

Once the reservoir was completed, it did not take long before people found out that this was a good place to swim and soak up the sun. The Puddingstone Reservoir and the surrounding land has become a large regional park and remains a very popular place during the summer months.

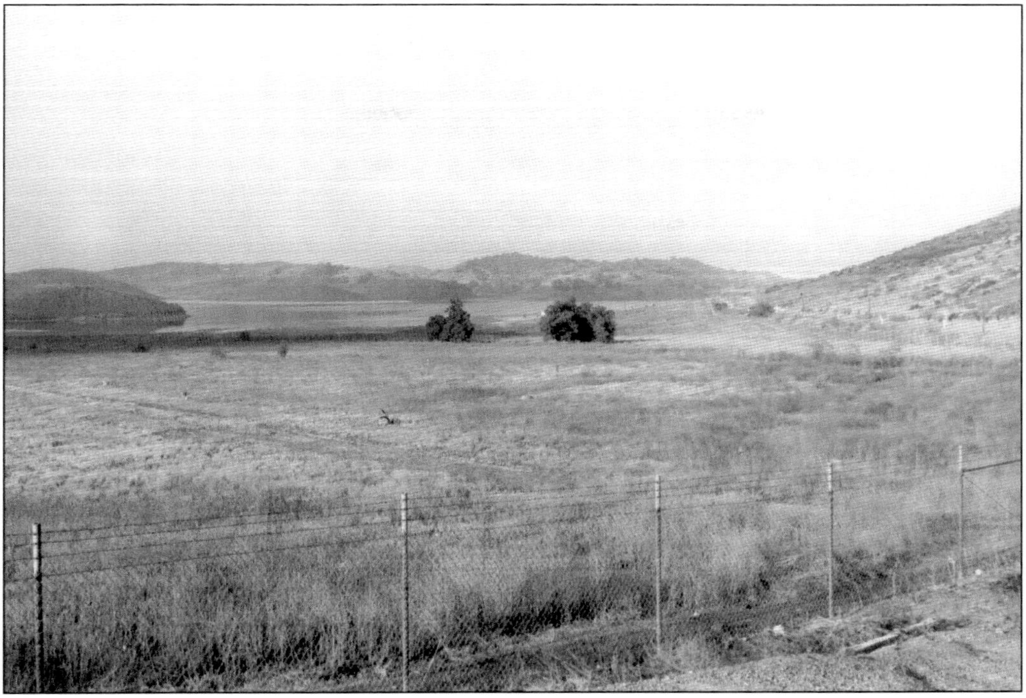

This view looks west across the valley that forms the site of the Puddingstone Reservoir. Before the land was purchased for the flood control reservoir, it was planted with citrus and fruit trees. The site still looks like this today except for homes built on the hills.

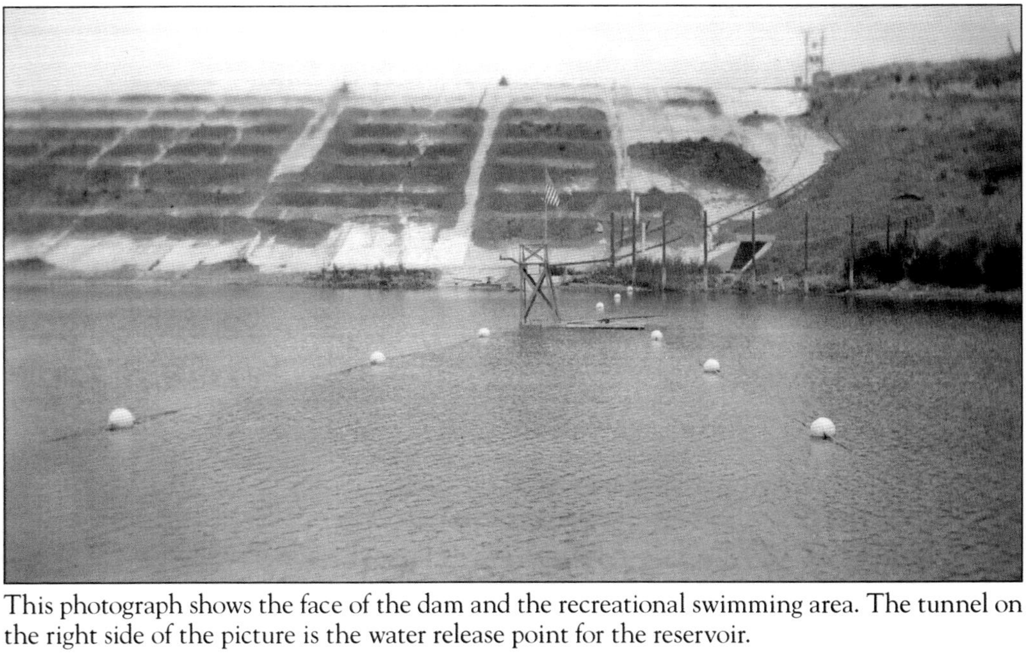

This photograph shows the face of the dam and the recreational swimming area. The tunnel on the right side of the picture is the water release point for the reservoir.

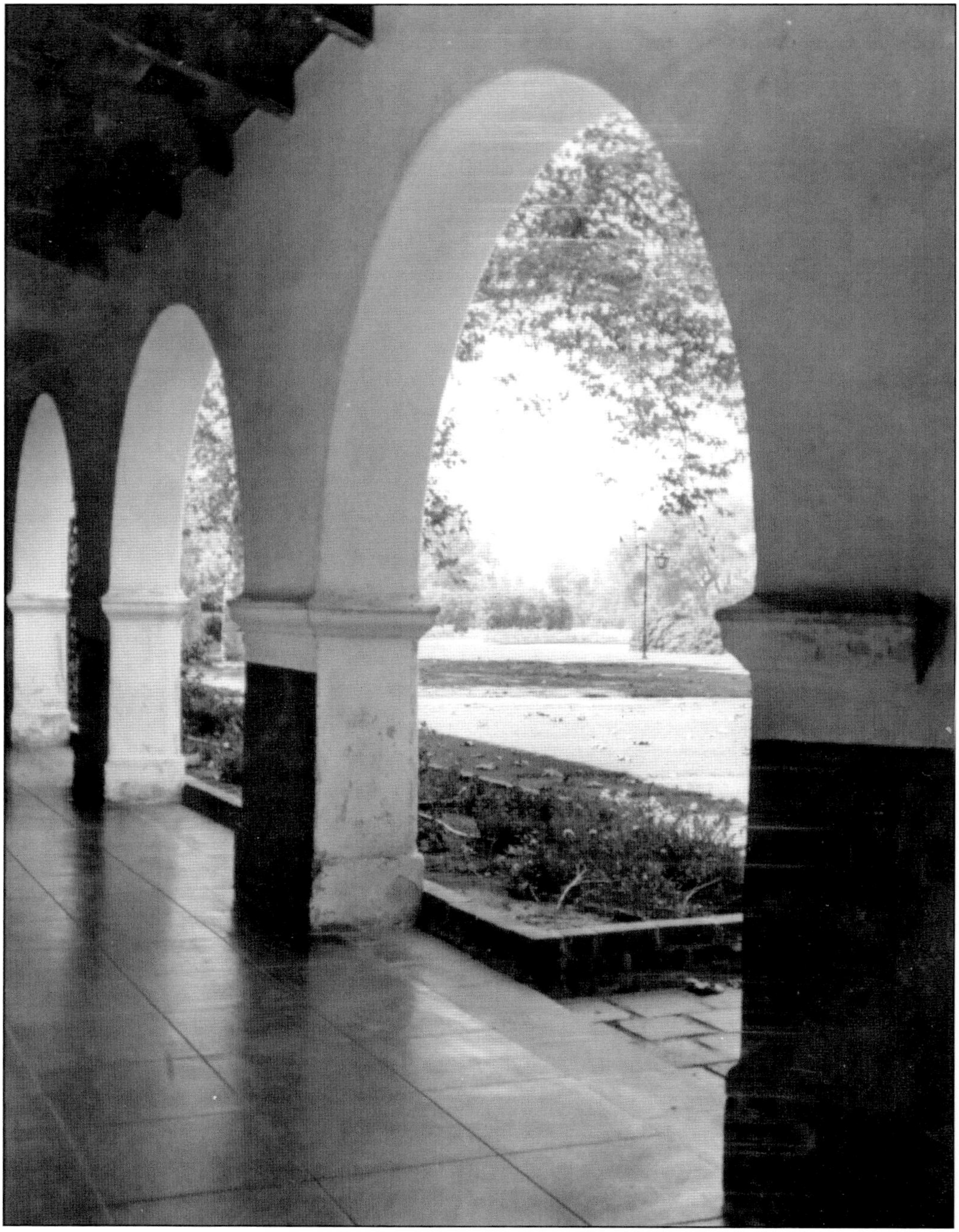

The arched approach to the administration building welcomed visitors to the Voorhis School for Boys, located along Walnut Creek in the southern part of San Dimas. Jerry Voorhis served as the headmaster of the school and later became a congressman in the 75th Congress of the United States.

Five

Voorhis School for Boys

Cal Poly Pomona, Voorhis Unit

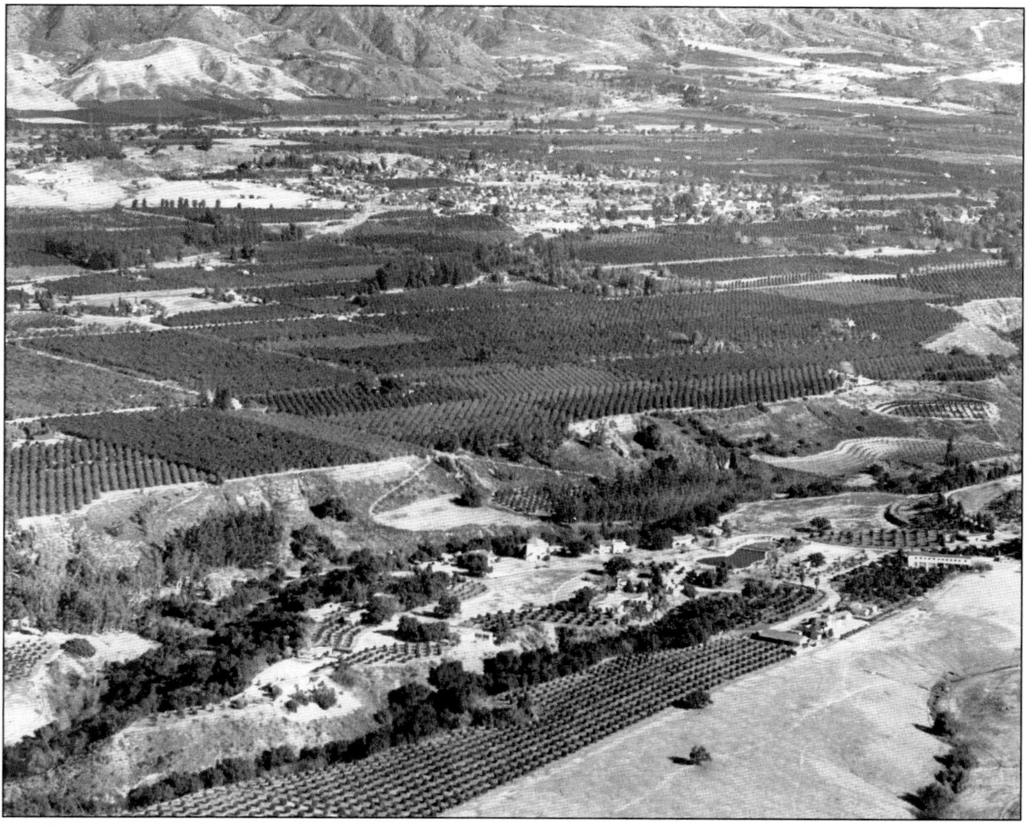

Nestled among the citrus groves along Walnut Creek, the Voorhis School for Boys was established in 1927. The school existed until 1938, when it was gifted to the State of California and became the Voorhis Unit of Cal Poly Pomona. The male students at Cal Poly (California Polytechnic State University) used this facility as their living spaces.

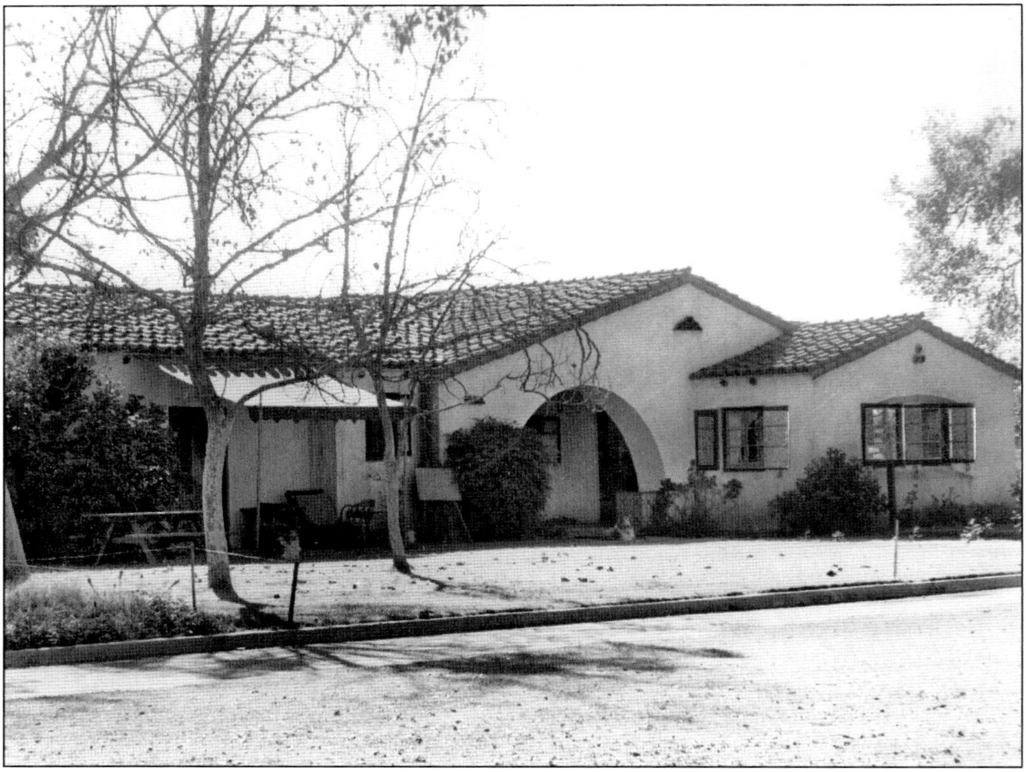

All the buildings at the Voorhis School for Boys were constructed in the Spanish motif. The sturdy construction has allowed the buildings to survive, and the facility is still in use today. One large building was constructed many years later when the property was a bible college; however, most of the area remains the same as when it was constructed.

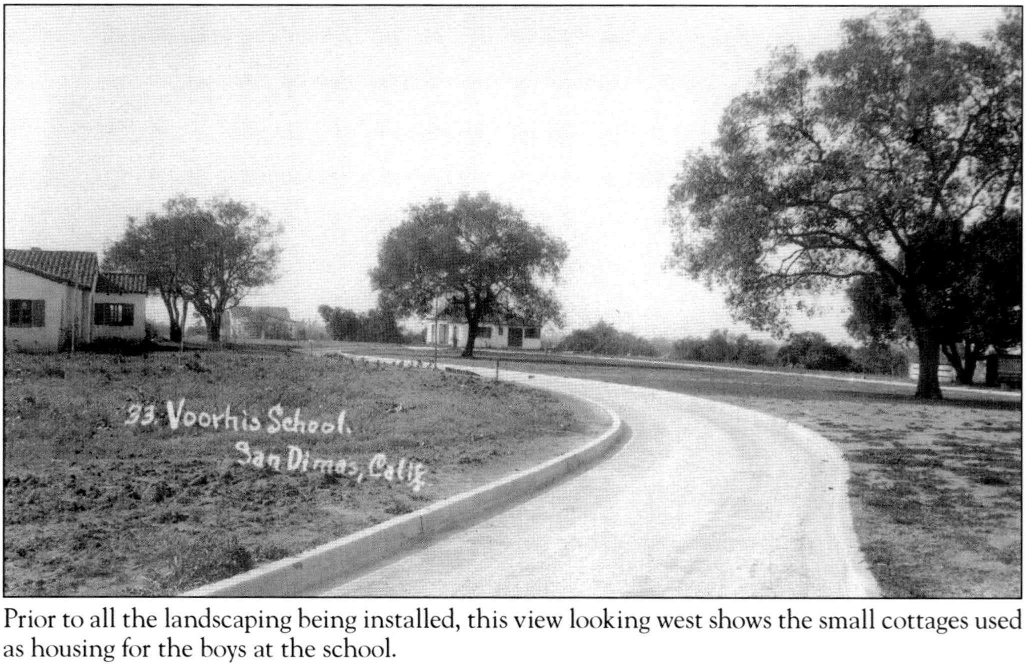

Prior to all the landscaping being installed, this view looking west shows the small cottages used as housing for the boys at the school.

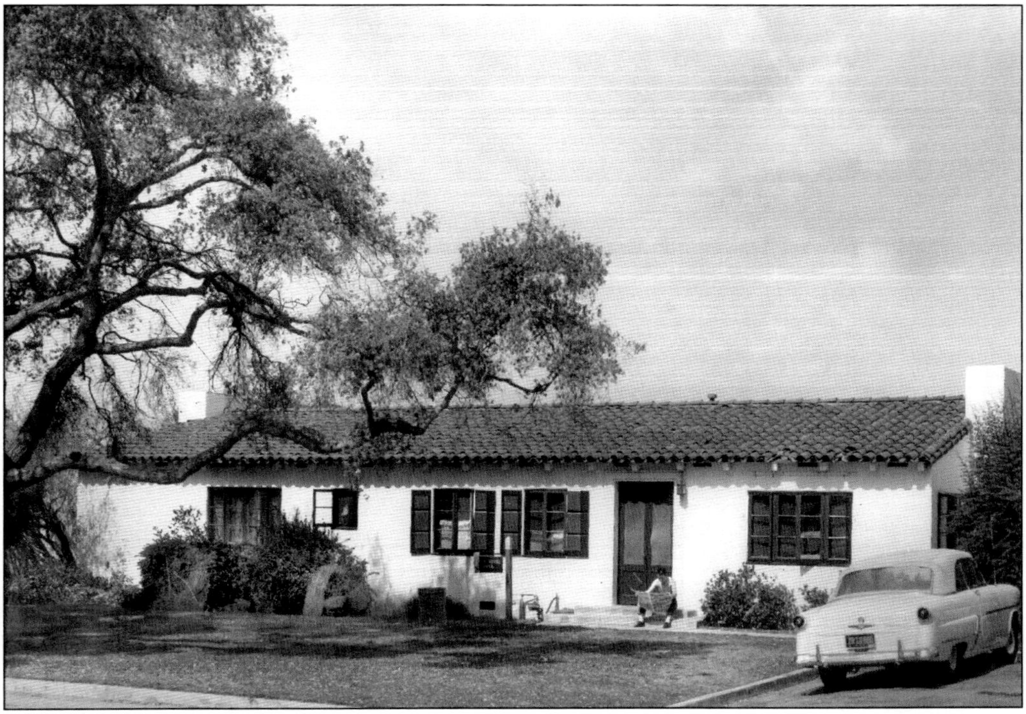

When the State of California opened the Voorhis Unit of Cal Poly, male students used the buildings as their living quarters and commuted to the campus in Pomona. Stories have been told of the young men trying to set a record on how fast they could drive the narrow winding roads to school and back.

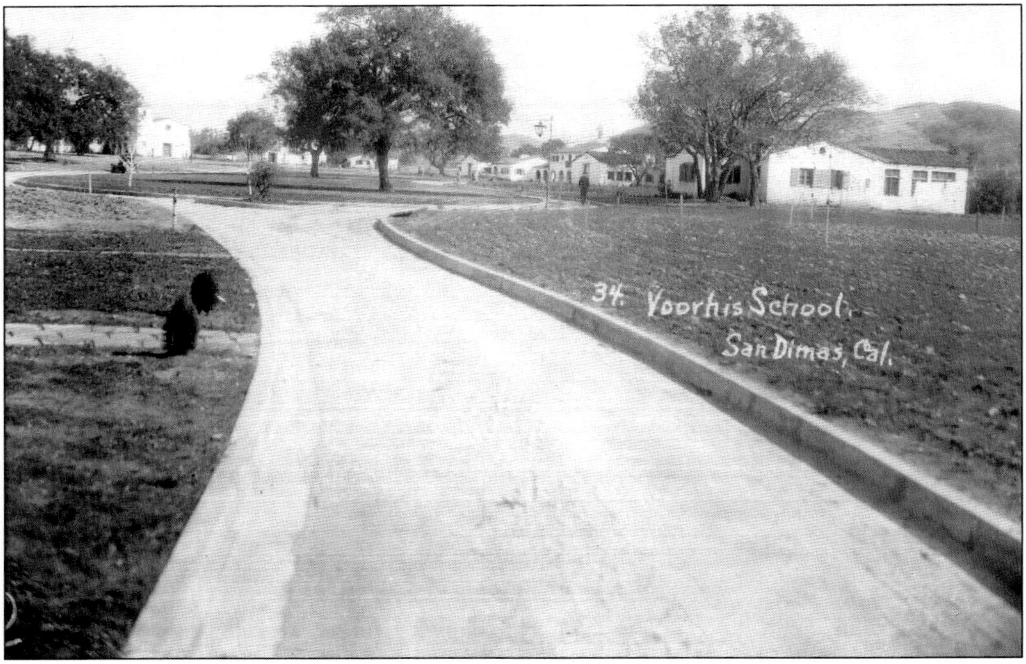

This picture shows another view of the open areas of the Voorhis School for Boys. The view is looking east with the chapel on the left side of the photograph.

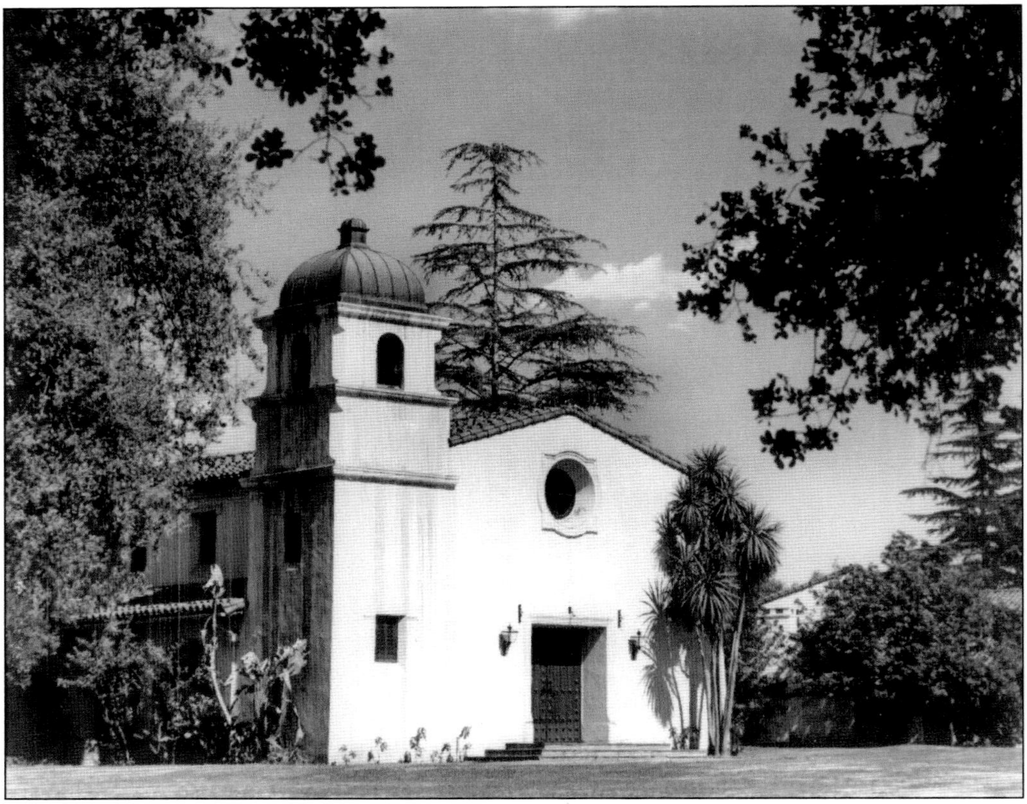

The chapel at the Voorhis site held services for the boys at the school and later for the students from Cal Poly Pomona. The building still exists and is used today.

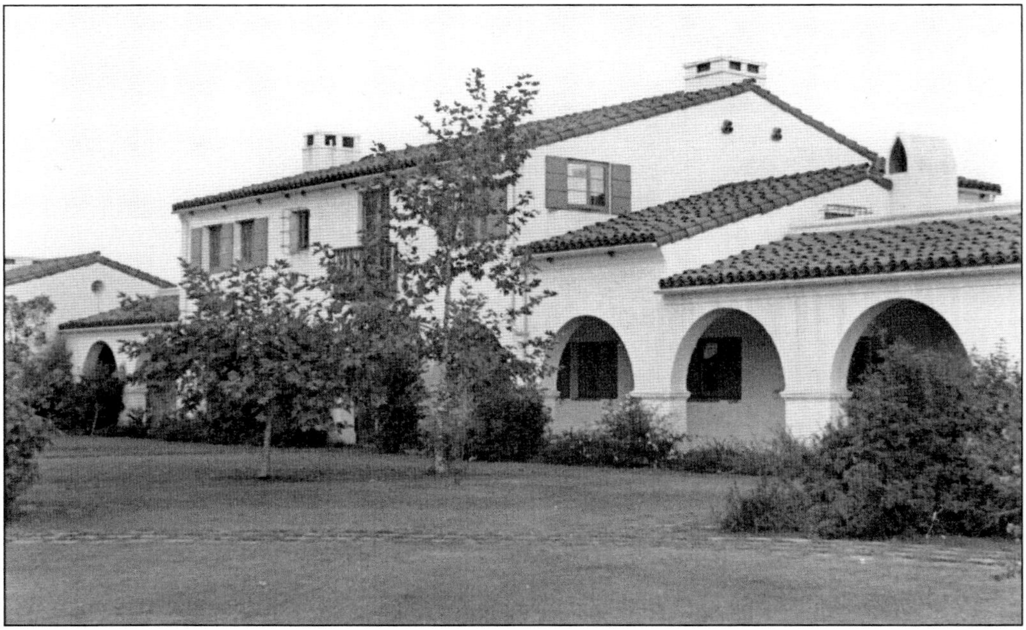

The large administration building on the campus is an imposing structure and the first to greet visitors to the center.

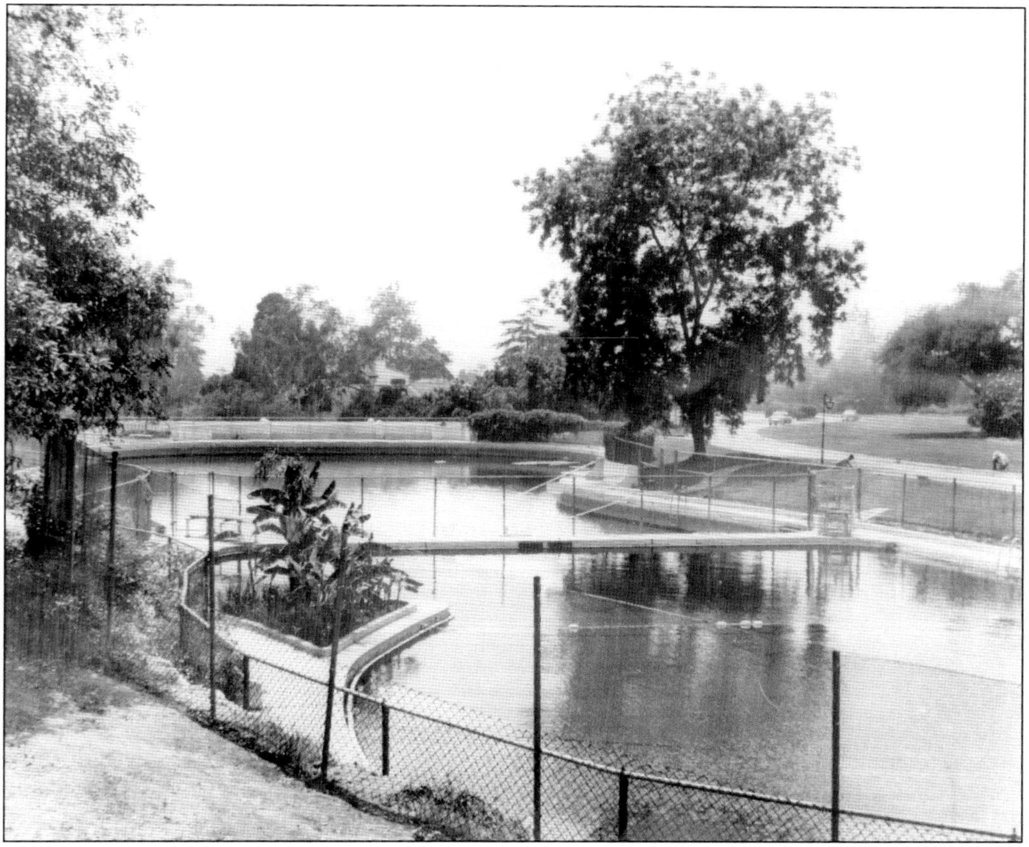

The water reservoir, or swimming pool, is in the center of the campus at Voorhis School. The story has it that Jerry Voorhis was able to get the "pool" built as a training facility for the 1932 Olympics.

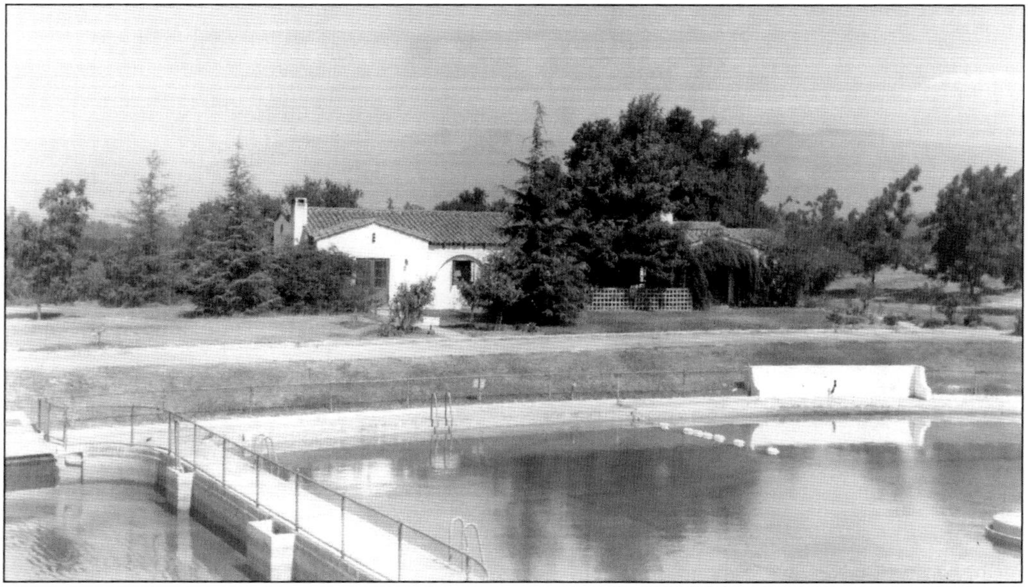

The San Gabriel Mountains make a beautiful background for the school's swimming pool.

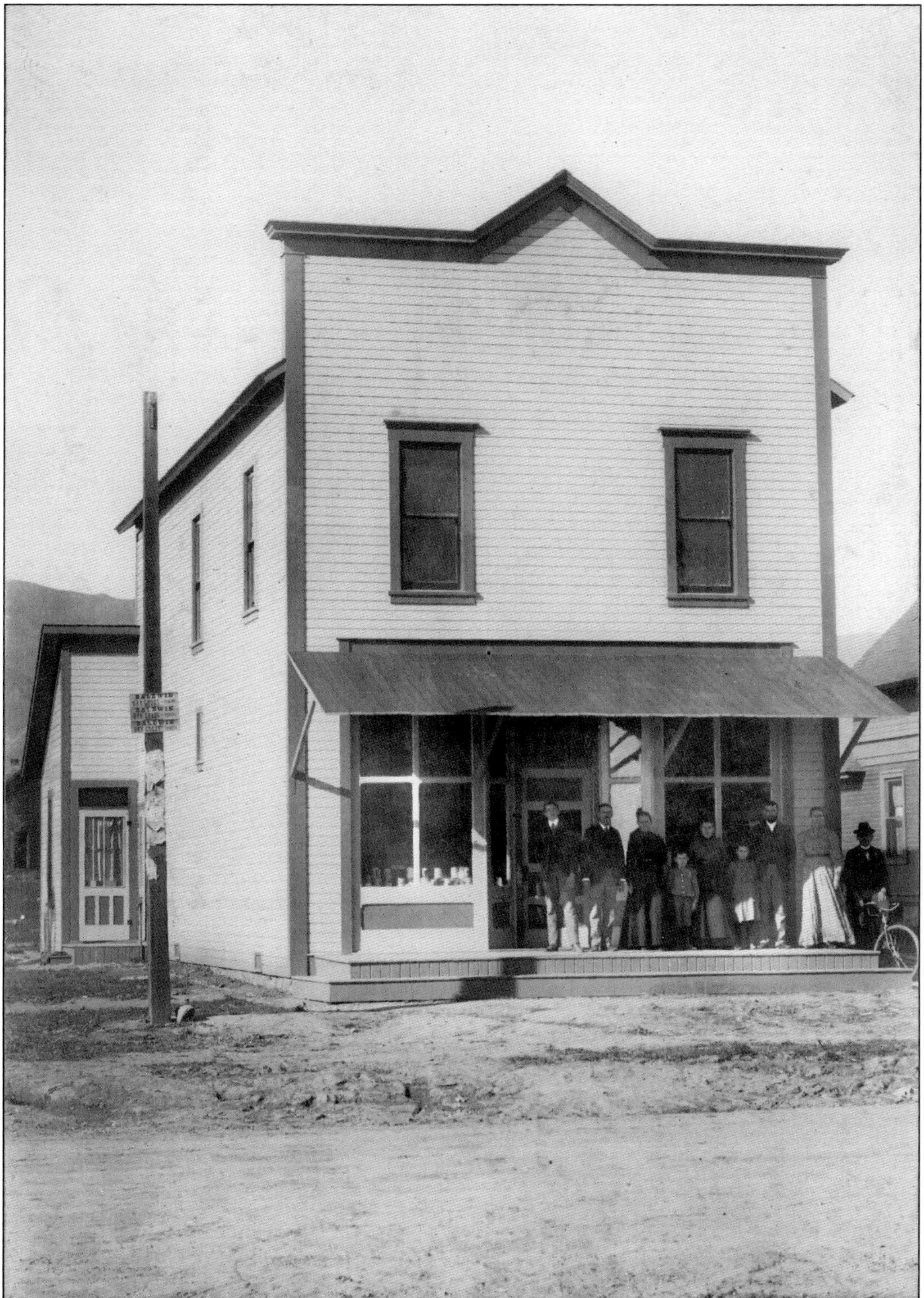

The first Neher Building, located at the corner of Bonita Avenue and Depot Street (today's Monte Vista Avenue), is seen here around 1901. It was later moved to allow a new building to be constructed.

Six

San Dimas 1887–1960

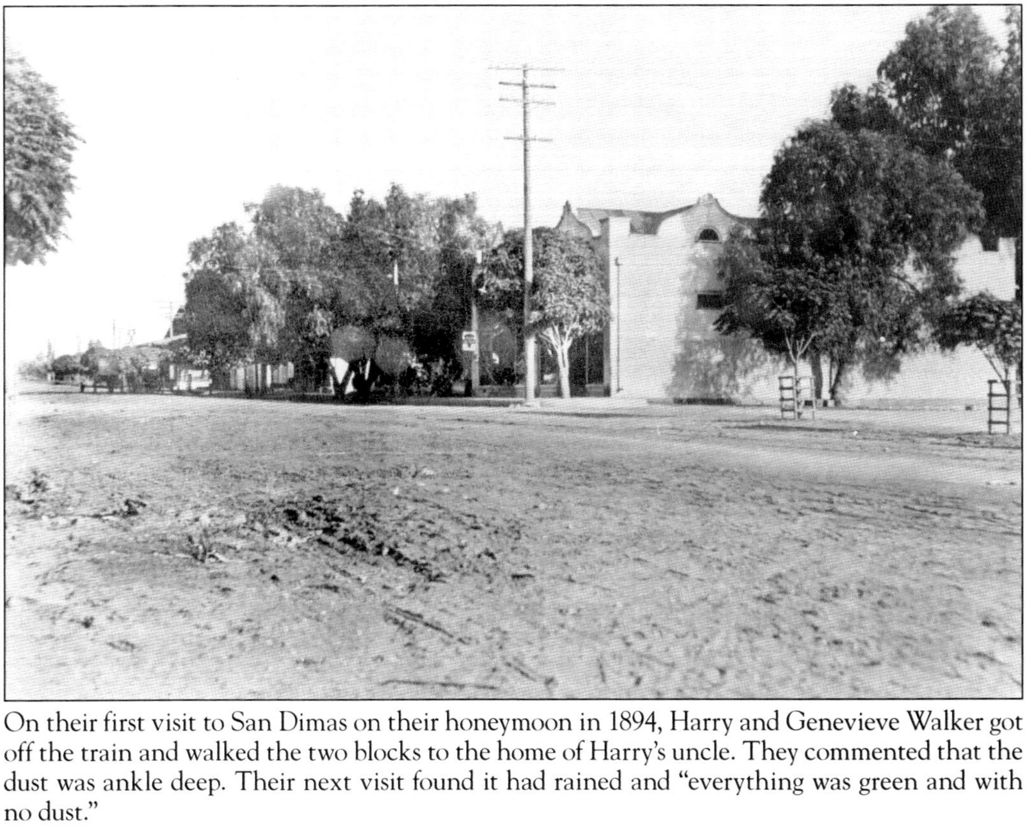

On their first visit to San Dimas on their honeymoon in 1894, Harry and Genevieve Walker got off the train and walked the two blocks to the home of Harry's uncle. They commented that the dust was ankle deep. Their next visit found it had rained and "everything was green and with no dust."

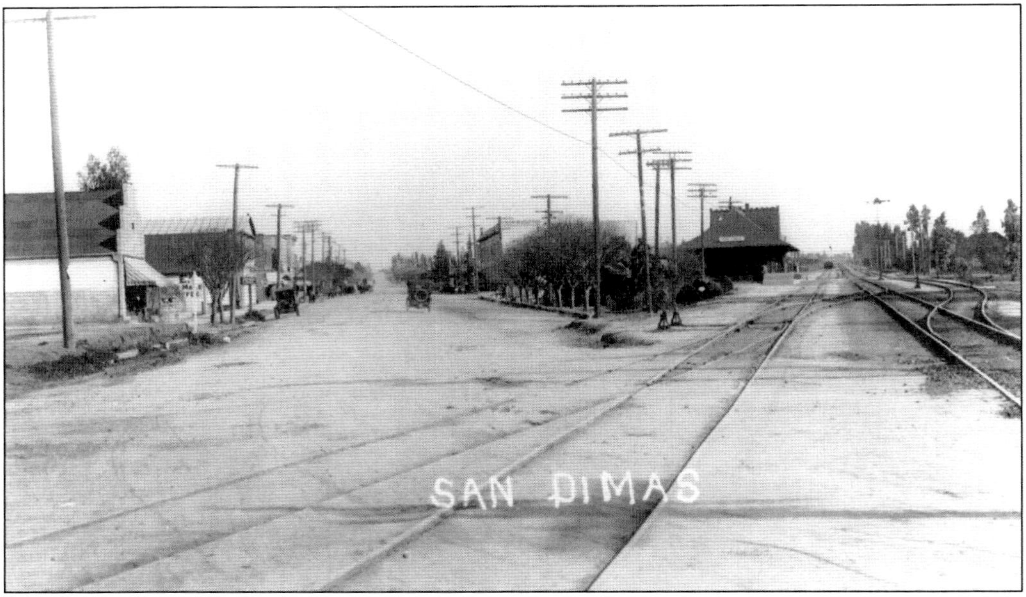

With the opening of the Santa Fe Railroad line through San Dimas in 1887, the town began to grow, although with dusty streets and few residents. In this photograph, the new train station can be seen in the right center of the picture.

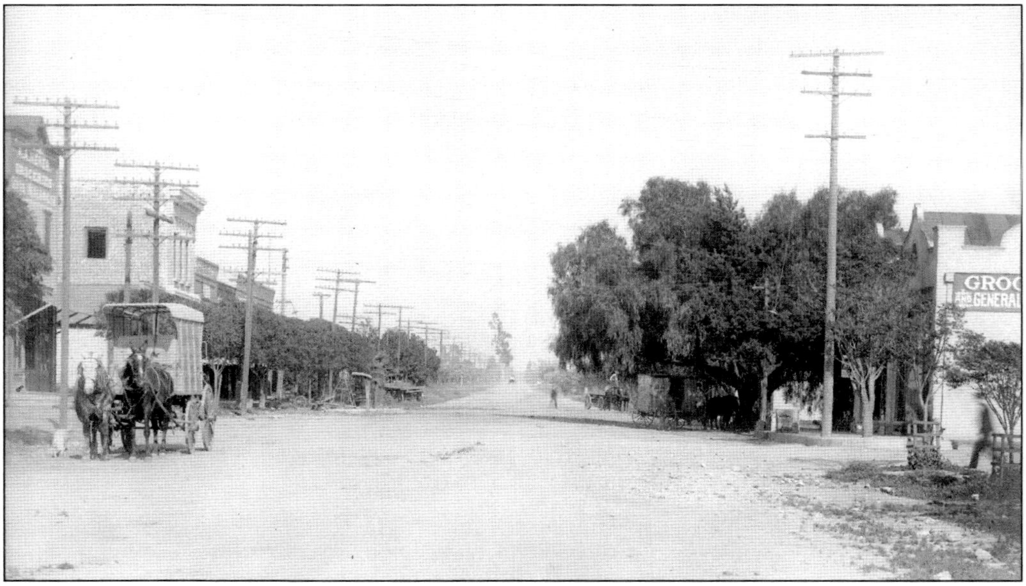

This picture shows the center of town with little activity. Most of the townspeople were busy establishing the new citrus groves and had little time to spend visiting.

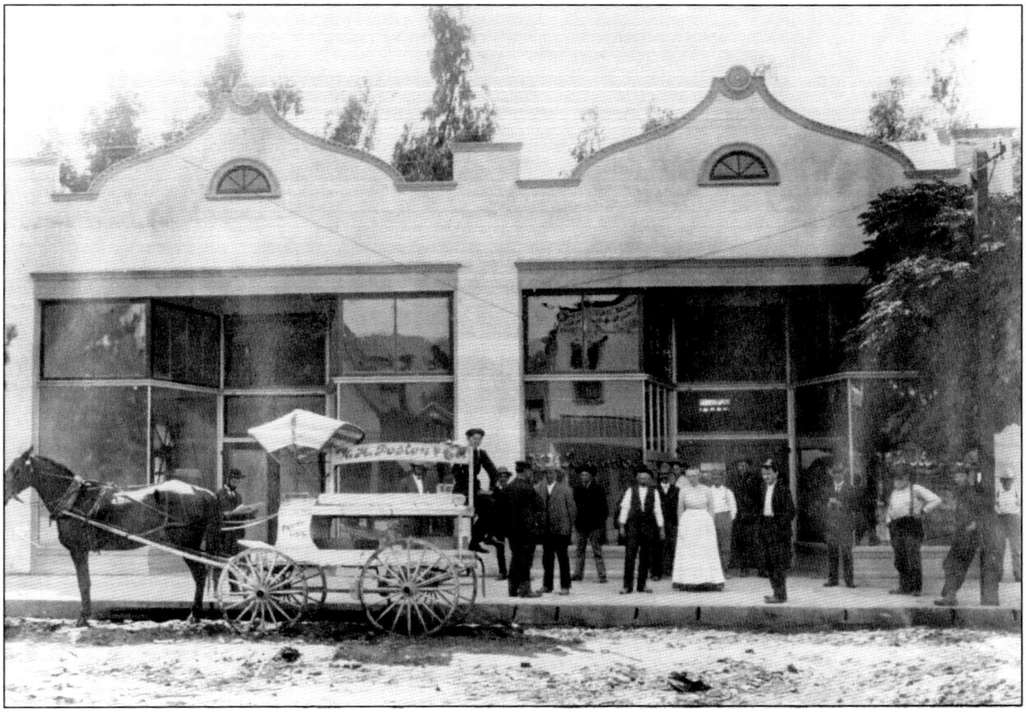

Poston's grocery store was located at the southeast corner of Bonita Avenue and Depot Street (now Monte Vista Avenue). Mr. and Mrs. William Macy, managers of the store, are in the foreground. The building lasted from 1902 to 1910.

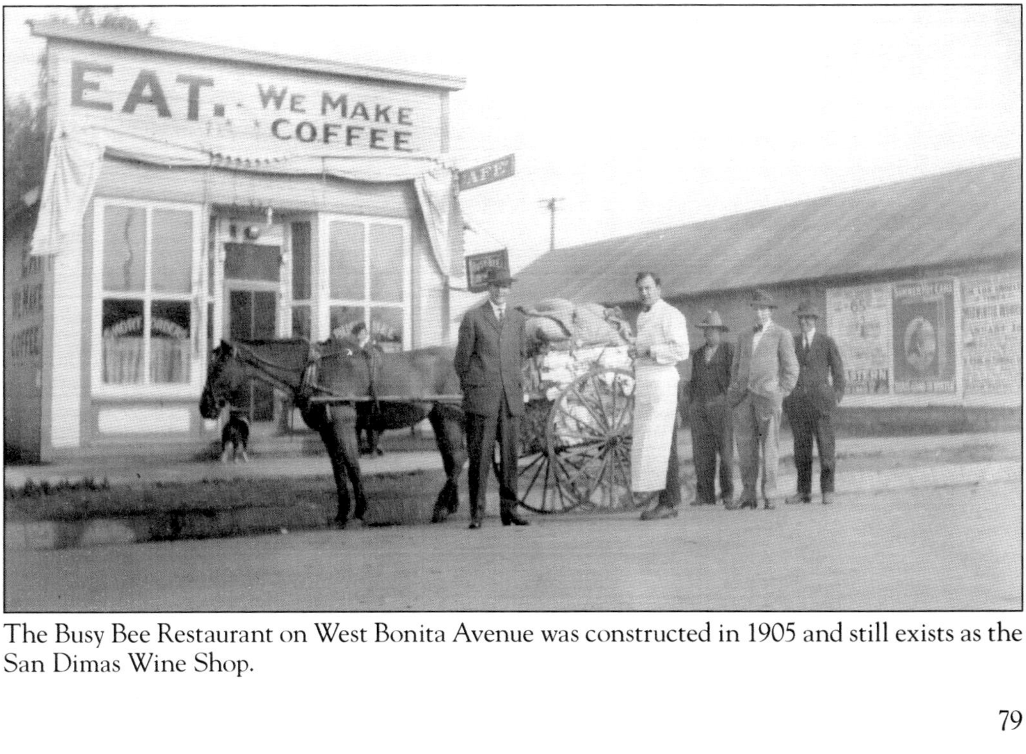

The Busy Bee Restaurant on West Bonita Avenue was constructed in 1905 and still exists as the San Dimas Wine Shop.

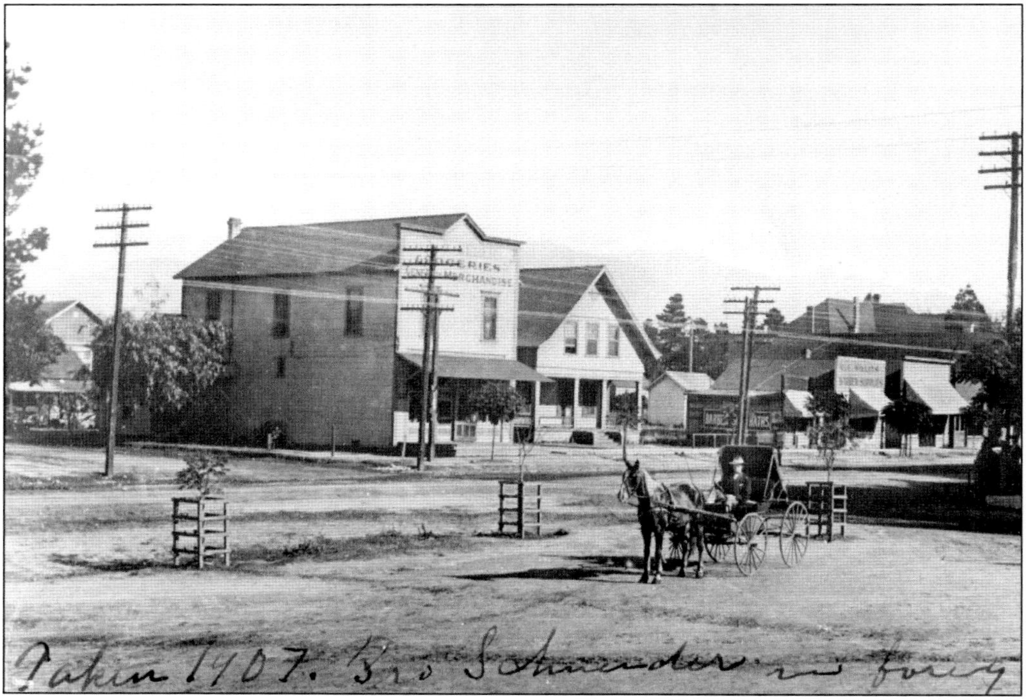

This photograph shows the original Neher Building, the boardinghouse, Uncle Ben's Jewelry, the barbershop, and Schneider's Grocery. Mr. Schneider sits in his horse and buggy in the foreground c. 1907.

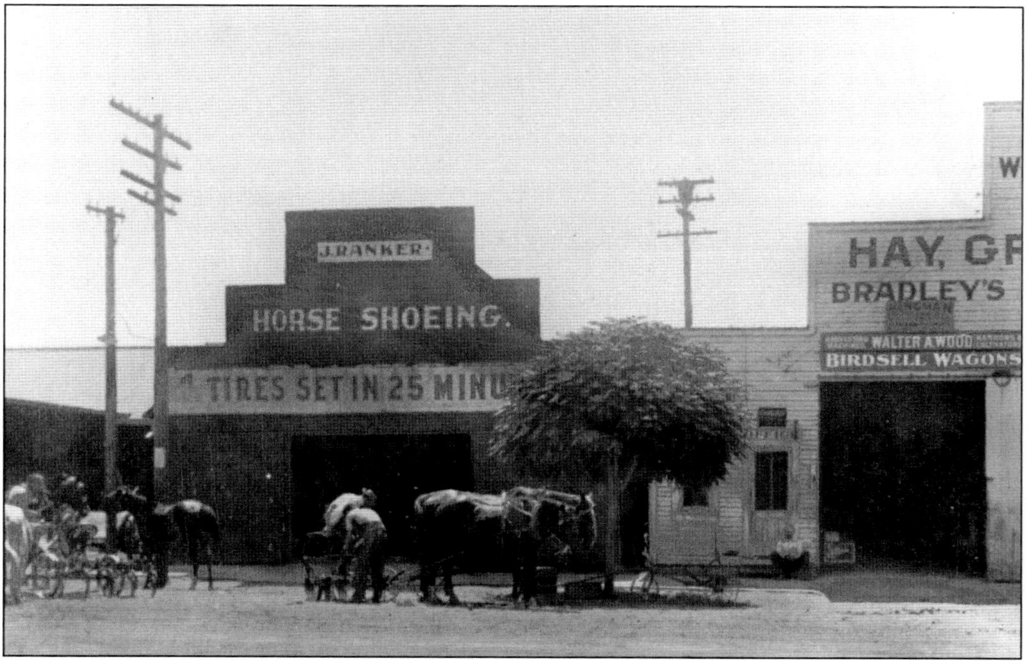

This 1907 photograph shows businesses along the south side of Bonita Avenue. Buildings such as this did not last too long, while many of the old brick buildings still exist today.

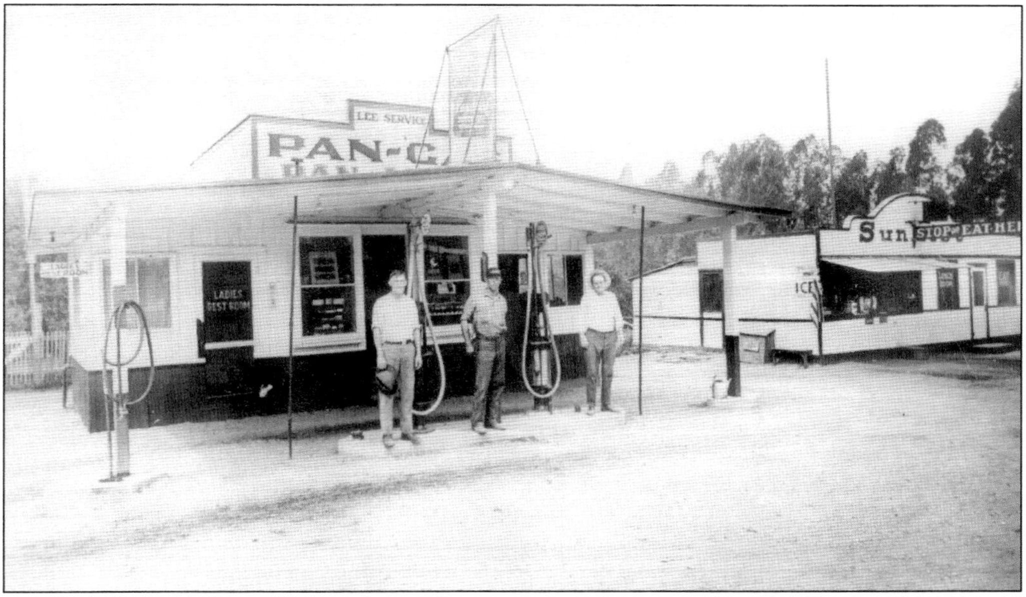

The gas station at the corner of Cataract and Bonita Avenues had a small diner located next door. Various versions of these buildings stood here over the years but are now gone.

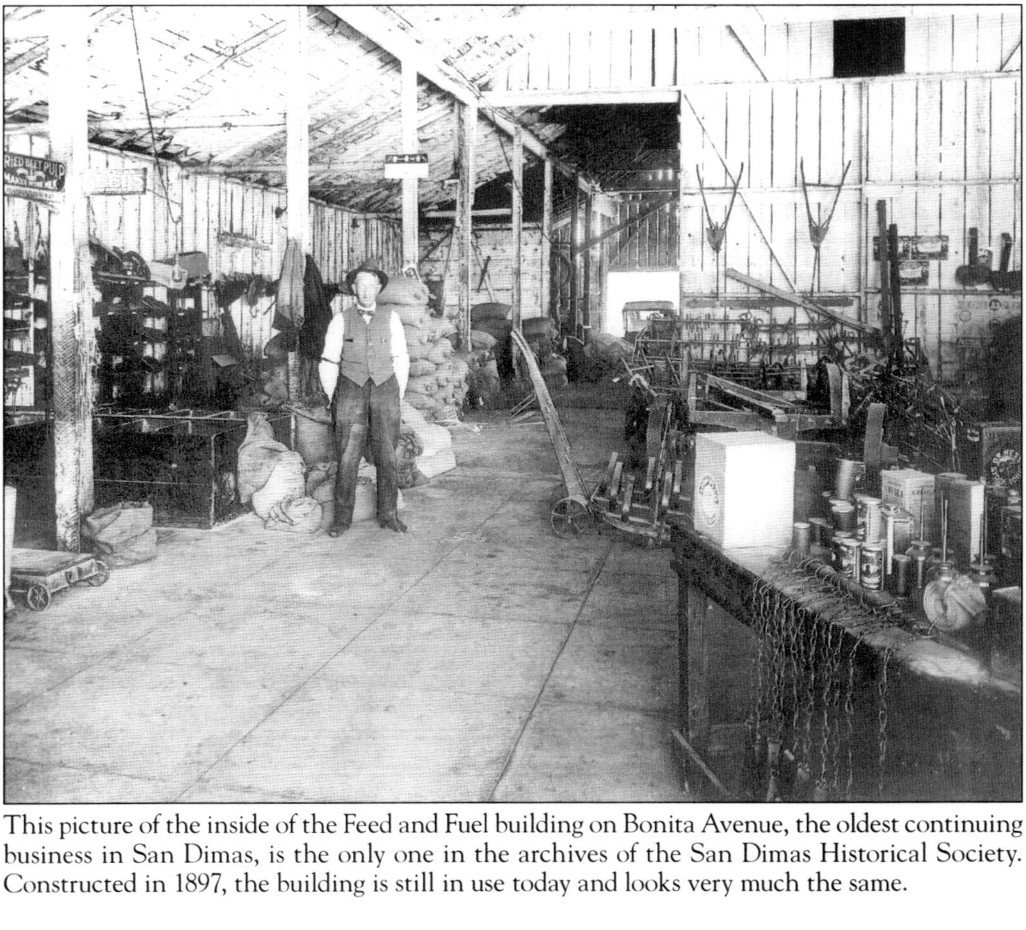

This picture of the inside of the Feed and Fuel building on Bonita Avenue, the oldest continuing business in San Dimas, is the only one in the archives of the San Dimas Historical Society. Constructed in 1897, the building is still in use today and looks very much the same.

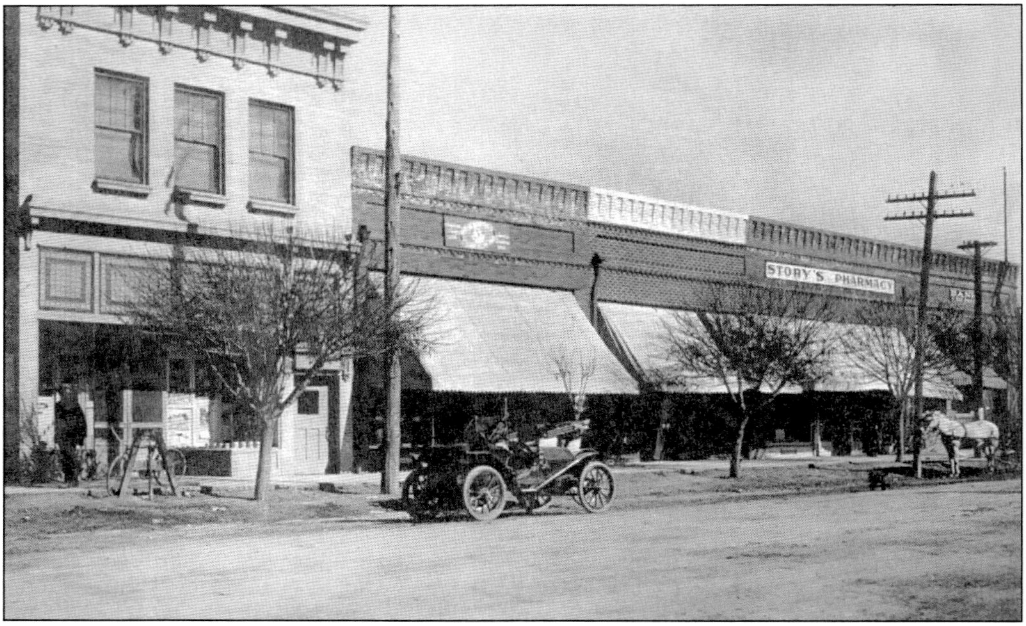

This photograph shows the north side of Bonita Avenue in the center of town in 1911. The brick buildings in the picture are still in place today, although with newer cars parked in front.

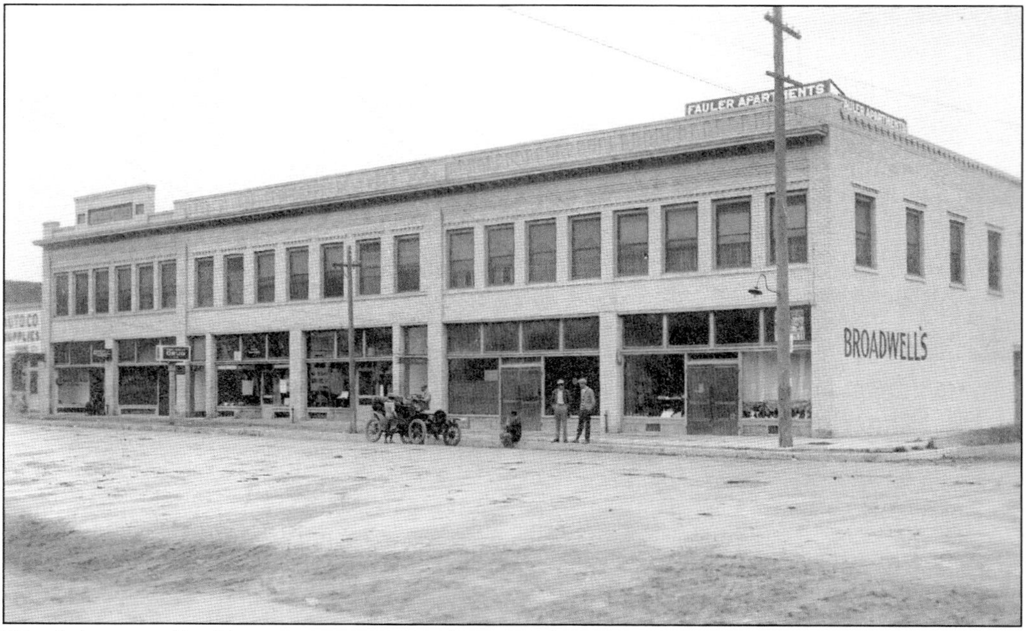

The Johnstone Building was constructed in 1910 by James A. and William A. Johnstone. A drugstore, restaurant, grocery stores, barbershops, and many other businesses have occupied the main floor over the years. The second story was used as office space and apartments. The building also has a basement. The structure still stands and houses the popular Roady's restaurant.

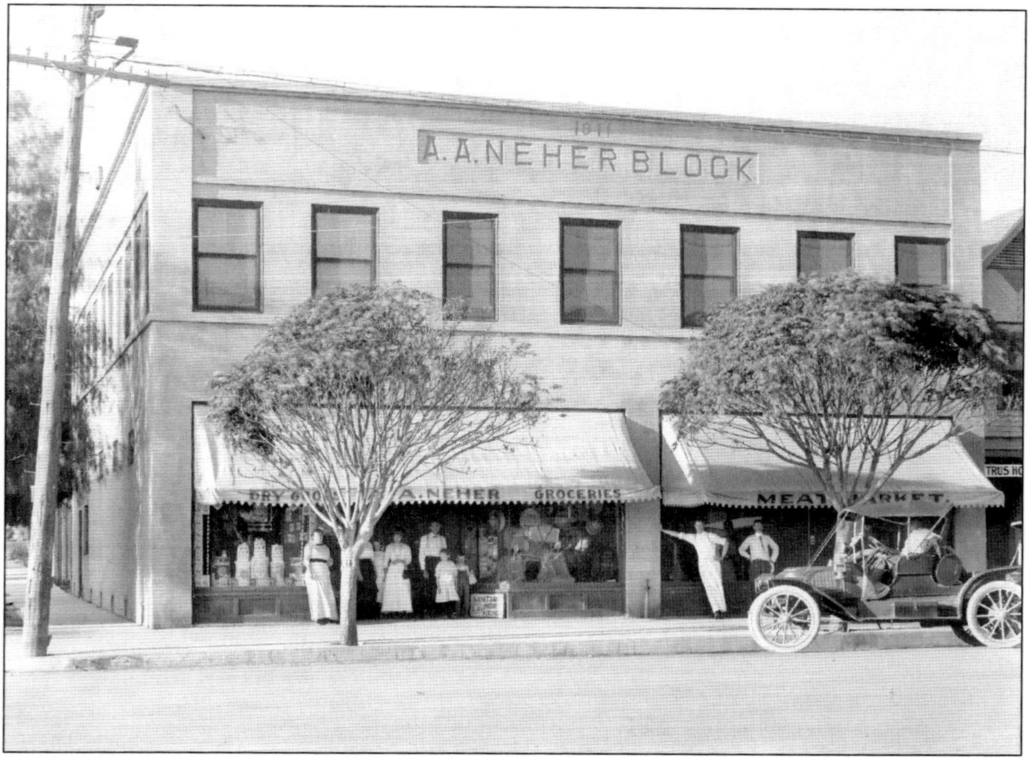

The second Neher Building, constructed in 1911, was used as a grocery store and many other ventures. The building is still in use today as an import-export business.

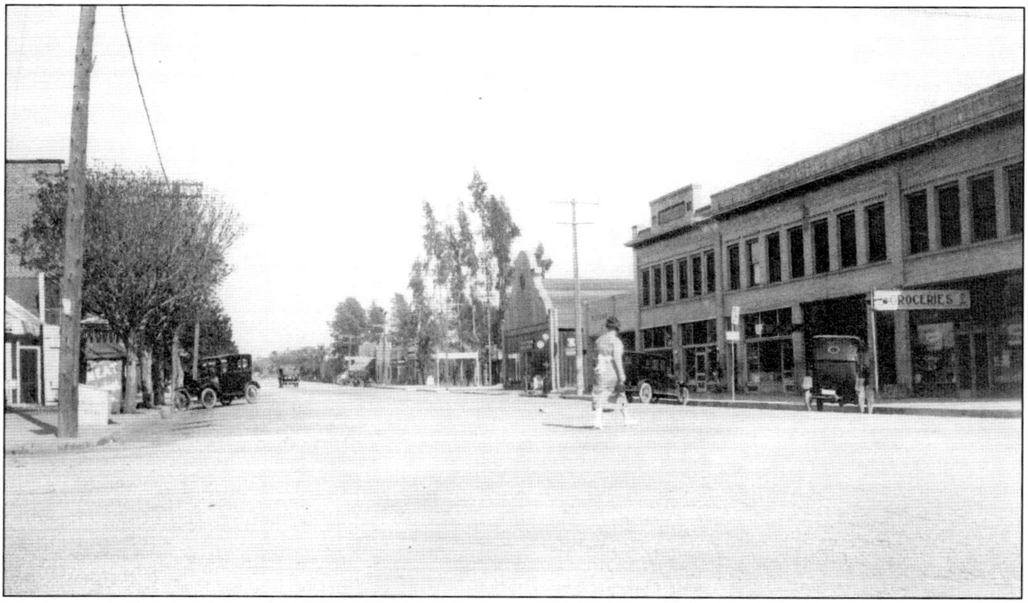

An eastward view from the corner of Bonita Avenue and Depot Street on April 14, 1922, shows a typically busy day in San Dimas. The two larger buildings on the right side of the picture still stand today.

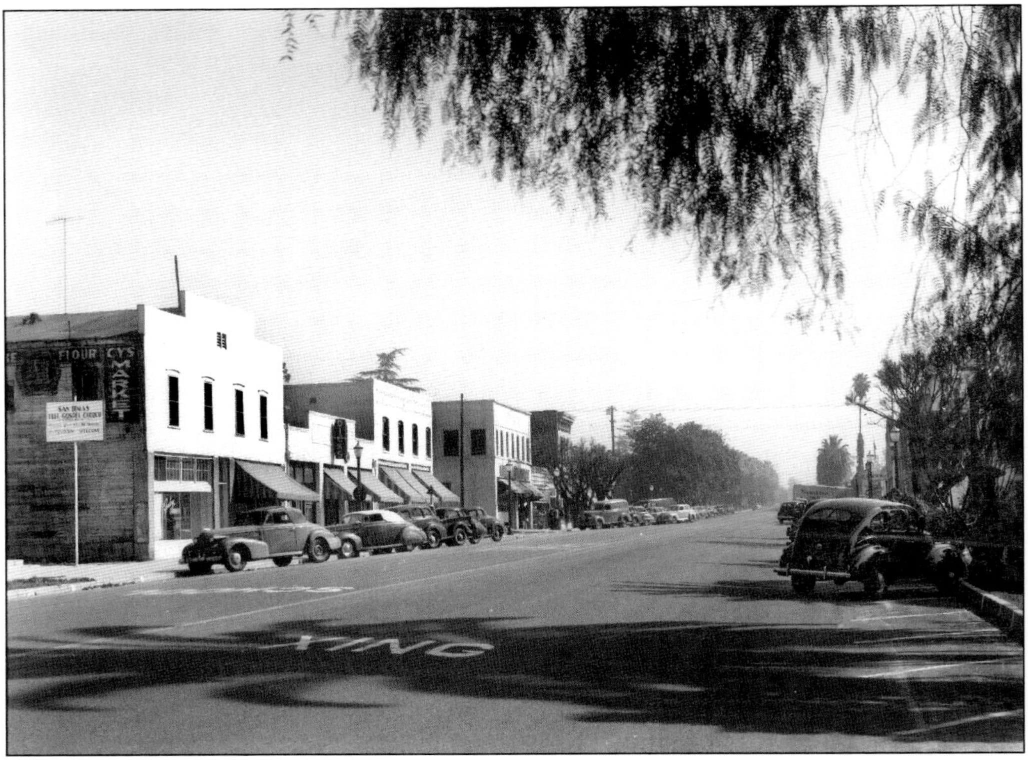

A 1940 picture of downtown San Dimas looks east from Rhodes Park. Nearly all the buildings seen in this picture still exist.

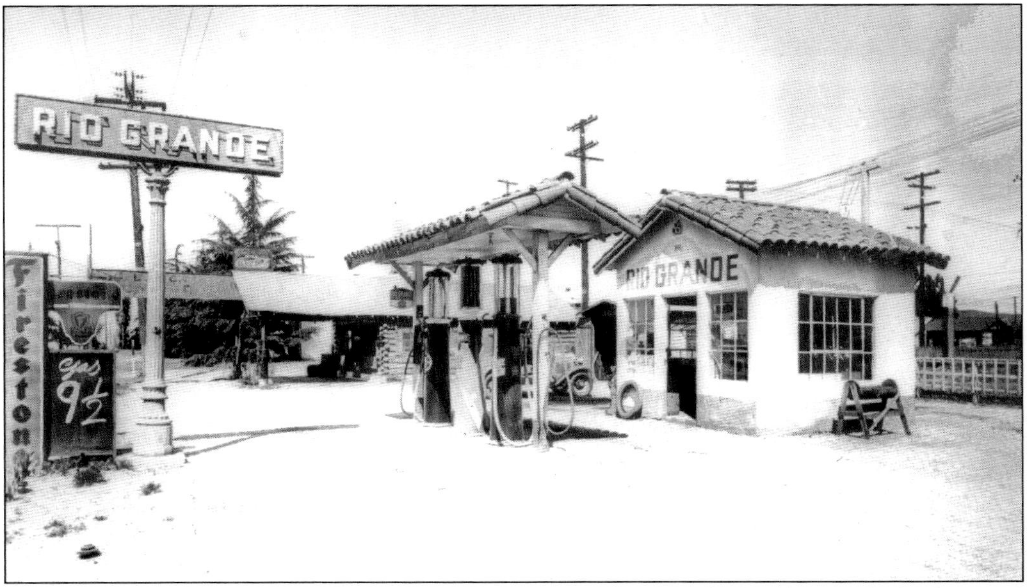

The c. 1932 Rio Grande gas station was operated by Walter Davis. The building in the background is the Old Log Cabin beer joint. Note the price of gas—9.5¢ per gallon.

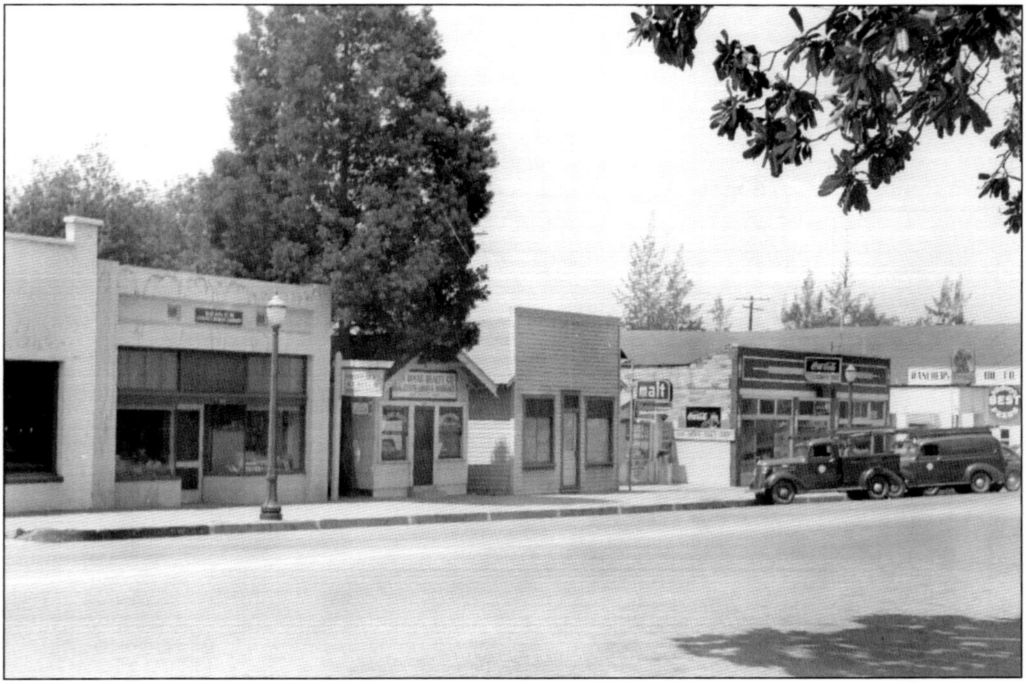

This picture is an early view of the south side of Bonita Avenue, the main street of San Dimas, looking west. The buildings behind the vehicles are now gone, replaced by new businesses. The building on the left side of the picture was the library and is now a restaurant.

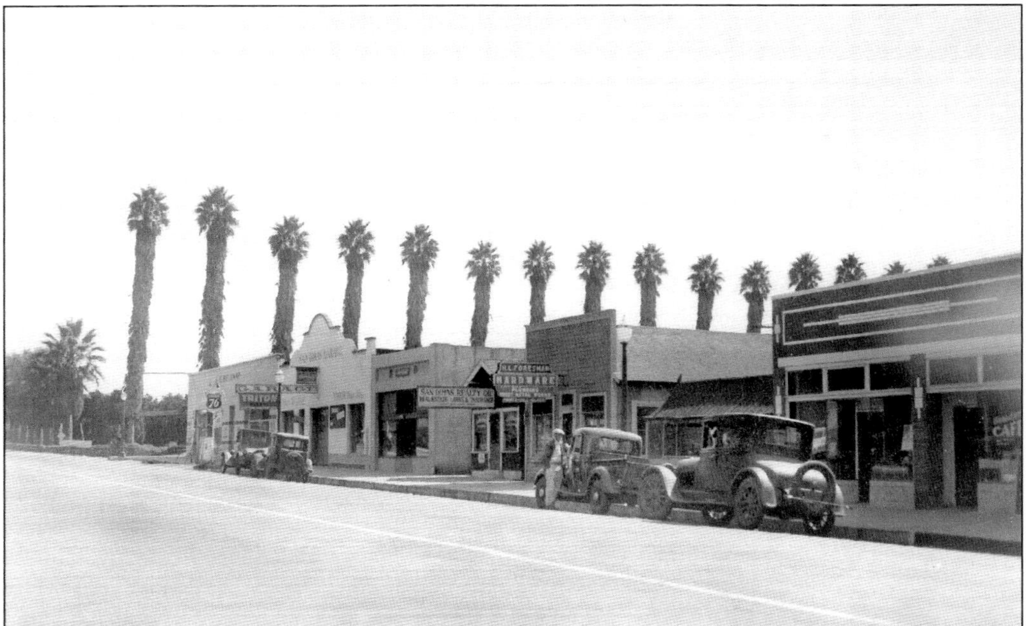

The south side of Bonita Avenue looking east with the Ford dealership on the corner is not much different from the westward view. The last three buildings on the left side of the picture remain while the others have been replaced.

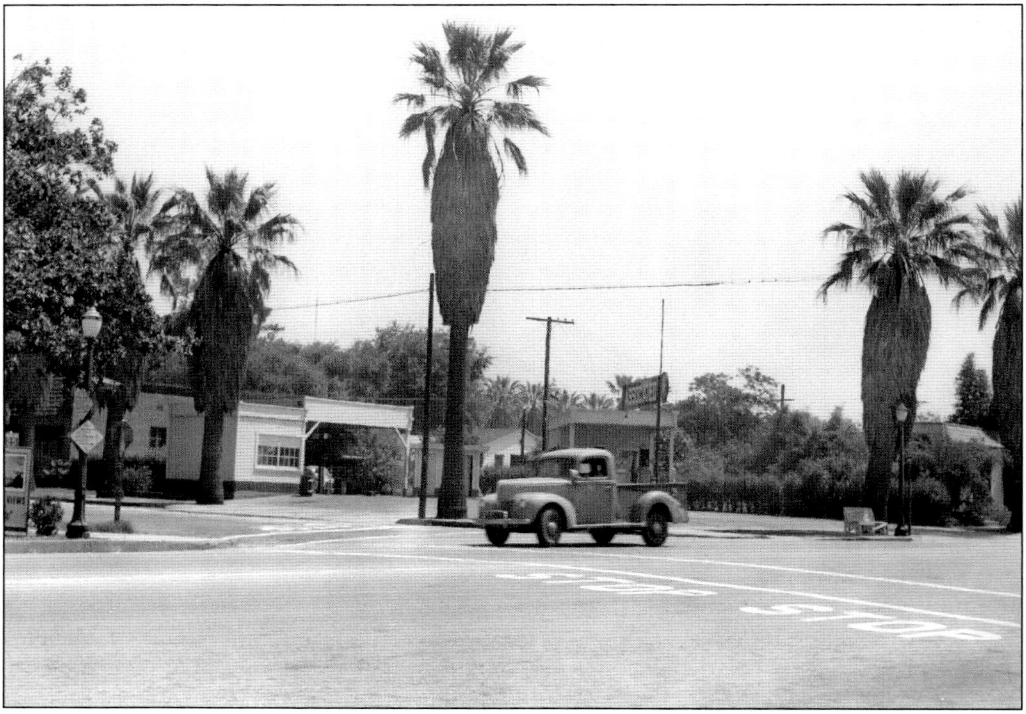

This is the intersection of Bonita and San Dimas Avenues in the 1950s. The intersection today is the "center" of town, with much more traffic. The old gas station is gone.

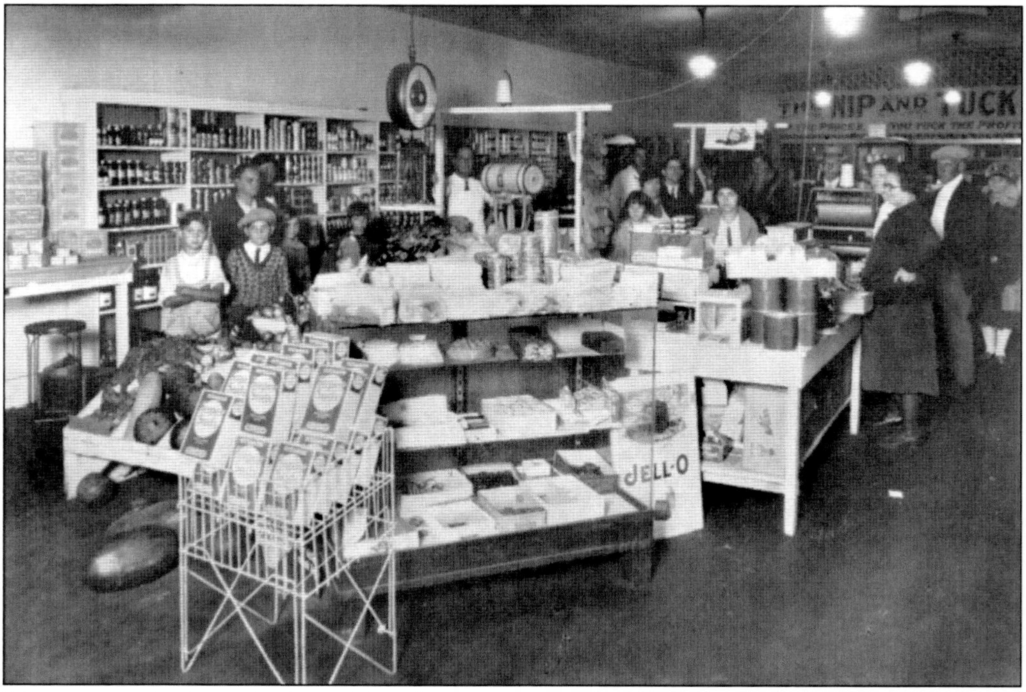

The markets in the early days of San Dimas were much more enjoyable to shop in. They were not the large stores of today; however, shoppers were able to obtain whatever they needed. This is the Nip and Tuck Market.

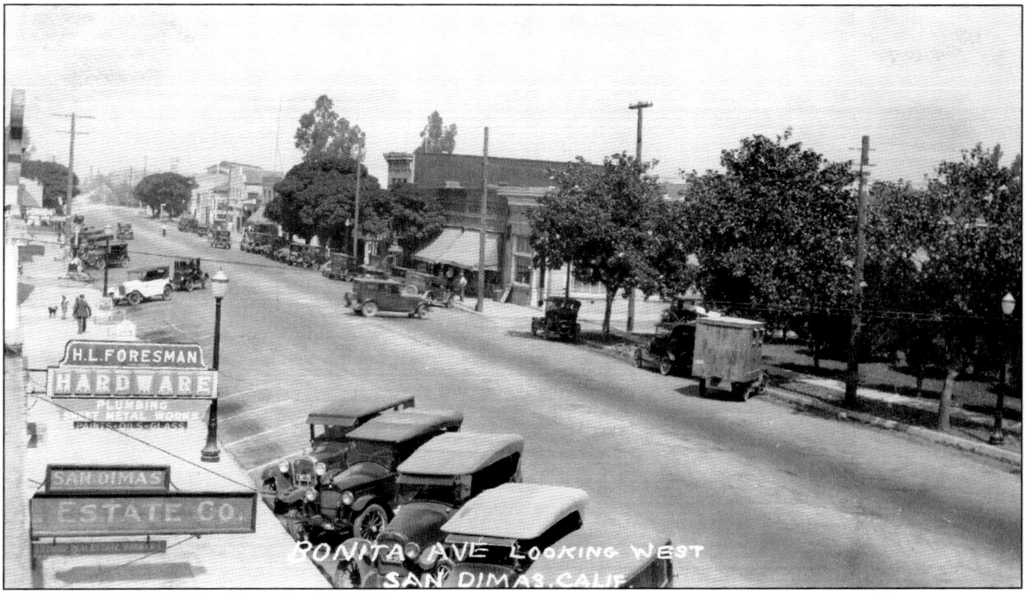

This is a *c.* 1928 view of Bonita Avenue looking west from atop the San Dimas Garage. The orange grove at the upper right side of this picture is now the site of the Bank of America.

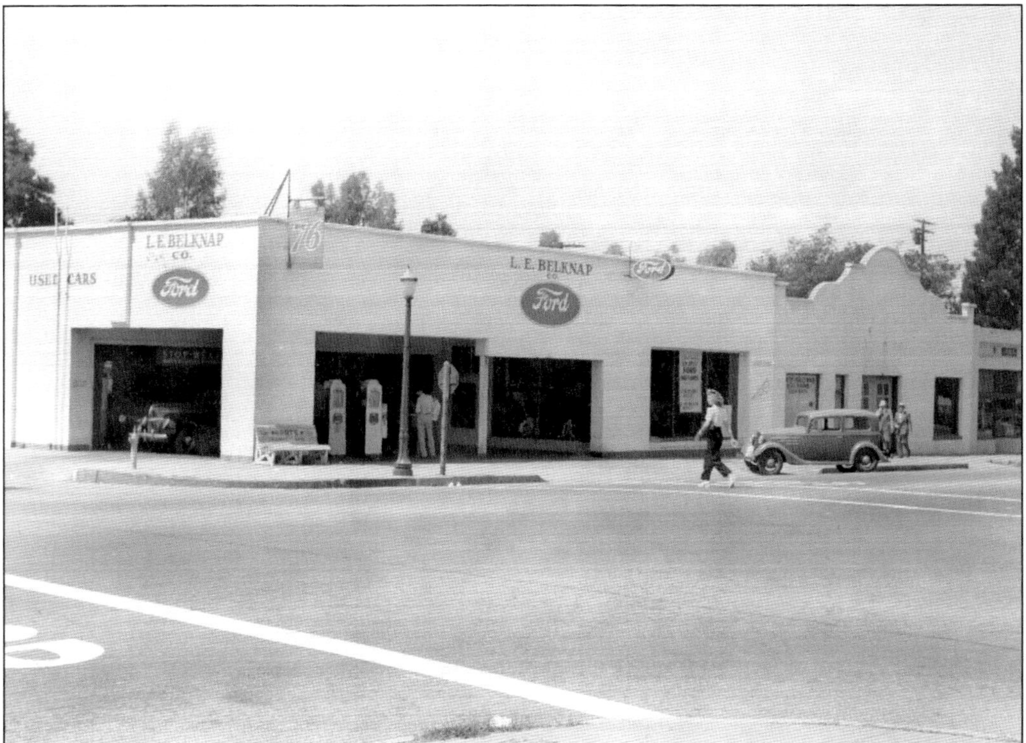

The Belknap Ford agency lasted in town for many years, and the building is now used as the Goodyear Tire business. The building to the right, with the fancy facade, is the old San Dimas Garage, constructed in 1910. It now appropriately houses the Old Ford Parts store. This is the southwest corner of Bonita and San Dimas Avenues around 1940.

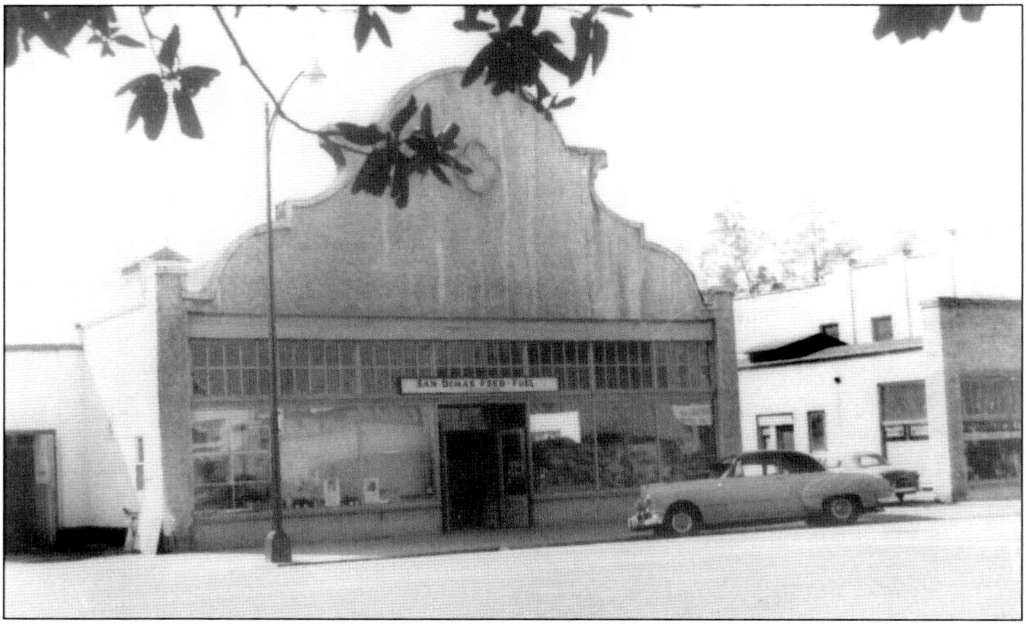

The San Dimas Feed and Fuel, now know as the Feed and Grain, is the oldest continuously operating business in San Dimas. The building was constructed in 1897 by William A. Johnstone and has served San Dimas and the surrounding area since that date.

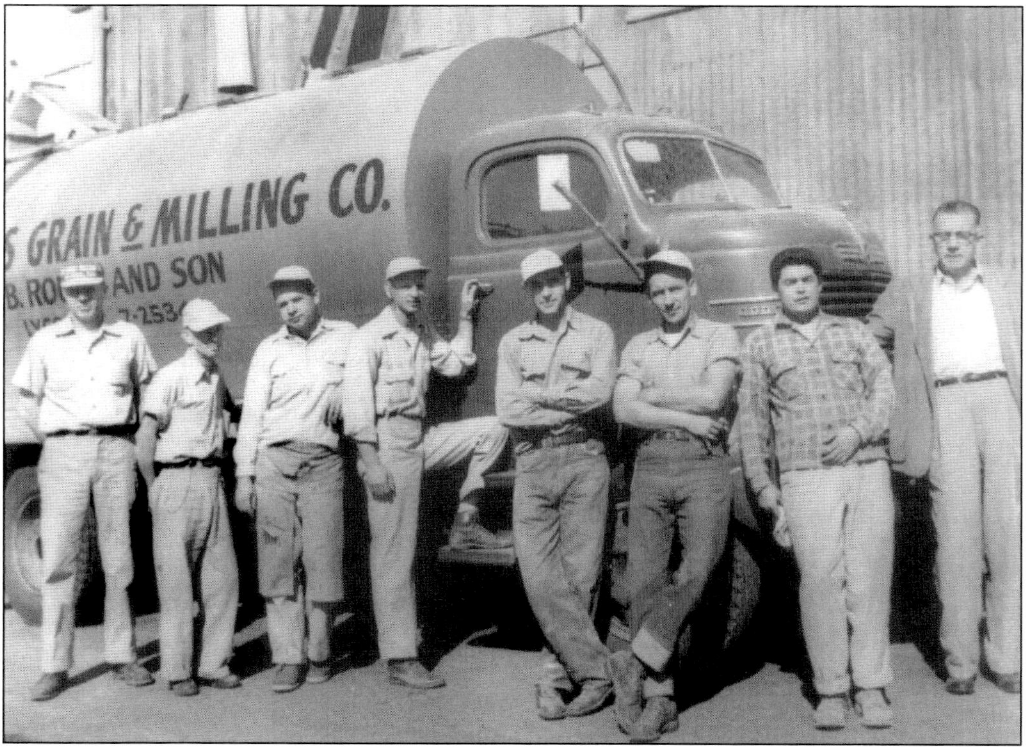

The crew of the San Dimas Grain and Milling Company, located on Bonita Avenue, is pictured around 1950. From left to right are Lloyd Rouse, ? Stevenson, Dick Meyhew, Art Dilly, Loa Thomas, Tip Goforth, unidentified, and Sanford Rouse (the owner).

On August 15, 1956, the Metropolitan Water District began a project of installing a 72-inch-diameter pipeline to transport a large amount of water from their filtration plant in La Verne to a new reservoir in Montebello. The project went right through the middle of San Dimas and closed Bonita Avenue for several weeks. The pipe is made of steel and was placed approximately 30 feet below the street level.

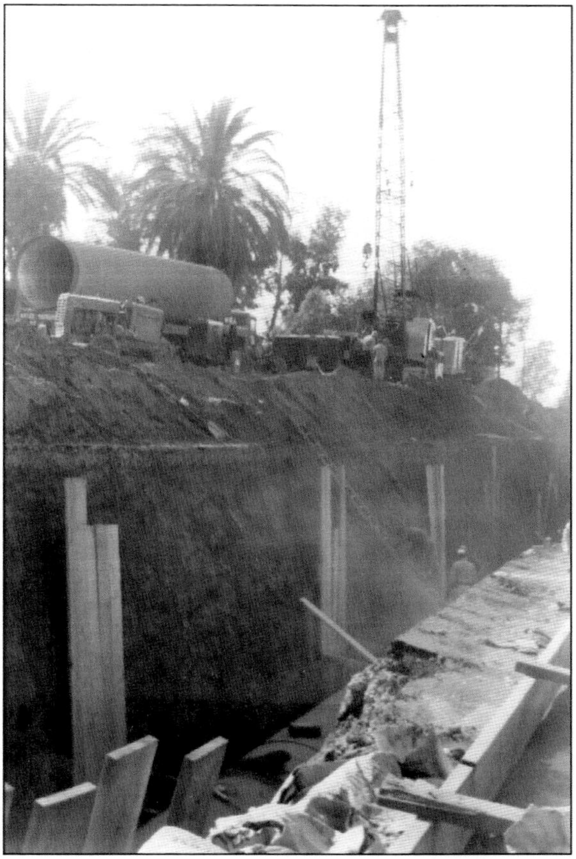

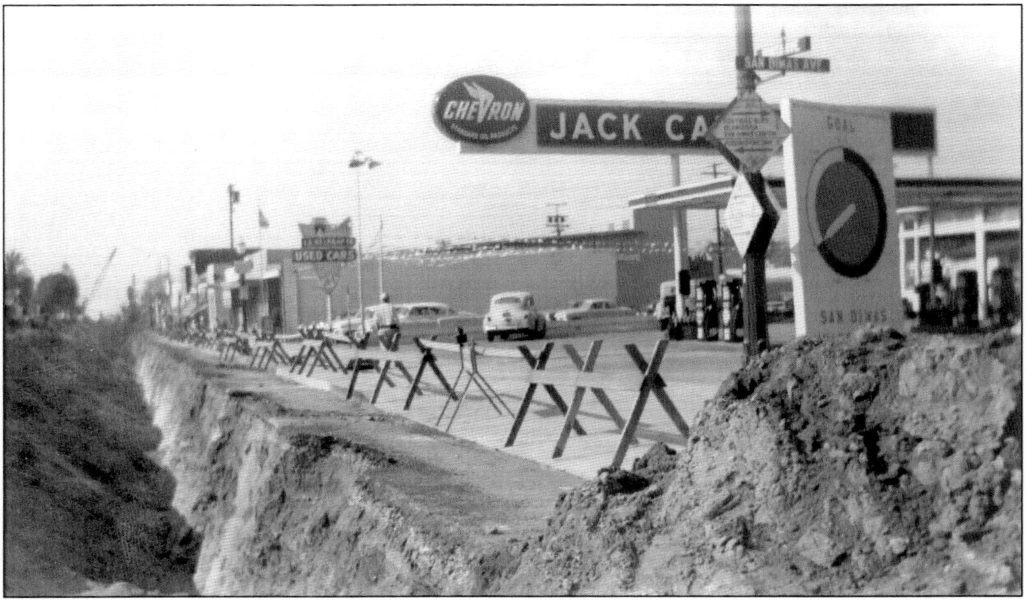

One has to wonder how the local businesses survived while the main street in town was torn up. The gas station on the corner was owned and operated by Jack Carruthers, who lived in the J. W. Walker house, just next door.

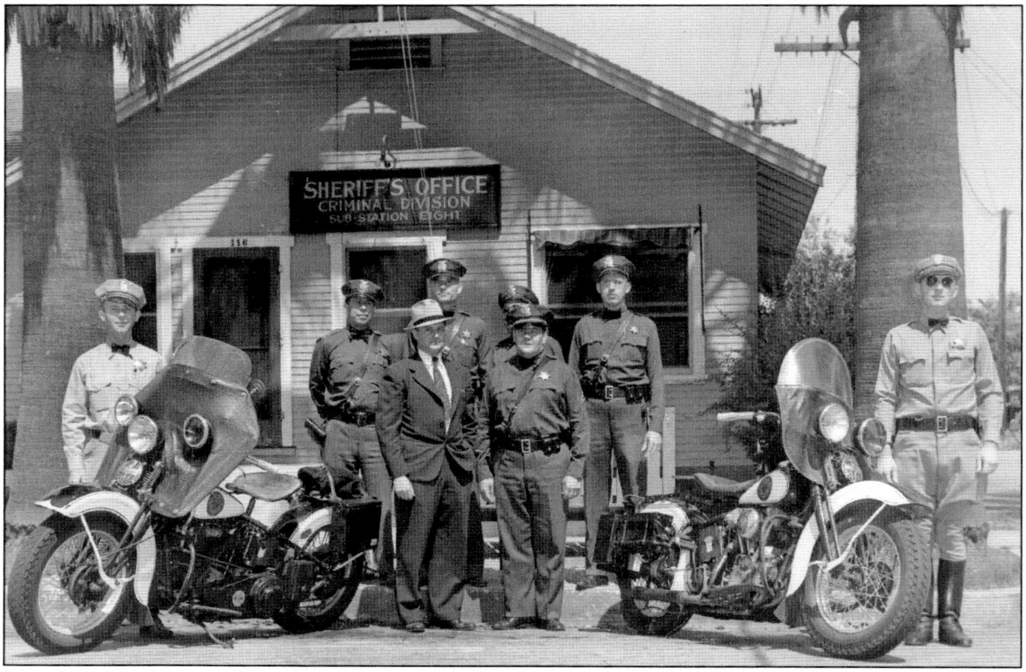

The first San Dimas sheriff station opened in July 1927. It was located at 116 North San Dimas Avenue. In 1949, the building was moved to make way for a new station and is now a single-family residence.

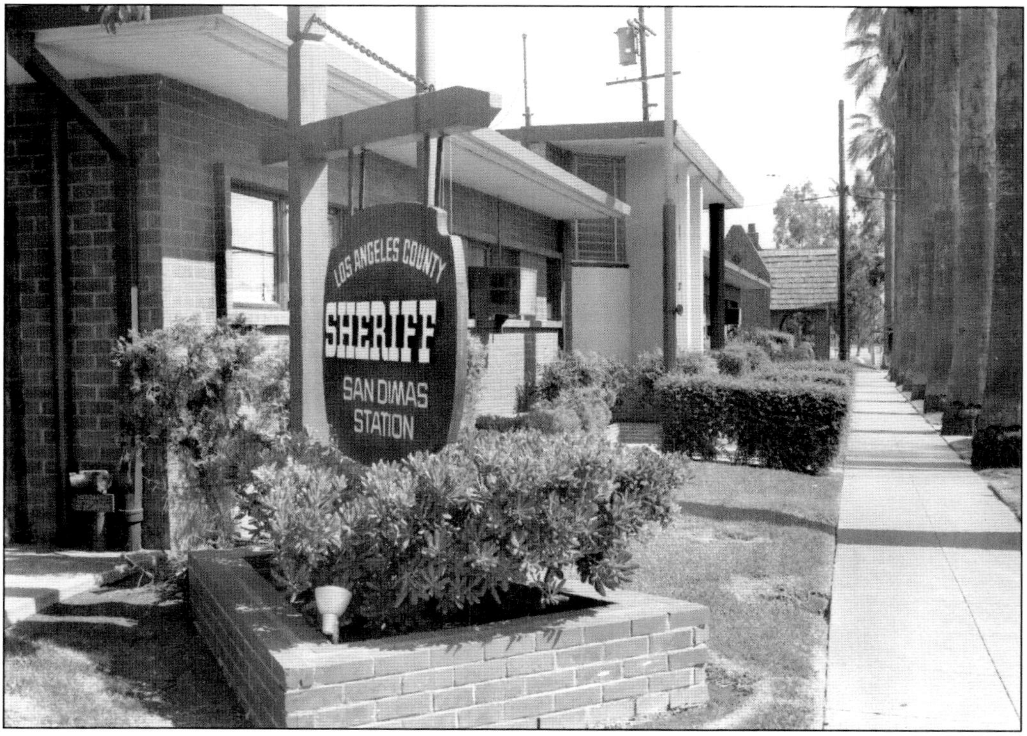

The second San Dimas sheriff station opened in 1950. It has since been replaced with a new station but remains in place.

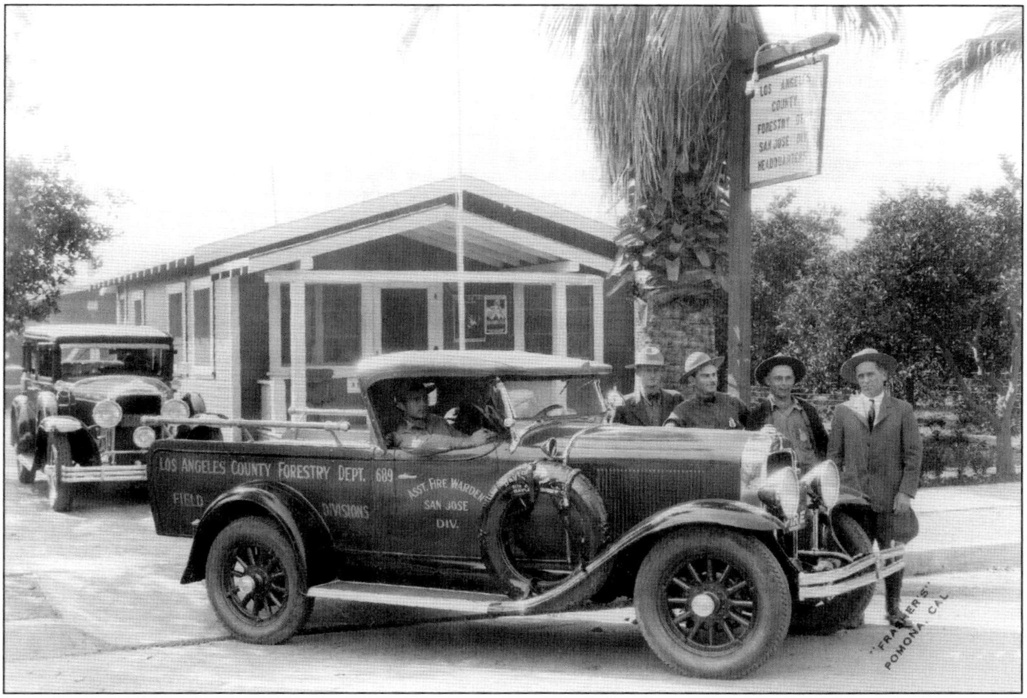

The Los Angeles County Forestry Department established the San Jose Division to provide fire protection for the area of San Dimas. The land for the station was donated by R. M. Teague.

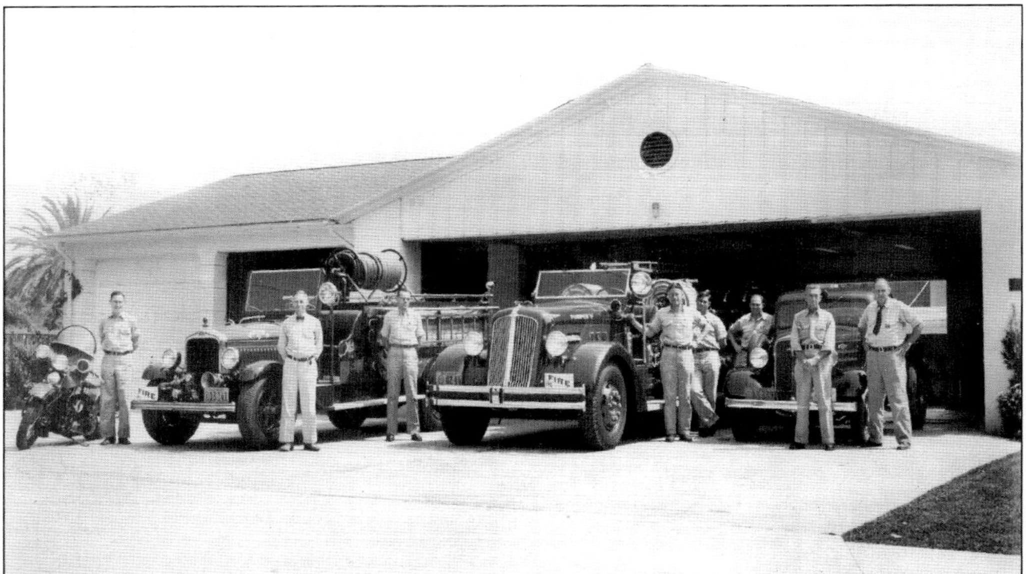

Firefighters stand ready in front of fire equipment at the Los Angeles County Fire Department Station 64 in San Dimas around 1935. The city's fire station is now located on South Walnut Avenue.

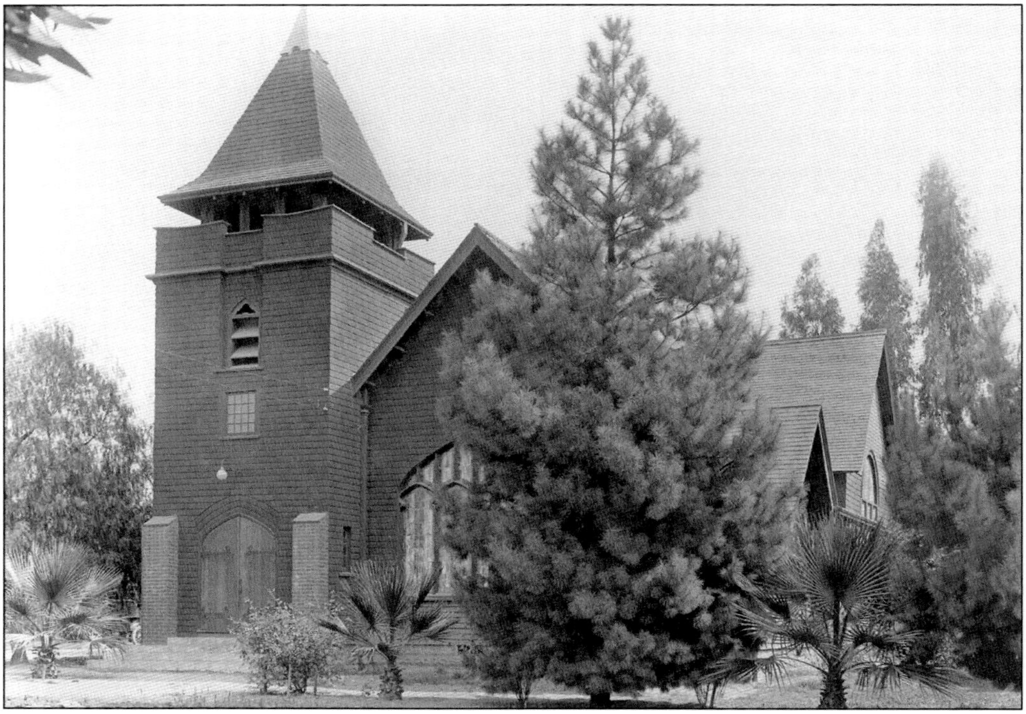

The First Baptist Church of San Dimas was established in 1898 on the west side of town. The building later moved to its current location at the corner of San Dimas Avenue and Second Street in 1908.

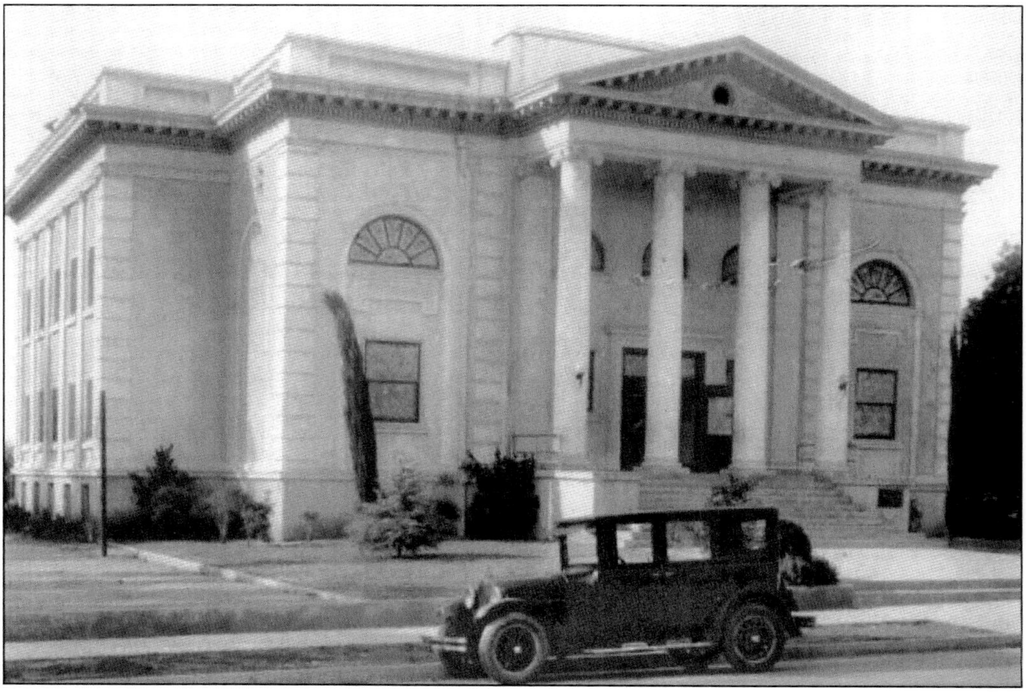

The First Christian Church was a beautiful building and was constructed in 1913 at a cost of $30,000. It burned on October 12, 1955—a terrible loss to the town.

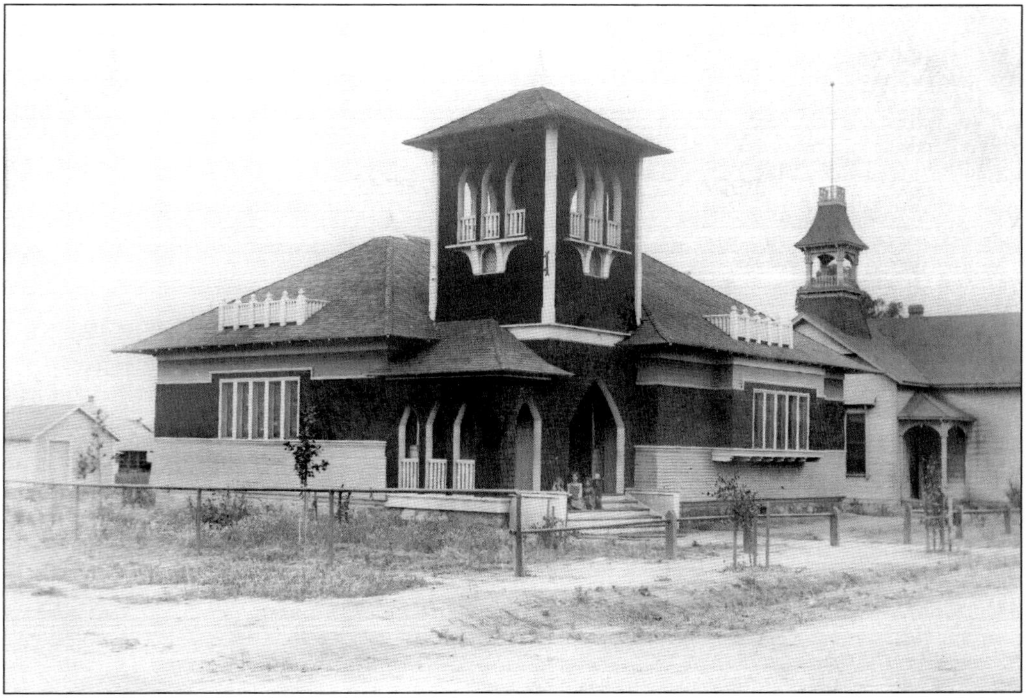

The United Methodist Church was built in 1901 and is still in use. A fire in 1999 heavily damaged the building, but it was reconstructed in a short period of time.

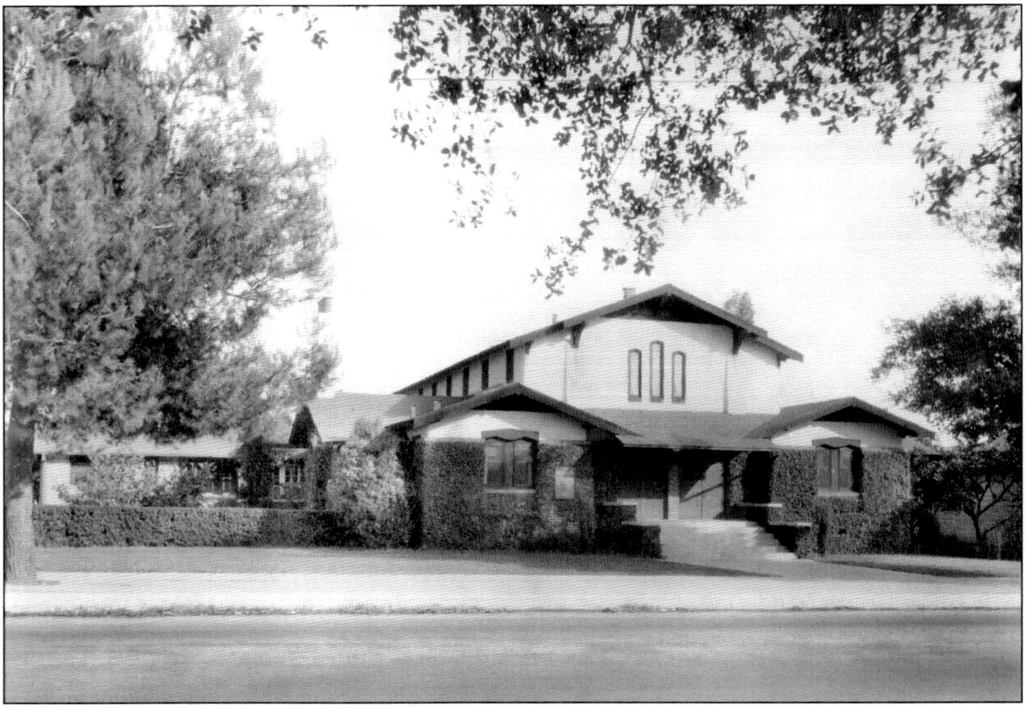

The United Church of Christ began as the Union Church and was organized in 1912. Their church was dedicated in 1917 and remains in service.

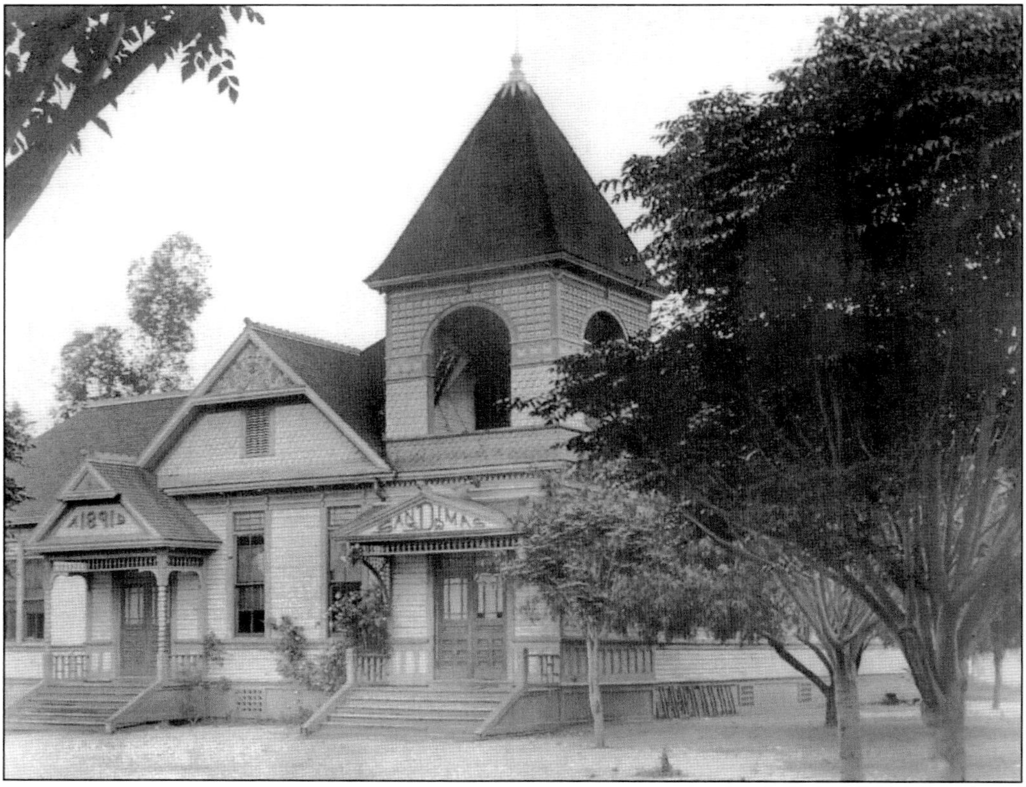

The first grammar school in San Dimas was built in 1891. The wood structure lasted until 1908, when it was replaced by the second grammar school.

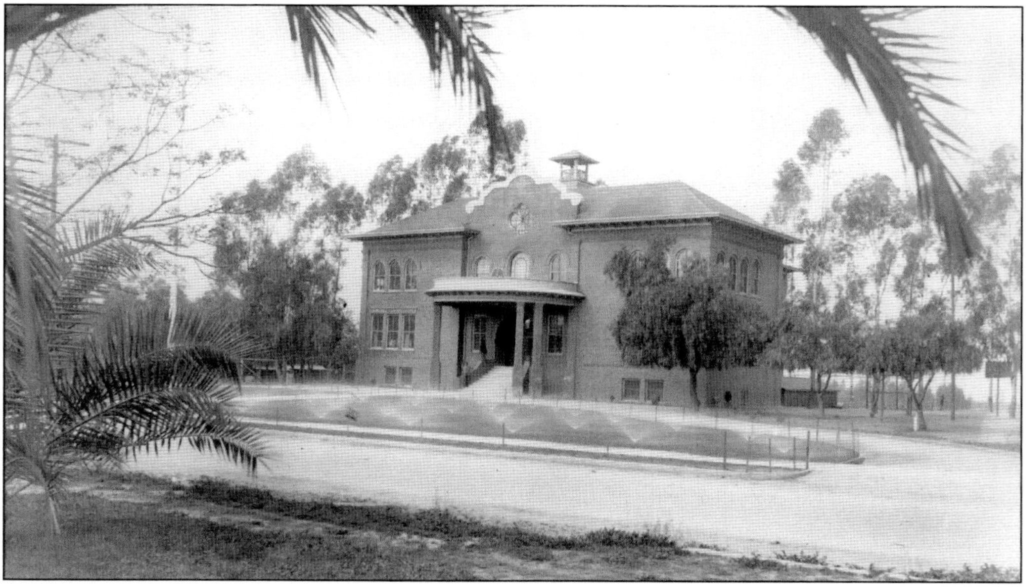

This is the second San Dimas grammar school, located on Cataract Avenue on the site of the first school. The brick building would last until 1930, while an auditorium was constructed on the right side of the building. In these days, schools were segregated and a separate building was built to teach the Mexican children.

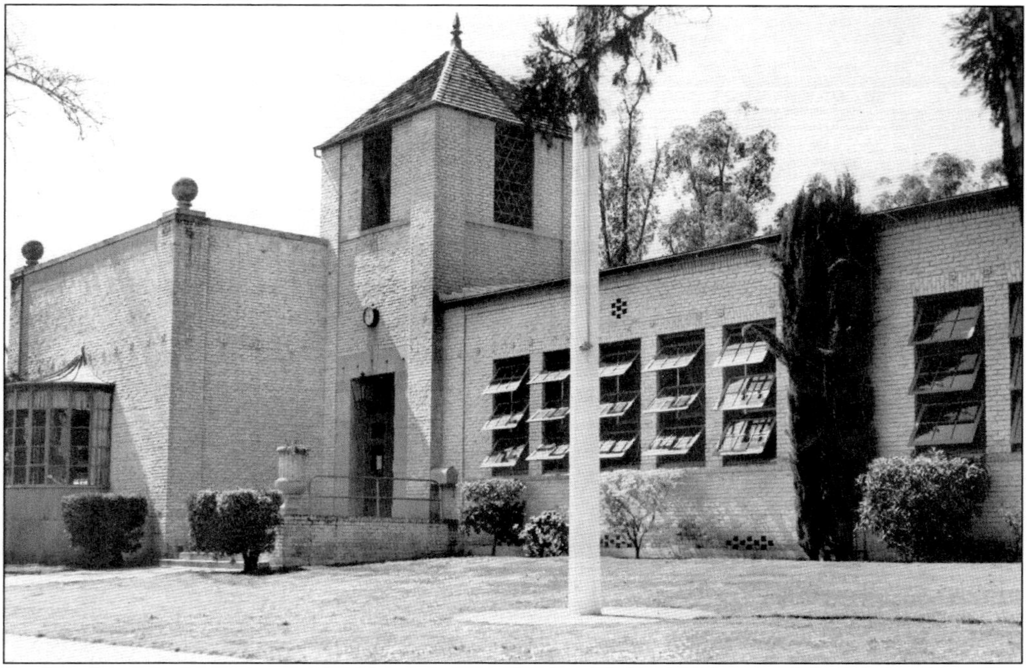

The third, and last, grammar school to be built on the site was constructed in 1930 and lasted until 1960, when it was deemed unsafe in case of earthquakes. The site is now a park.

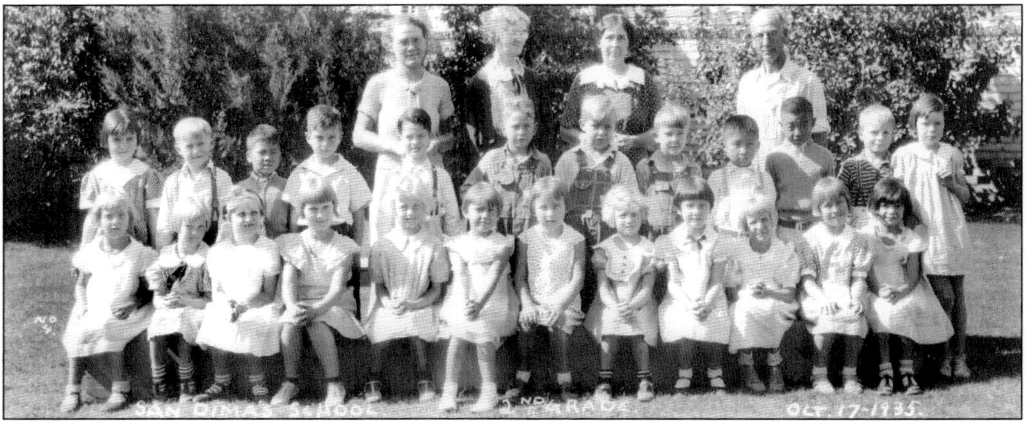

The San Dimas Historical Society is fortunate to have many class photographs from the years of the early grammar school. This is a second-grade class of San Dimas Grammar School on October 17, 1935.

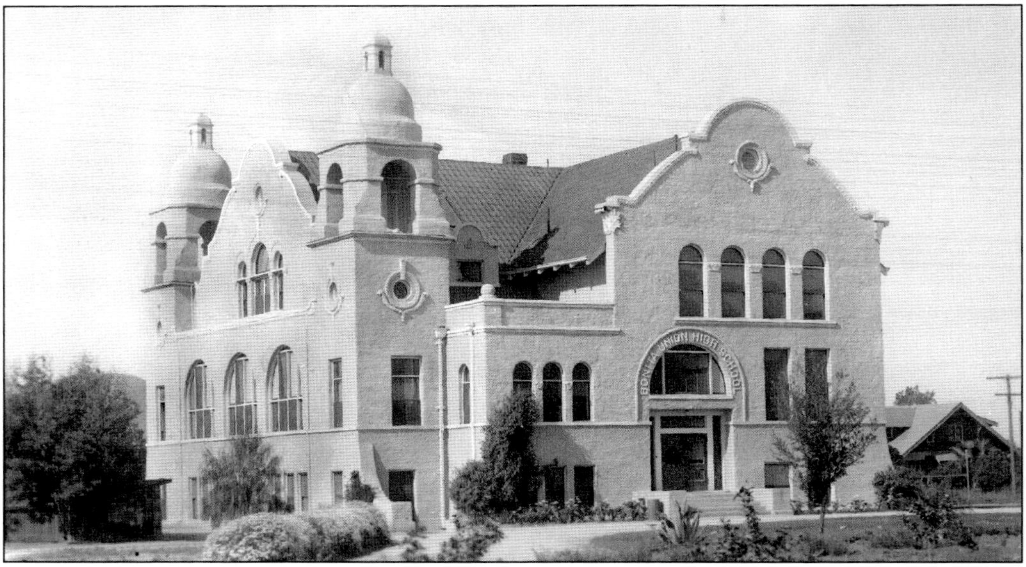

High school students attended Bonita Union High School—located between the towns of San Dimas and La Verne. The building was completed in 1904 and provided a quality education for students from both towns.

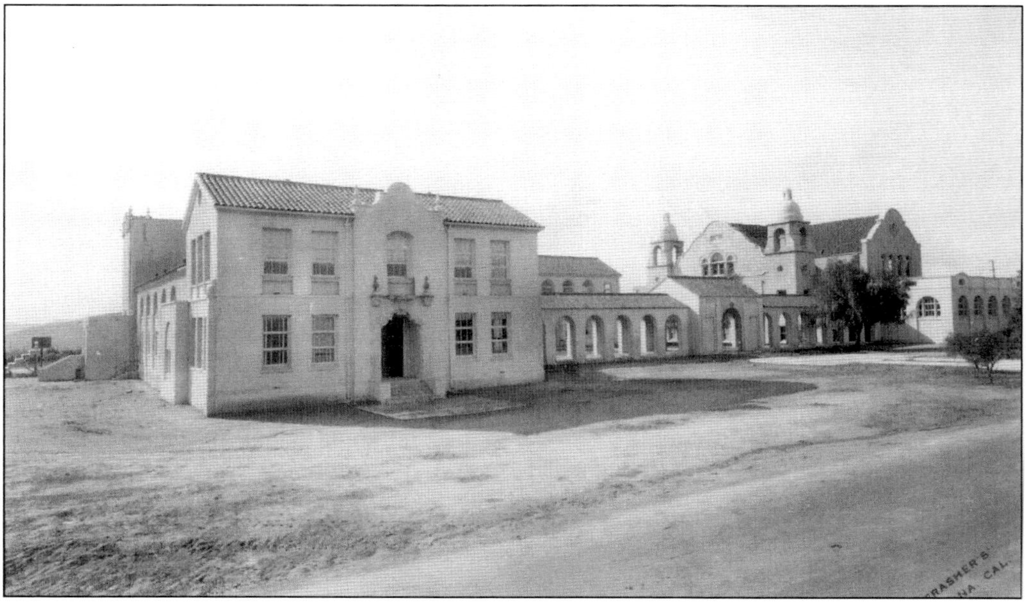

Over the years, many additions were made to the buildings as the need for more classrooms arose. The building is still in use as Damien High School, a Catholic high school.

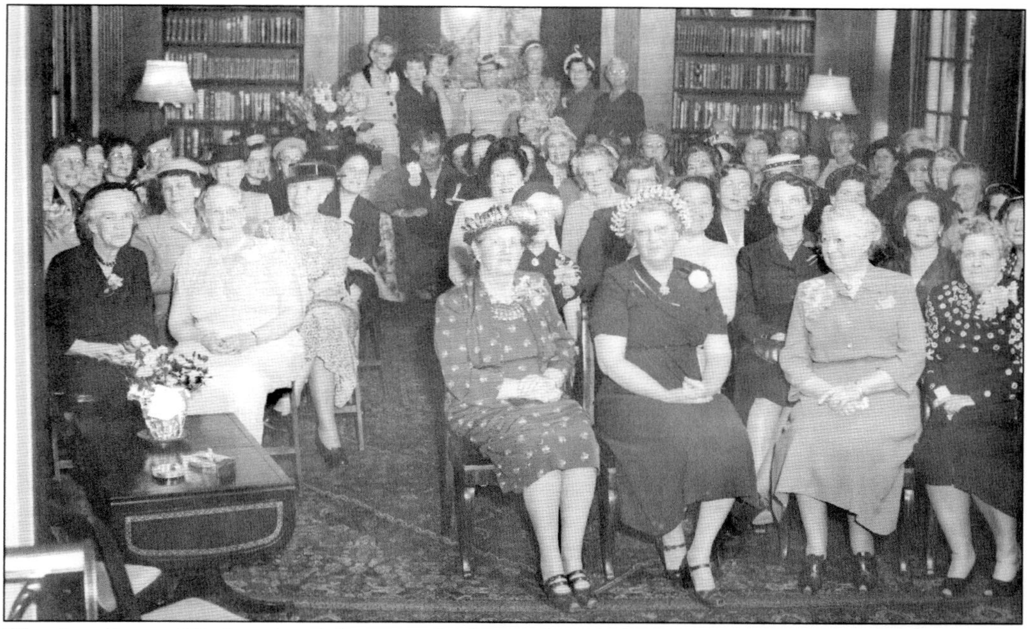

The San Dimas Wednesday Afternoon Club was founded in 1902 and continues today. When the club was formed, women needed to be home during lunchtime to prepare a meal for their husbands. Following lunch, the men would return to work in their citrus orchards or other ventures and the women could meet for their afternoon get-together. This meeting, in celebration of the 50th anniversary of the club, was held at the home of Genevieve (Mrs. Harry) Walker.

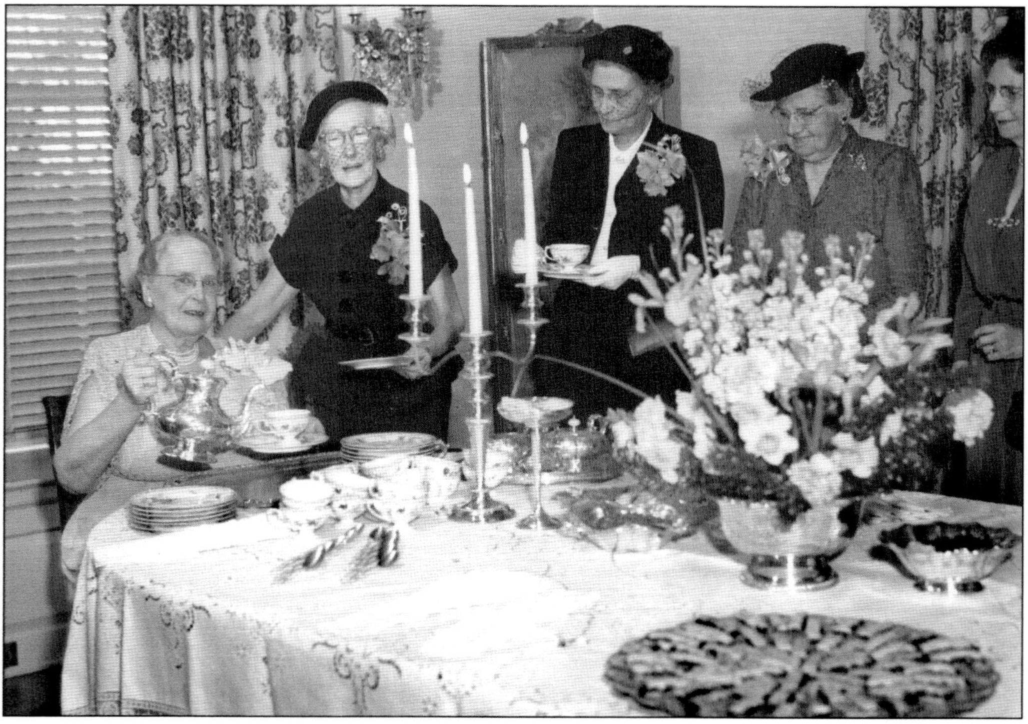

Genevieve Walker (seated) prepares to serve tea to members of the club during the dinner at her home. Today the club meets seven times a year and is limited to 35 members.

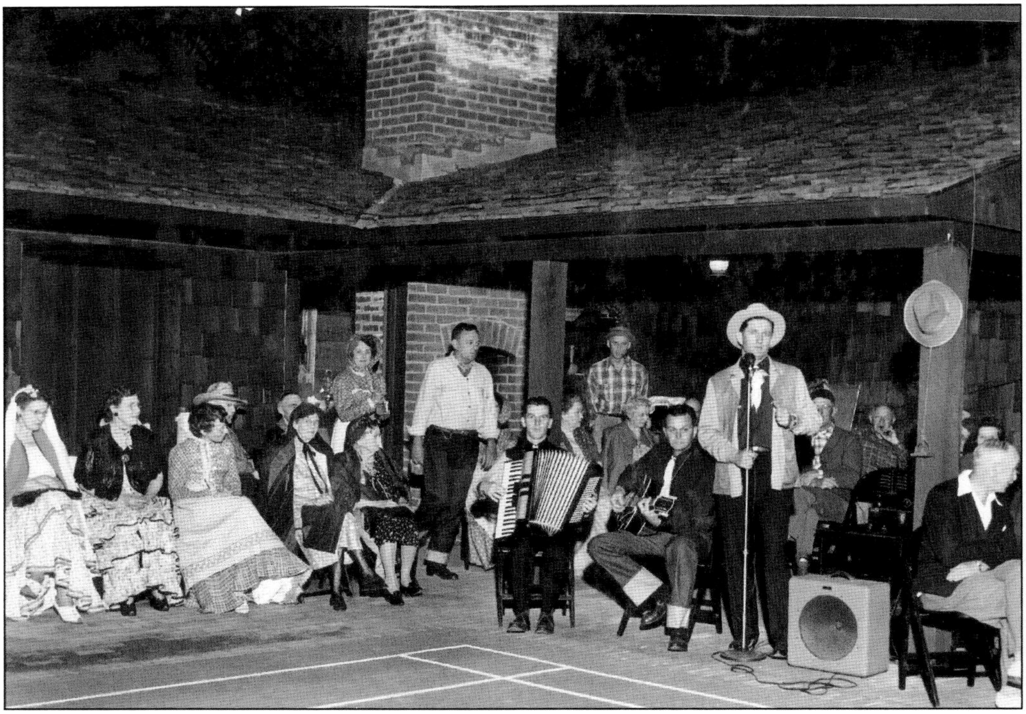

The Wednesday Afternoon Club held this party at the home of Fay and Clarice Marchant. At one time, the club had evening events that included their husbands. Notice the dress of the guests for this lavish western night of music and dancing. Besides being a social organization, the Wednesday Afternoon Club assists other organizations with cash donations once a year.

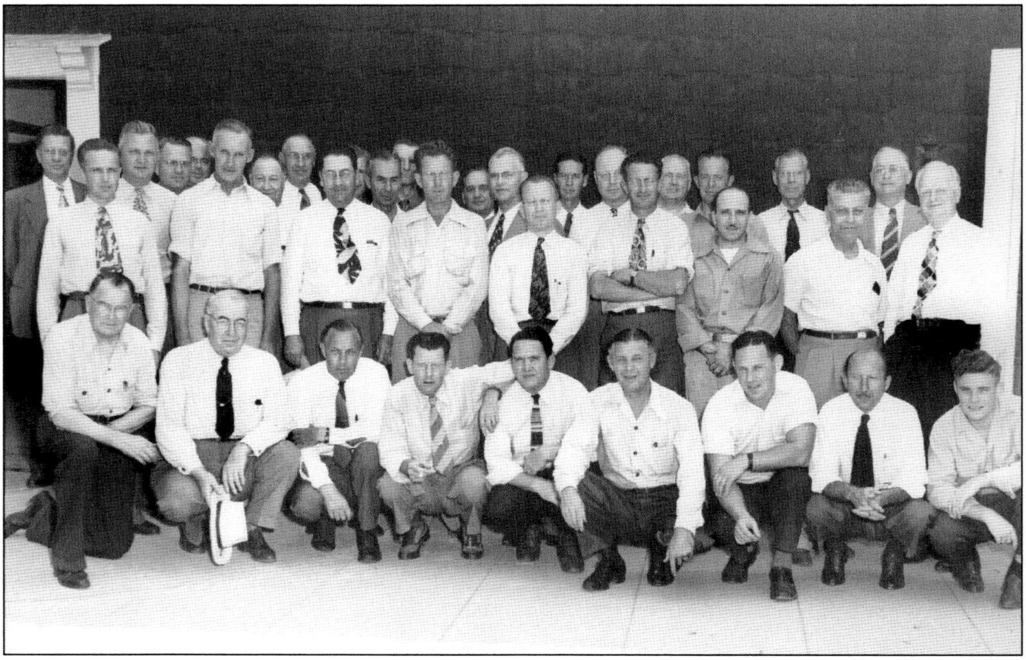

This is a picture of the San Dimas Service Club taken in 1947. Not much is known about the service club's activities; however, it appears it included about everyone in town.

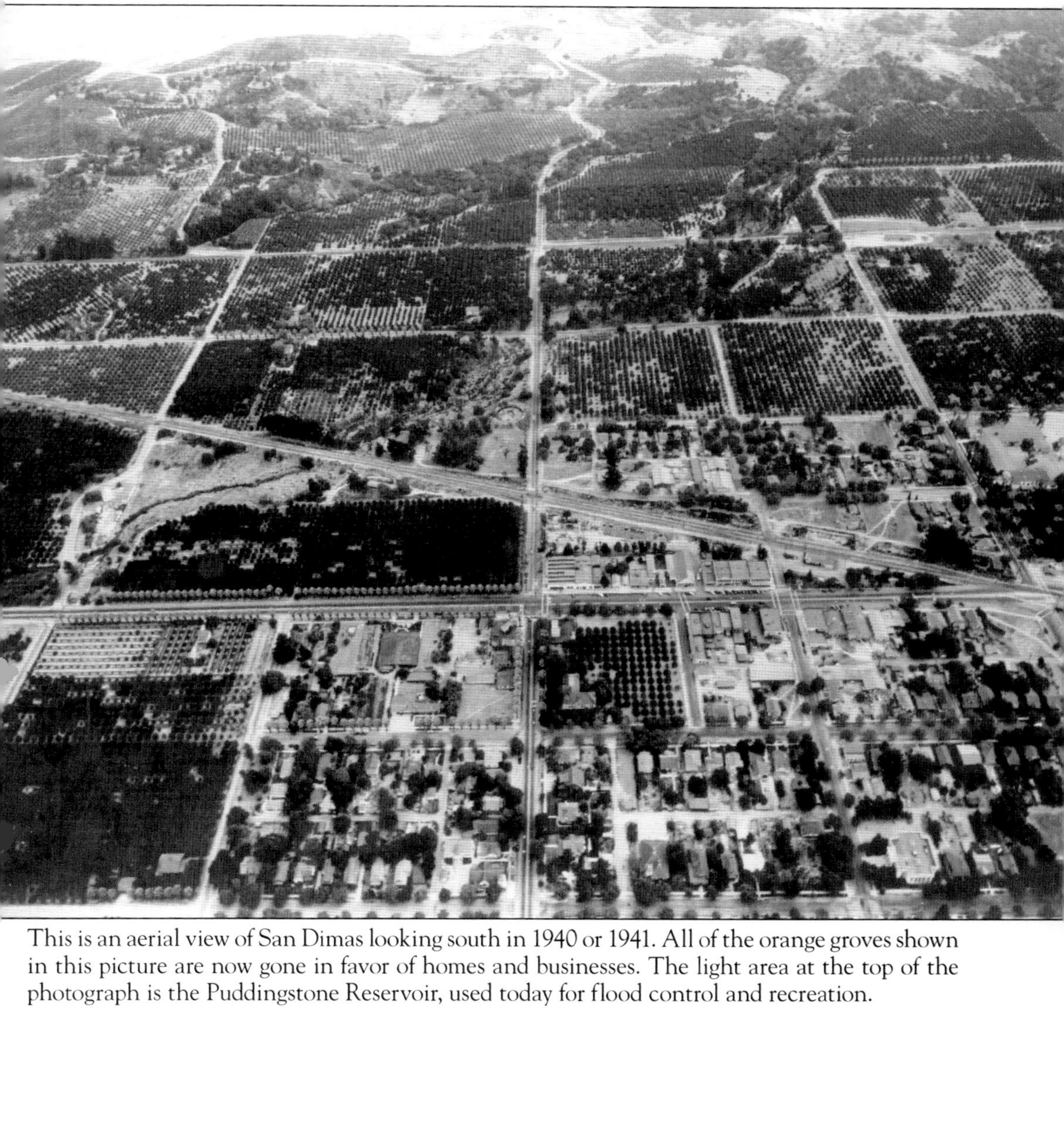

This is an aerial view of San Dimas looking south in 1940 or 1941. All of the orange groves shown in this picture are now gone in favor of homes and businesses. The light area at the top of the photograph is the Puddingstone Reservoir, used today for flood control and recreation.

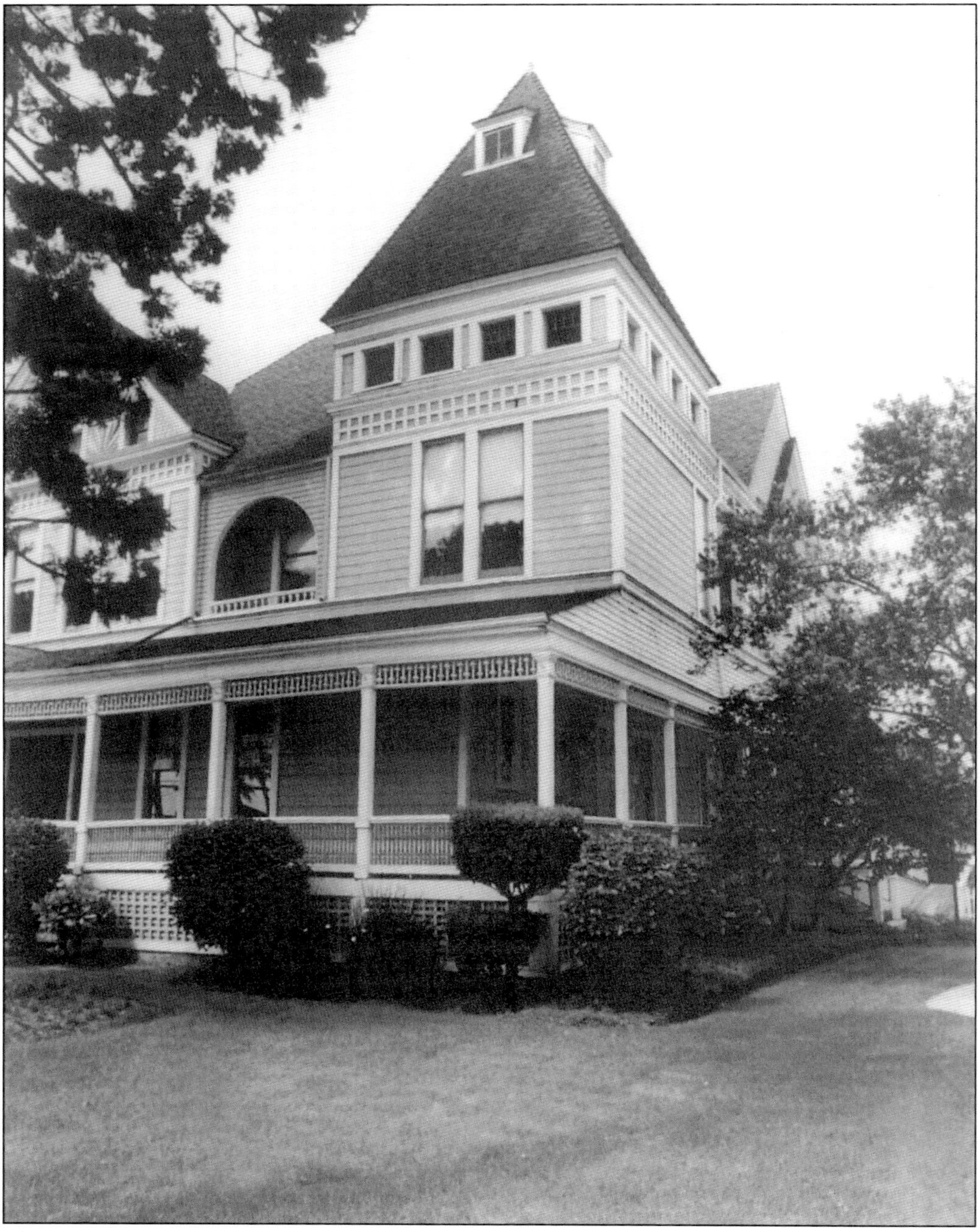

The J. W. Walker House was converted into a restaurant in the 1970s but was unable to stay in business. After sitting vacant for several years, the old hotel was purchased by the City of San Dimas and has undergone a major renovation to preserve this historic building.

Seven

The City of San Dimas
1960 to Present

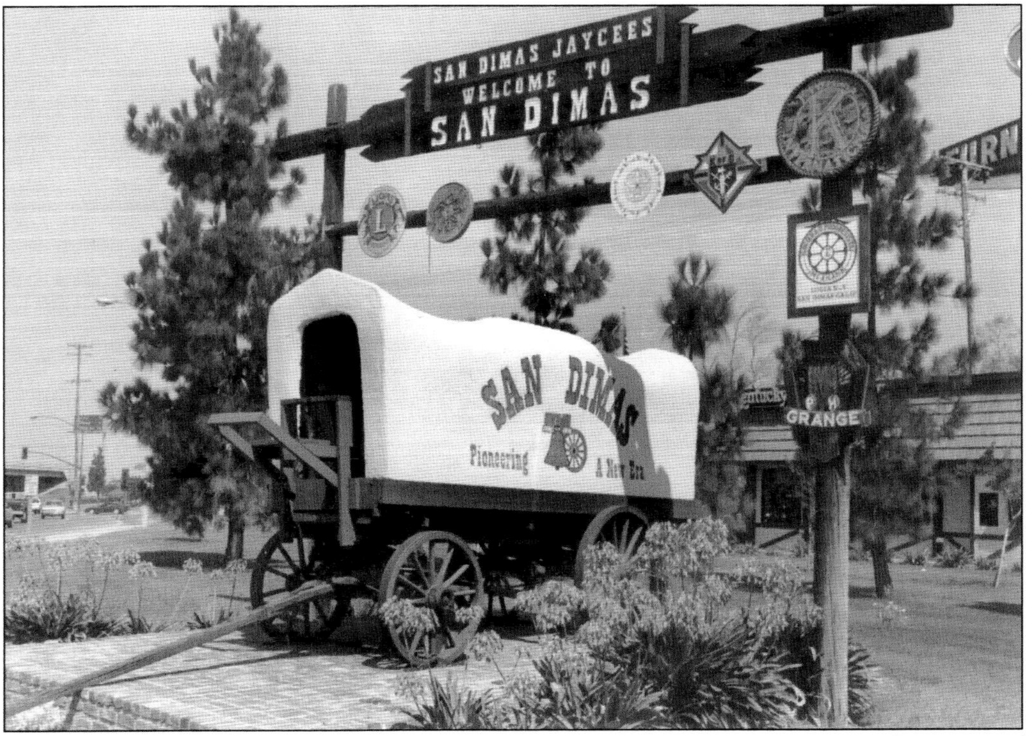

This picture shows the entrance into the historic downtown area of San Dimas at the corner of Arrow Highway and Bonita Avenue. The corner has gone through major renovations over the past several years; however, the old wagon remains.

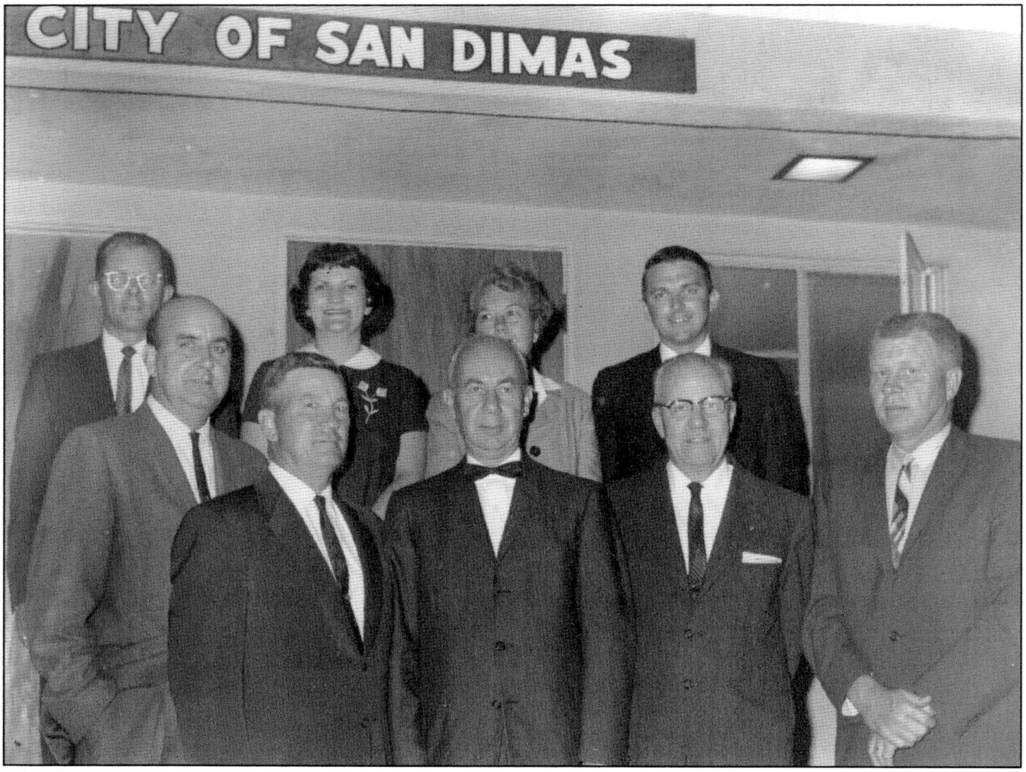

The first San Dimas City Council and officials included, from left to right, (first row) Vice Mayor Ted Glauthier, councilman Harry Whipple, Mayor Stanley Plummer, councilman G. F. Harbin, and councilman Lloyd Rouse; (second row) attorney John Larson, deputy clerk Patricia Gore, treasurer Lela Hathaway, and city manager Robert Carleson. The building was used as the first city hall and is today a church.

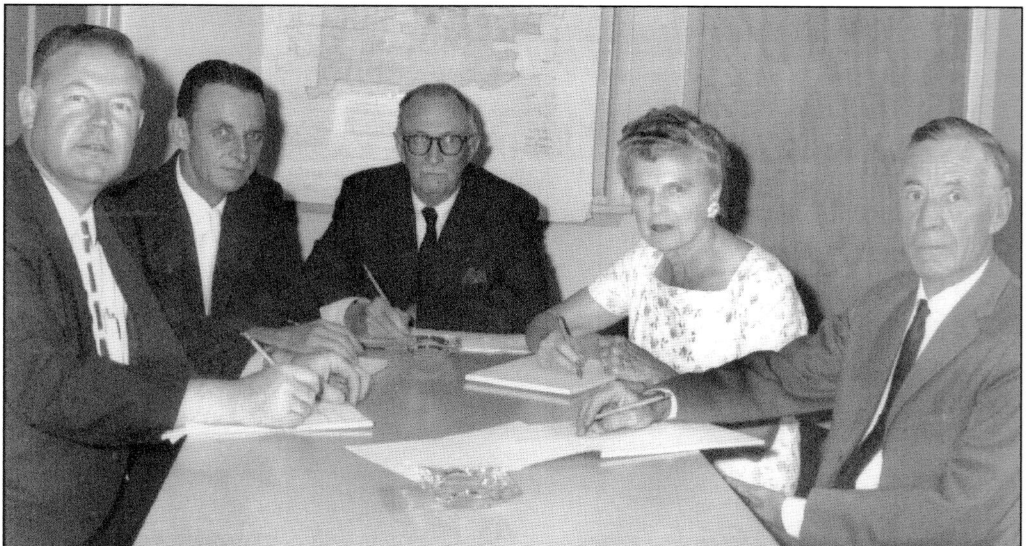

This is the first Planning Commission, including, from left to right, Joe Bauer, Carl Favre, Fred Kennedy, Clarice Marchant, and Robert Williams.

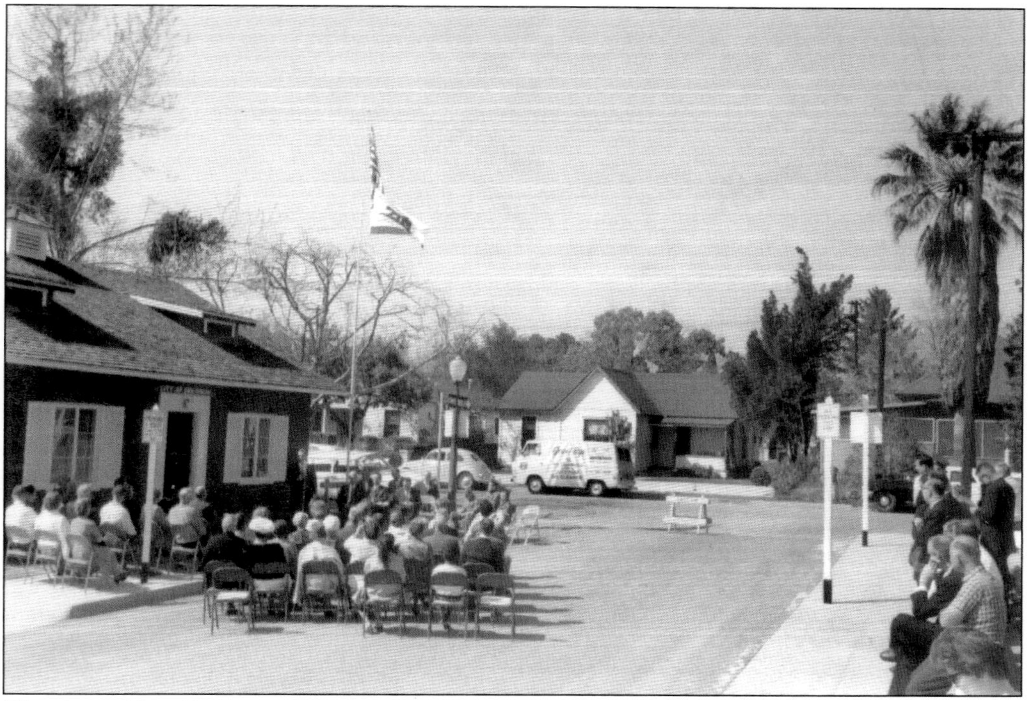

The City of San Dimas was incorporated in August 1960. The city established their second city hall in this building and had their dedication in May 1962. The building was on North Exchange Place and had been two other businesses before it became the city hall.

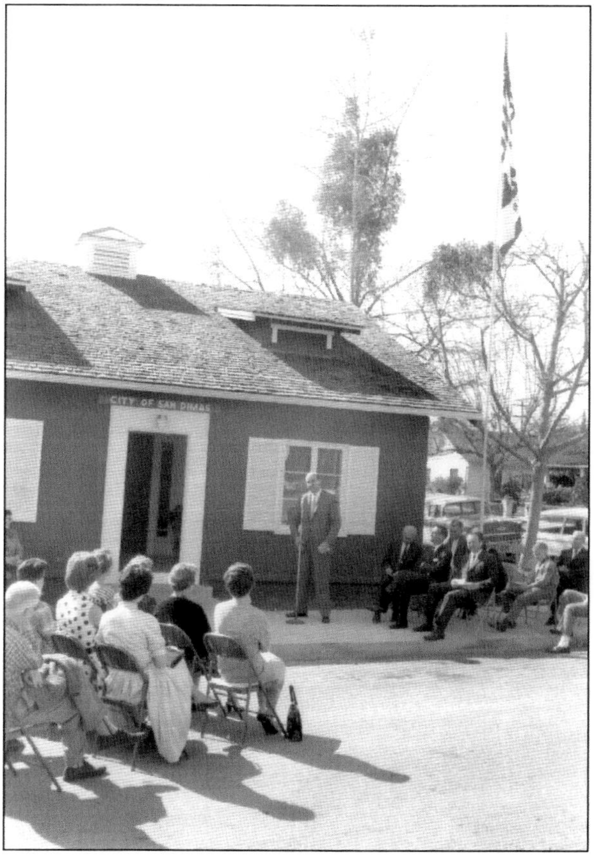

The city hall building has seen prior life as a funeral chapel and a doctor's office. The city would remain in this building until the new facility was completed in 1969. Following their move to the new civic center, this building was sold for $100 and moved to another part of town, where it is today a single-family residence. The area where the building sat is now a parking lot.

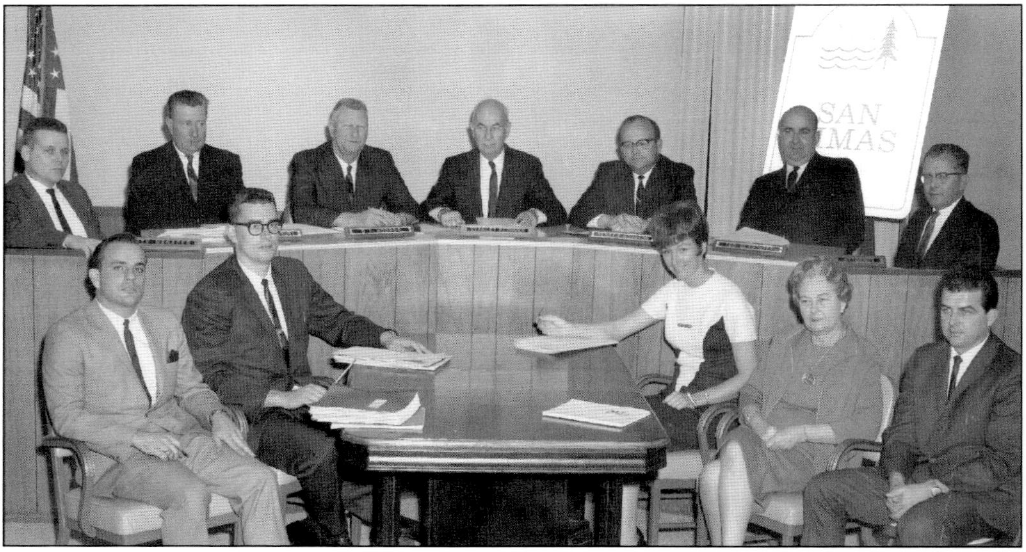

This is a picture of the city council and other officials taken in 1966. From left to right are (first row) planning director Jim Cooper, administrative assistant Norm Boehm, city clerk Barbara Henderson, treasurer Lela Hathaway, and director of public works Ron Kranser; (second row) city manager Bob Christofferson, councilman Loyd Salisbury, councilman D. F. ("Buck") Hooper, Mayor Stanley Plummer, councilman Hank Houston, councilman Ted Glauthier, and city attorney John Larson.

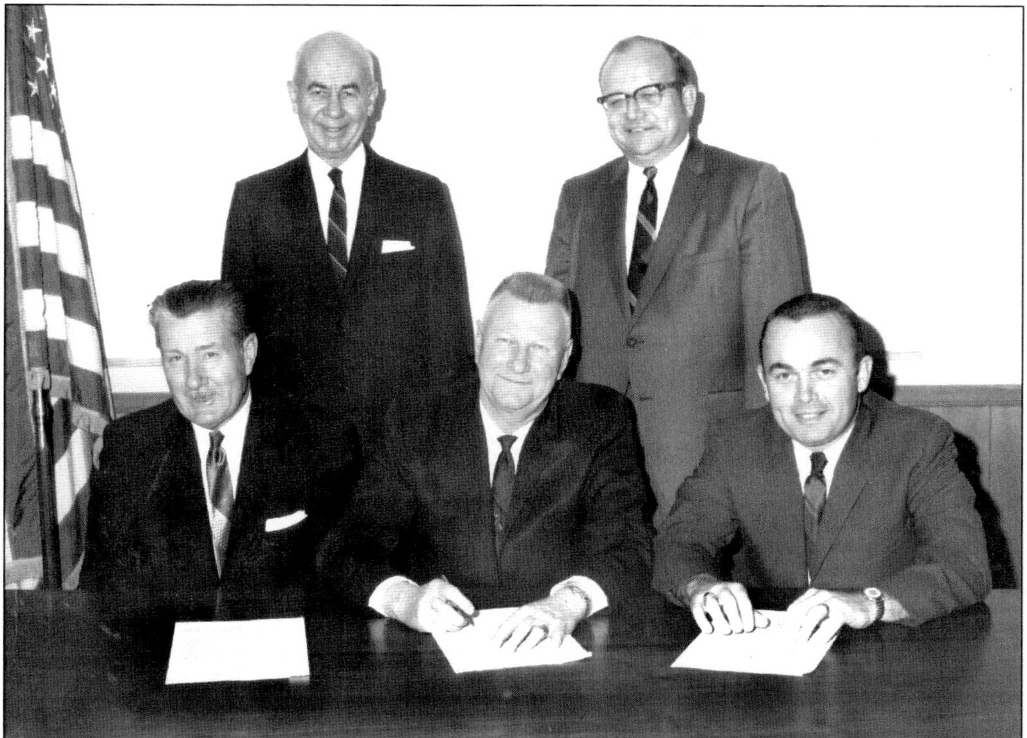

Taken in 1968, this photograph shows (seated) councilman Loyd Salisbury, Mayor Buck Hooper, and councilman Tom Nuss; (standing) councilmen Stanley Plummer and Hank Houston.

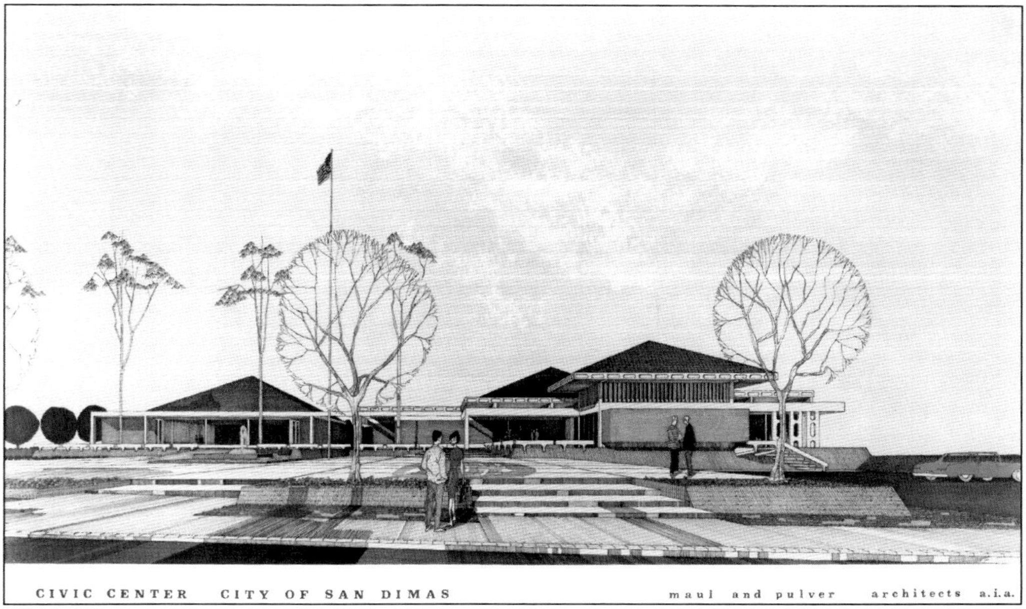

This rendering is of the new civic center to be constructed at the corner of Walnut and Bonita Avenues. The ground-breaking for the new 31,944-square-foot building was held in June 1968 and construction completed in October 1969.

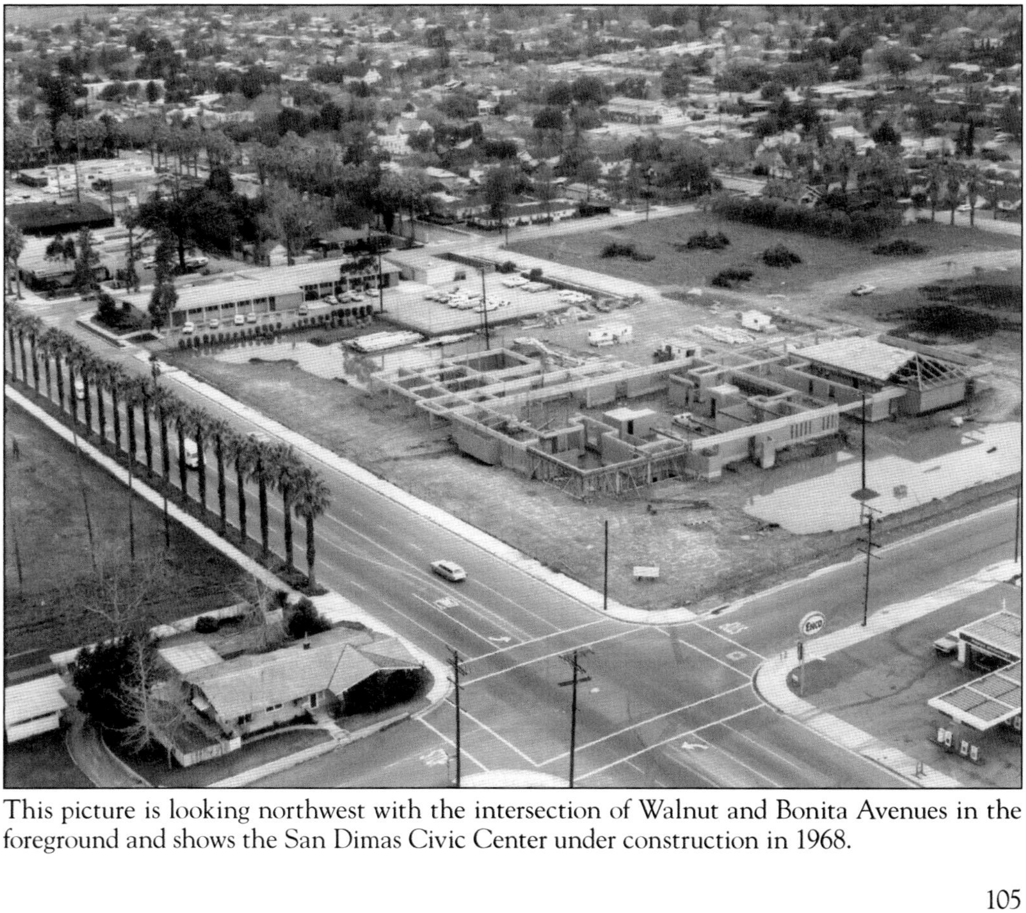

This picture is looking northwest with the intersection of Walnut and Bonita Avenues in the foreground and shows the San Dimas Civic Center under construction in 1968.

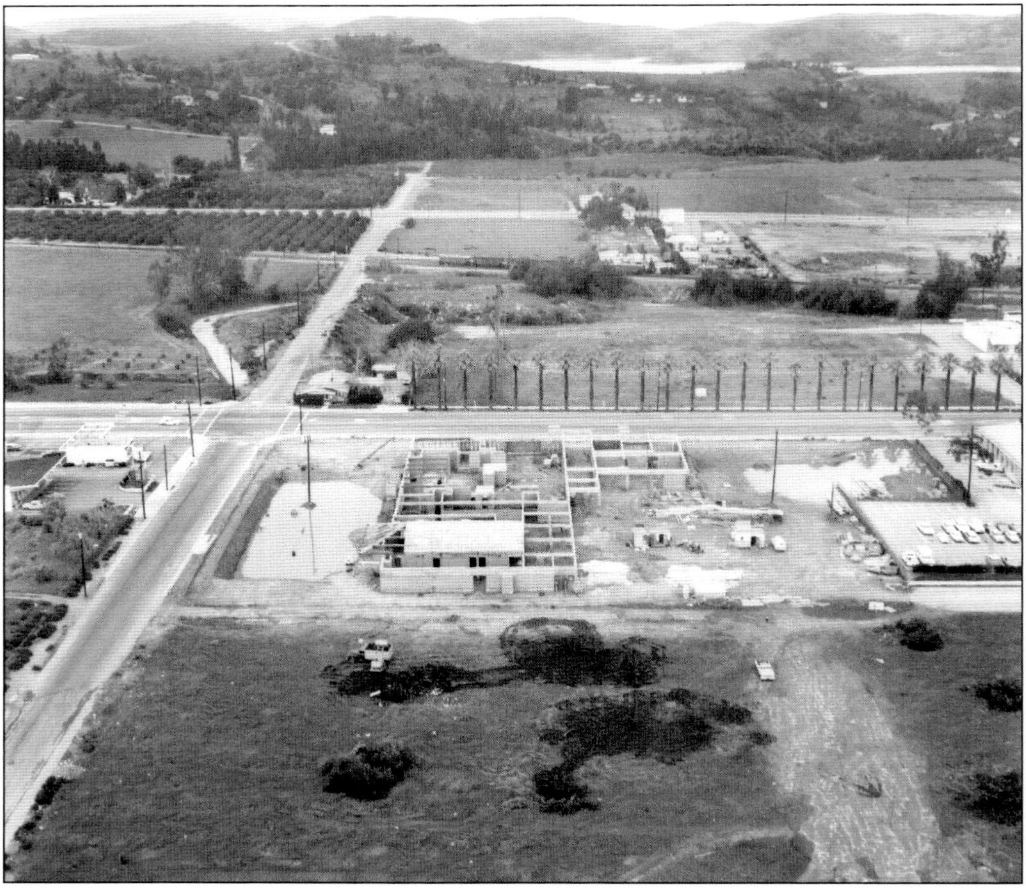

This is another view of the construction of the civic center, this time looking south with Bonita Avenue crossing the picture in the middle.

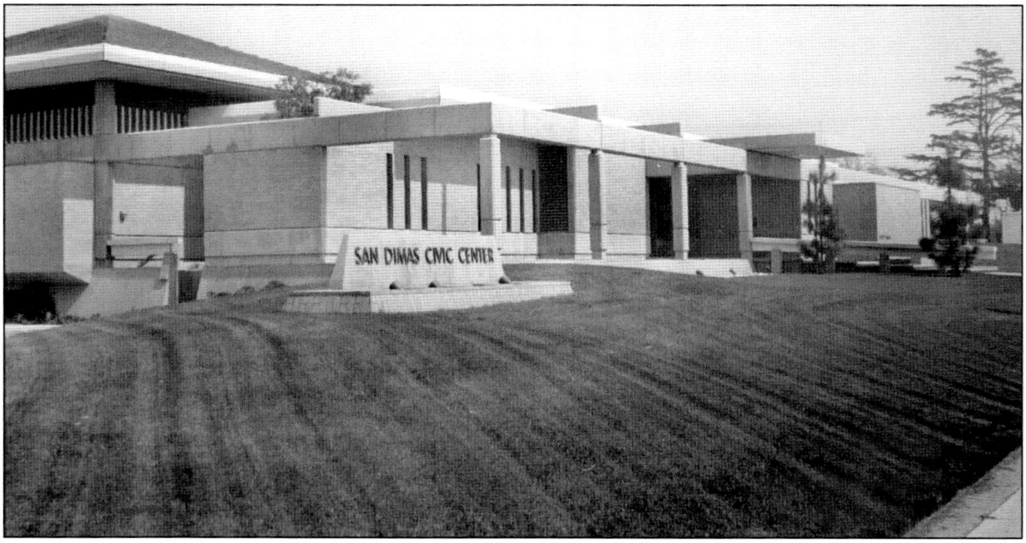

With the construction completed, the front of the new San Dimas Civic Center is ready for the dedication. The building looks much the same today and has served the city well.

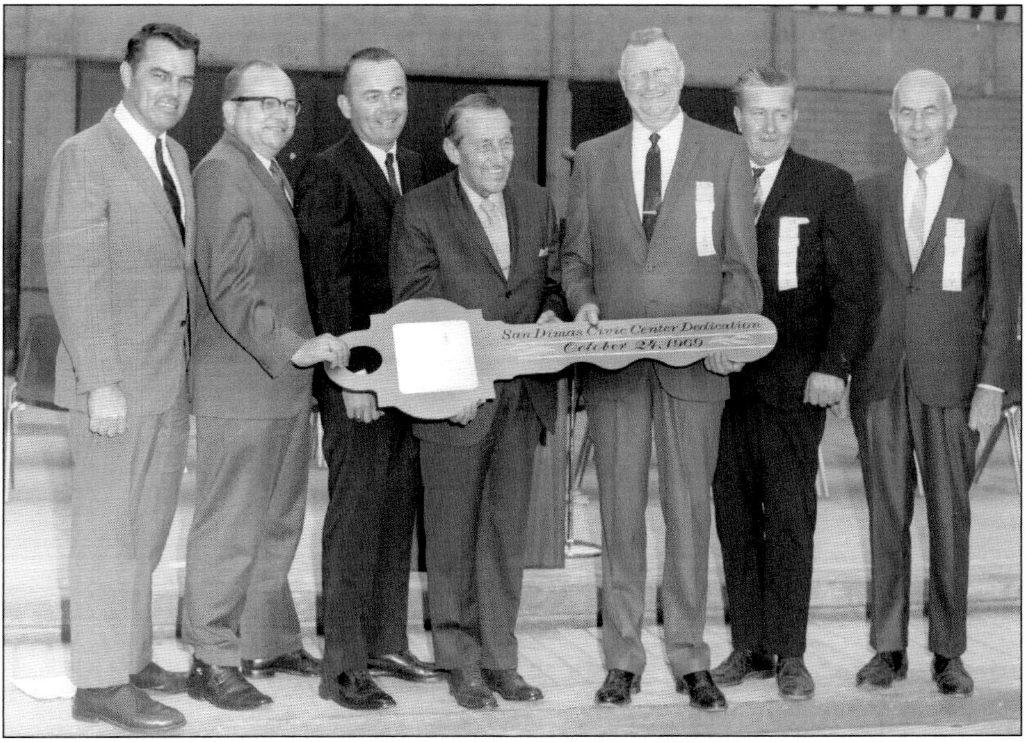

This is the dedication ceremony for the San Dimas Civic Center in 1969. From left to right are Pete Scharbarum, assemblyman; Hank Houston, councilman; Tom Nuss, councilman; Frank Bonelli, county supervisor; Buck Hooper, mayor; Loyd Salisbury, councilman; and Stanley Plummer, councilman.

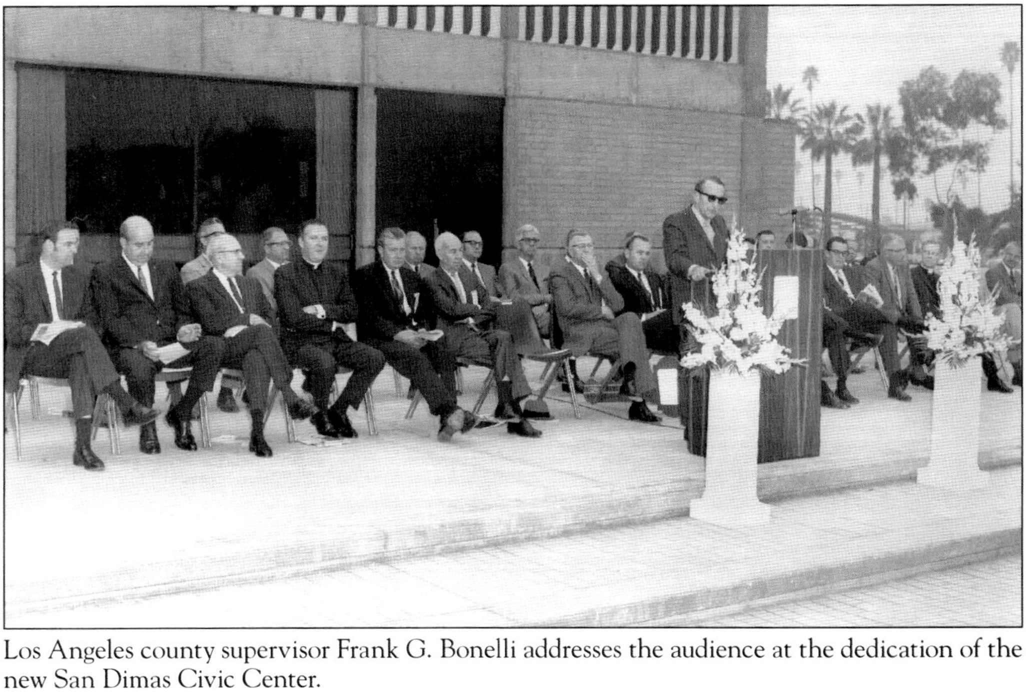

Los Angeles county supervisor Frank G. Bonelli addresses the audience at the dedication of the new San Dimas Civic Center.

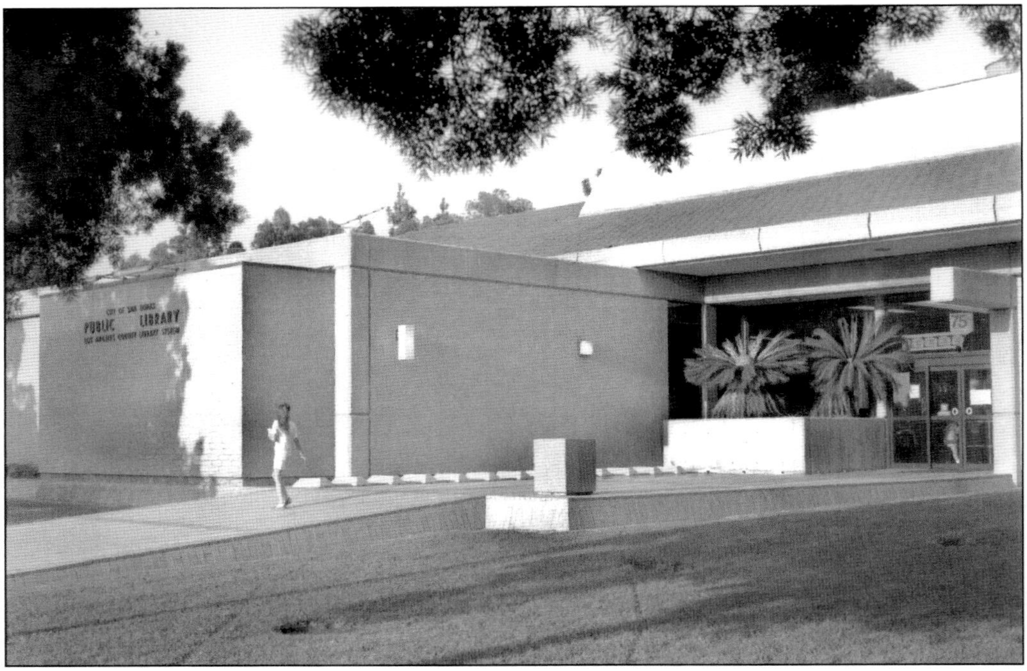

The Los Angeles County Library in San Dimas was constructed in 1970 and 1971 under a federal grant of $130,048, which was administered by the state library. It was dedicated on Thursday, April 8, 1971, with Mayor D. F. "Buck" Hooper acting as the master of ceremonies.

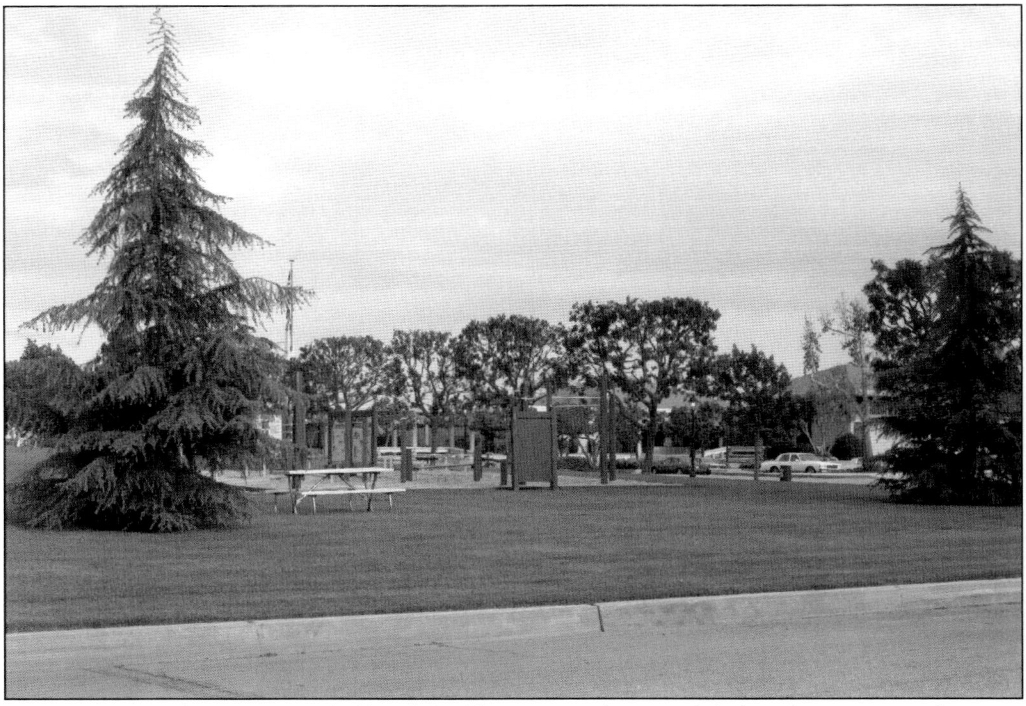

Civic Center Park, next to city hall and the library, provides a restful place for citizens and visitors alike. The park is also used for the summer "Music in the Park" series, which always draws a large crowd.

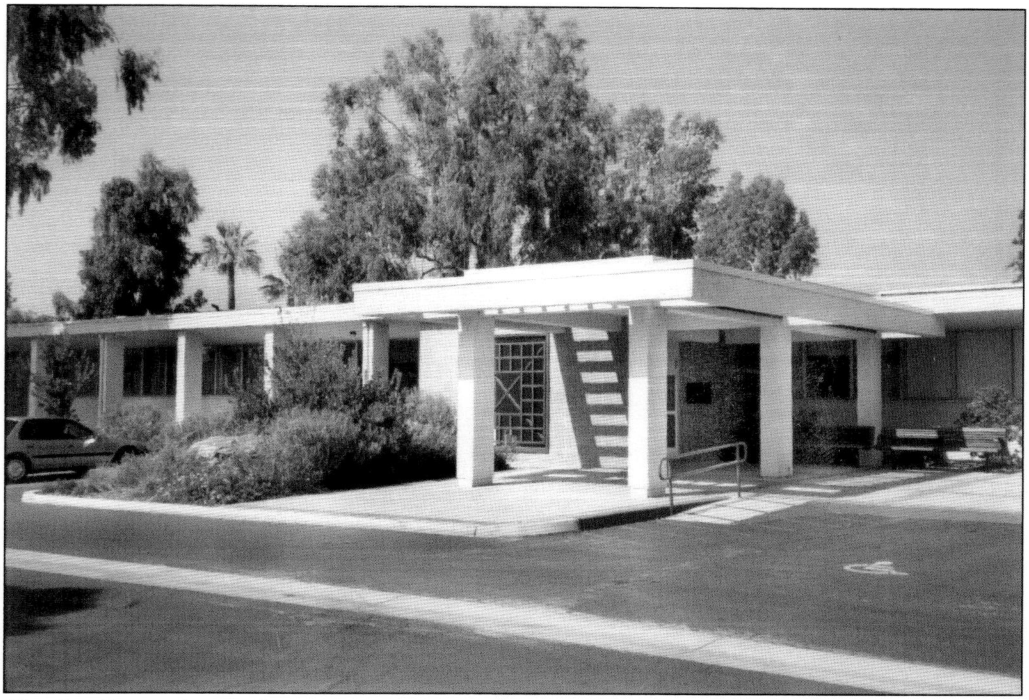

The San Dimas Senior Center was constructed as a Los Angeles County engineer's building and later converted to the senior center. It provides many programs for the city's senior citizens along with meeting facilities for various groups and a senior luncheon program.

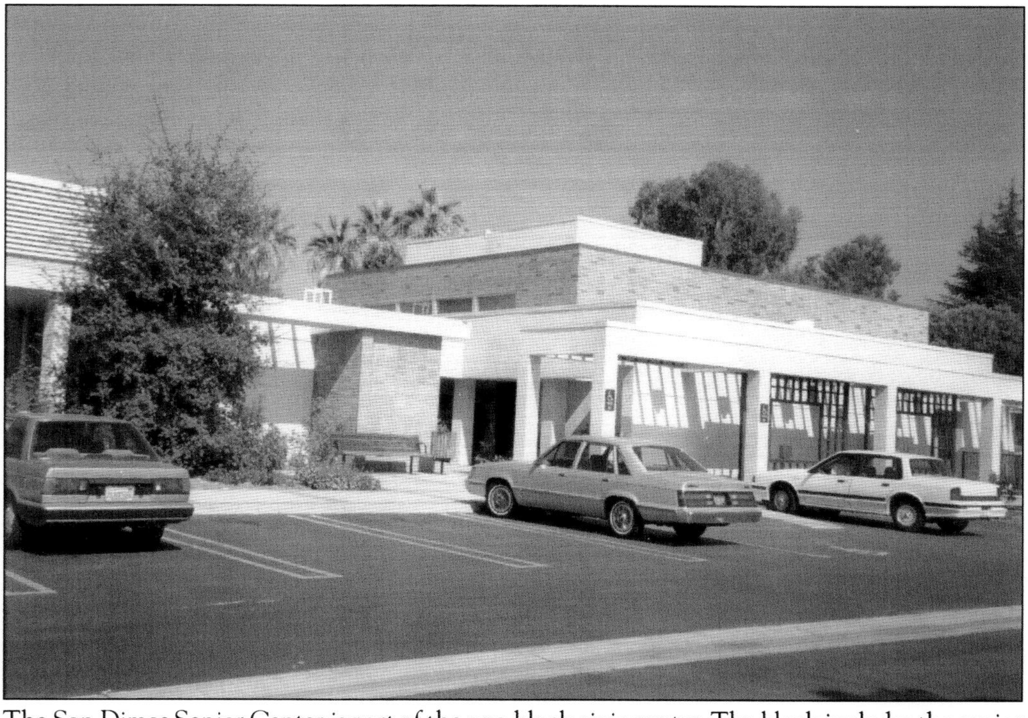

The San Dimas Senior Center is part of the one-block civic center. The block includes the senior center, city hall, library, community center, and park.

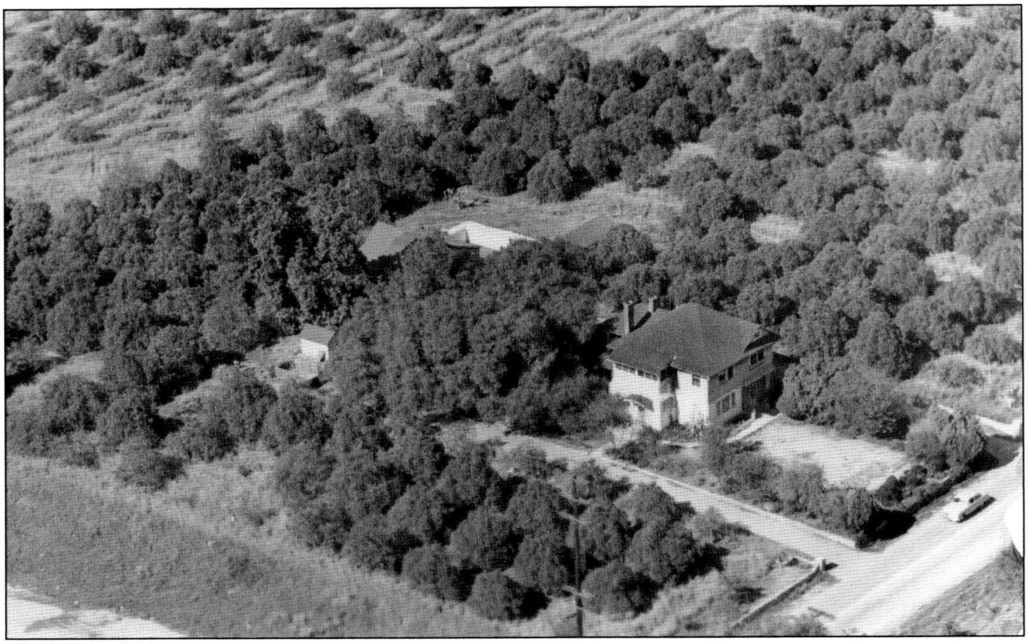

The home of William Martin was constructed in 1901 in its original location on Cataract Avenue in San Dimas. The building was donated in 1987 to the city and moved to its current location.

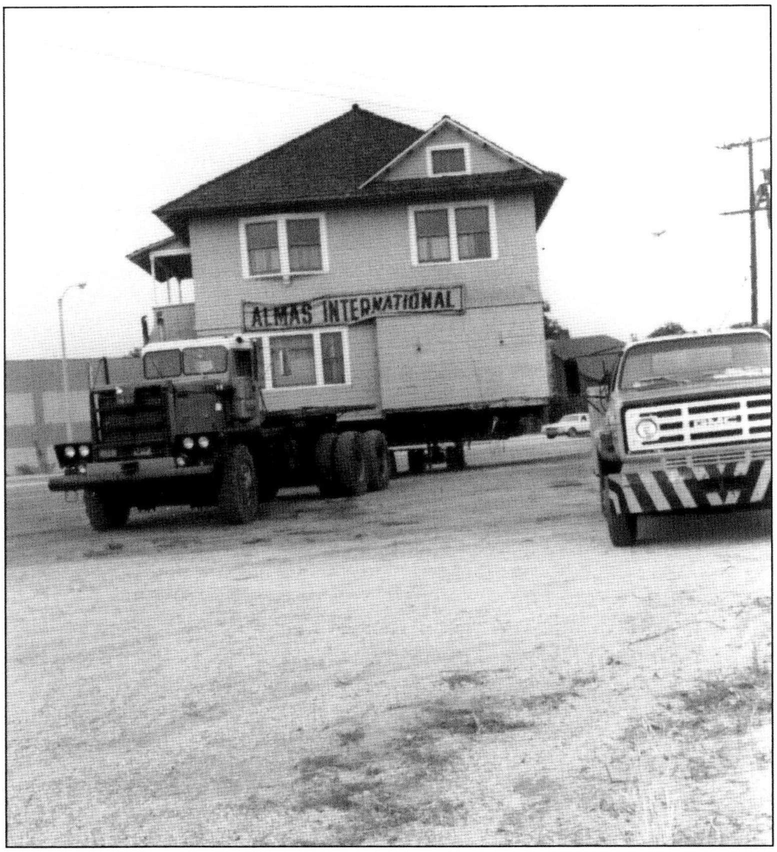

Here the movers are transporting the Martin House to its new location in 1987. One good thing about the moving of the building is that it went from a relatively obscure location to a place of prominence across the street from city hall.

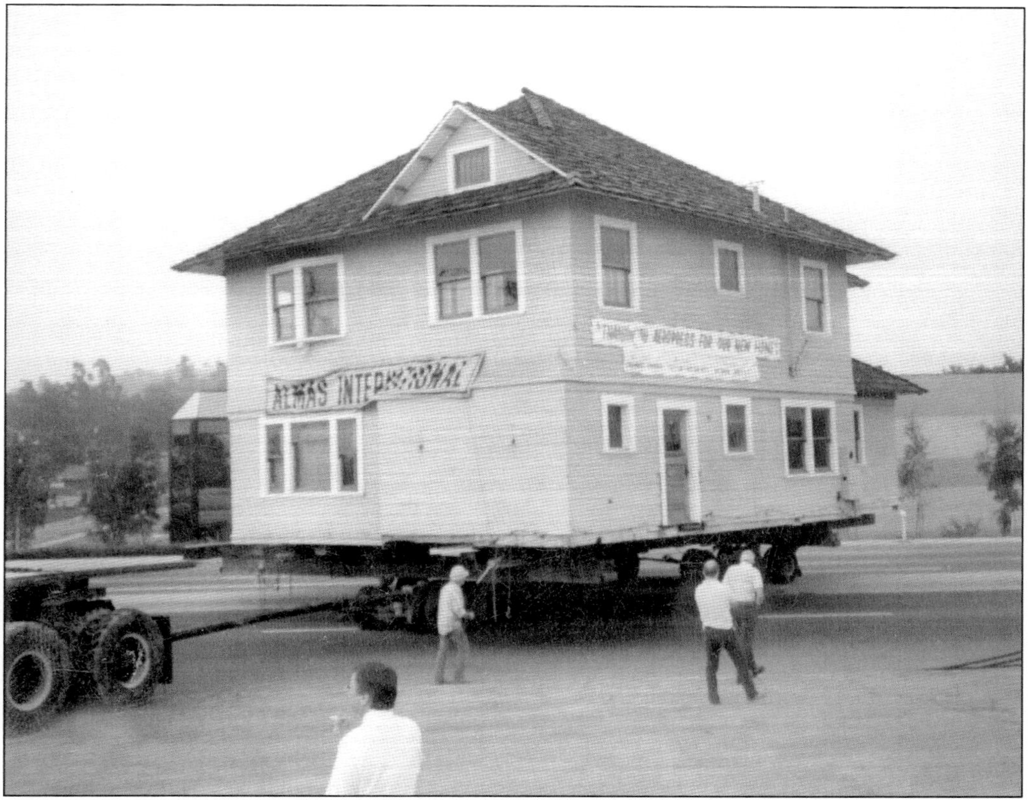

The old building withstood the move very well, which had to say something about its original construction. Although the city made some changes to the exterior, it is still a beautiful building and is used today by several civic groups.

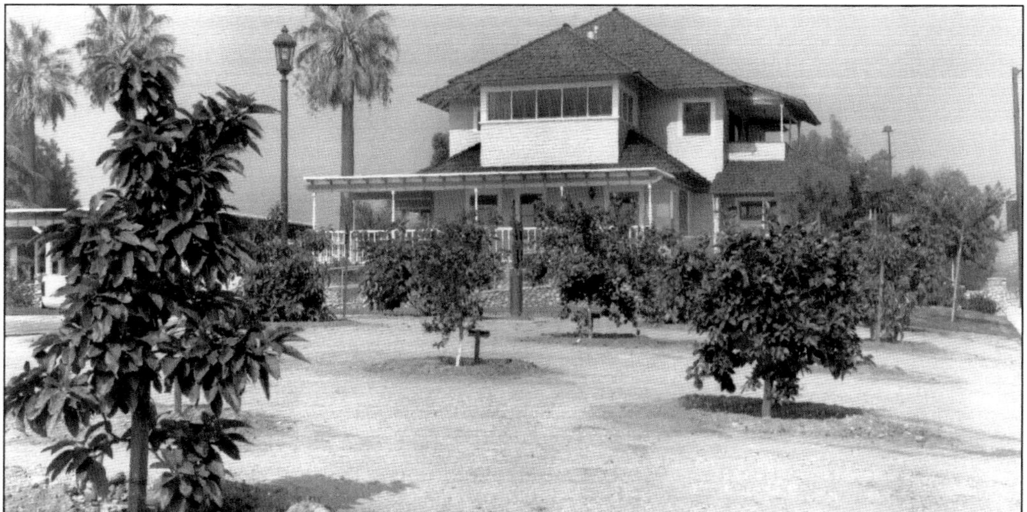

Dedicated in 1989, the Martin House is used today by the San Dimas Chamber of Commerce, the San Dimas Historical Society, and the San Dimas Festival of Arts.

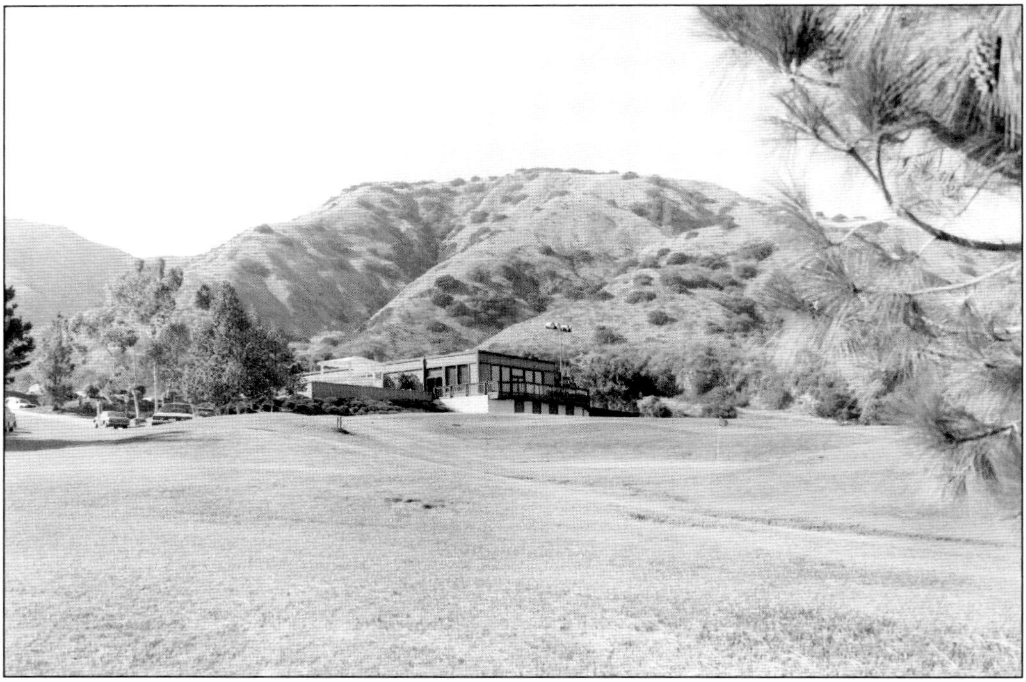

San Dimas Golf Course, located in San Dimas Canyon north of the city, was purchased by San Dimas in 1971. The facility is owned by the City of San Dimas and offers a room for functions such as the historical society's semiannual dinners.

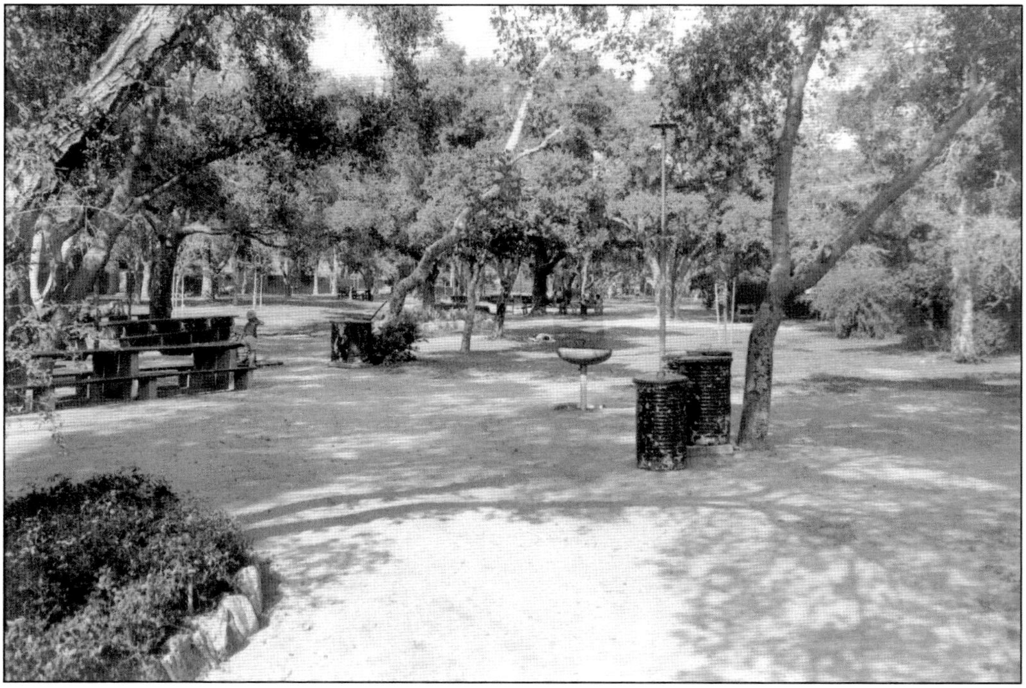

San Dimas Canyon Park is the oldest park in the city, having been developed by the County of Los Angeles Forestry Department in the 1920s. The park is one of 11 parks within the city of San Dimas and is operated by the County of Los Angeles.

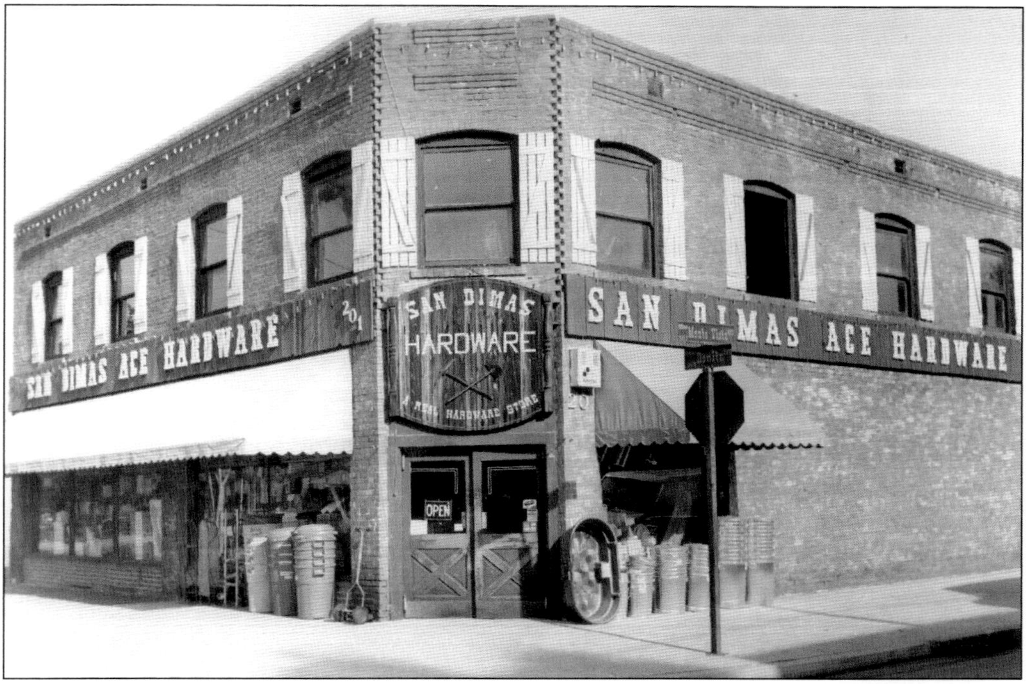

The San Dimas Ace Hardware store was originally constructed in 1904 by the Sipple brothers, merchants from Azusa. The building was completely rebuilt and finished in 1997 to look like it did when originally constructed. The top floor provides apartments for senior citizens.

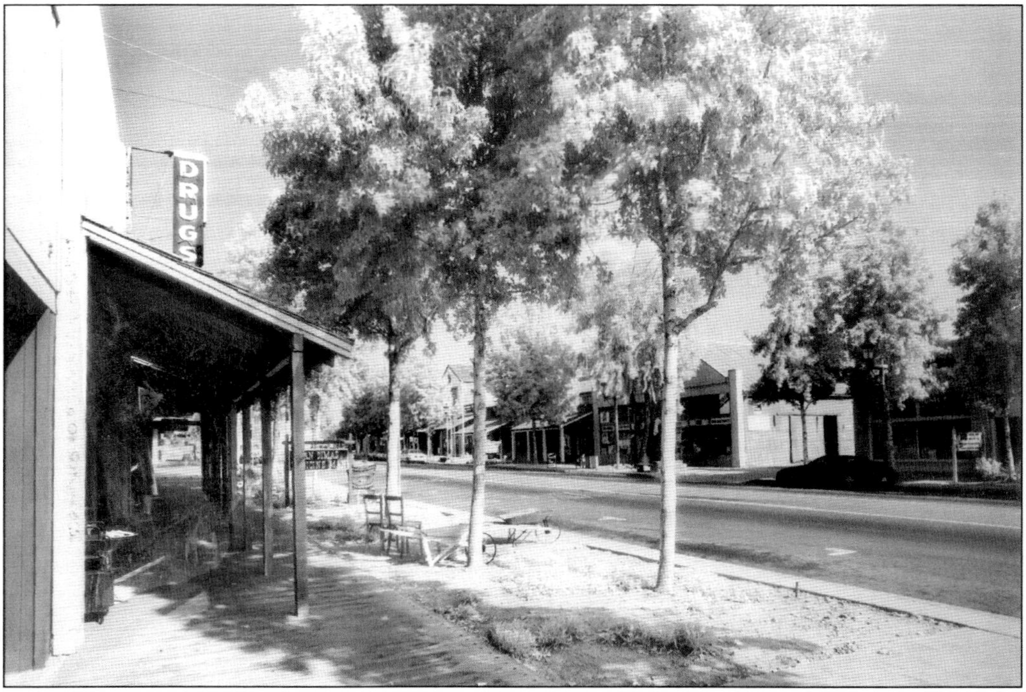

During the 1960s, the city decided to make the historic part of the town look like a western town along with wooden sidewalks. This appearance is still in existence, although the town was never a "western town."

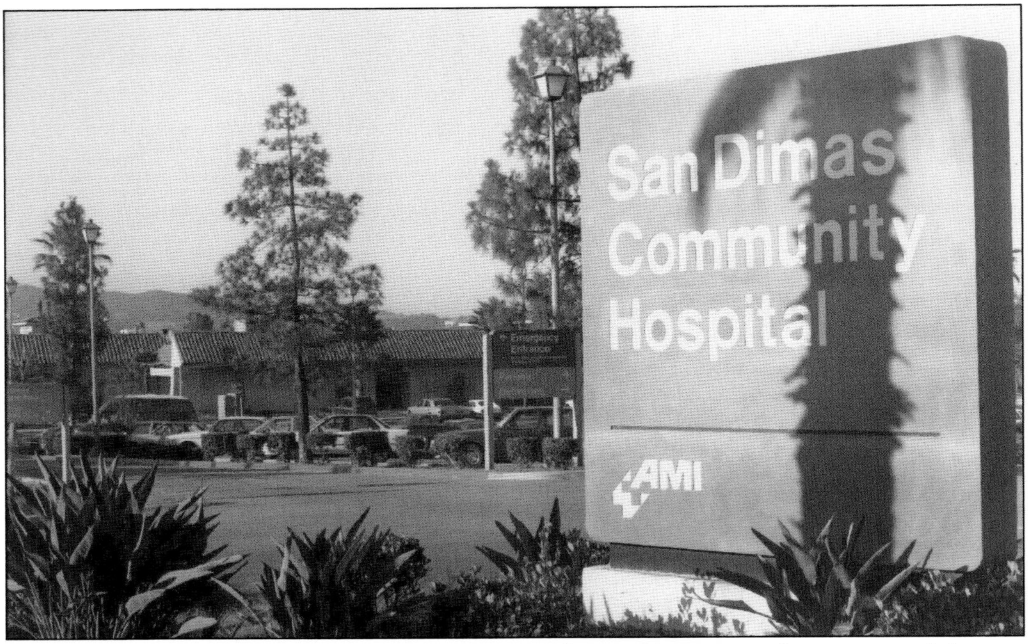

The San Dimas Community Hospital was opened in 1972 to serve the citizens of the city and the surrounding area. The 93-bed hospital provides 24-hour emergency service in a "family" atmosphere.

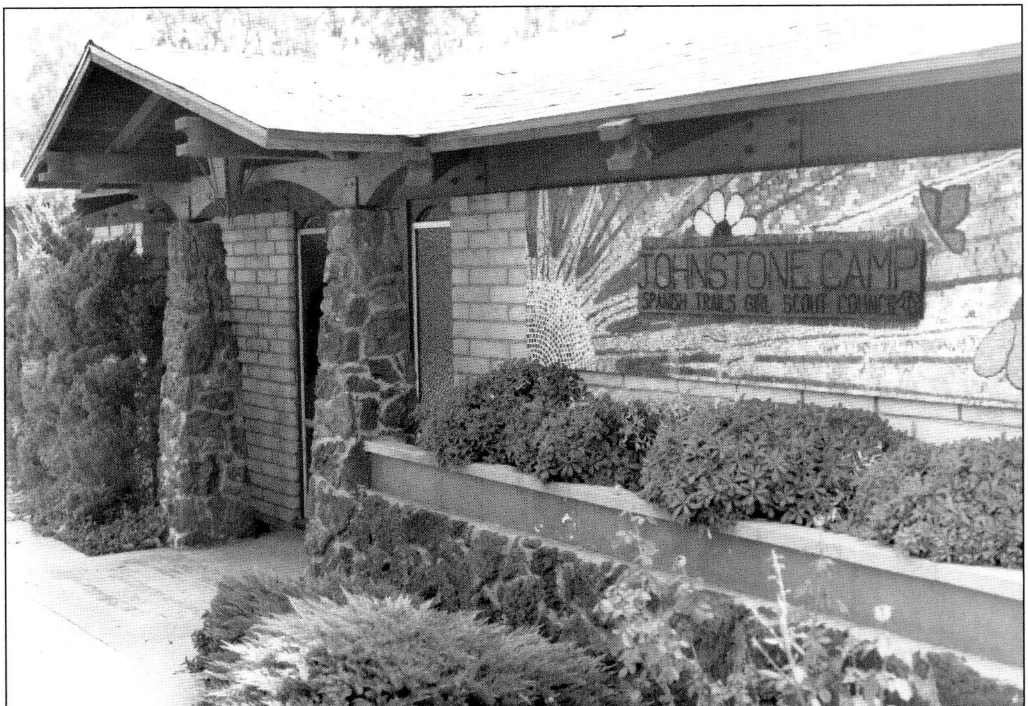

Johnstone Camp was built to replace the Scout House that burned in 1955. The camp has been named in honor of Alice Johnstone, who gave the initial property to the San Dimas Girl Scouts in 1937. Additional property was donated in 1964 by Robert and Jean Rimpau.

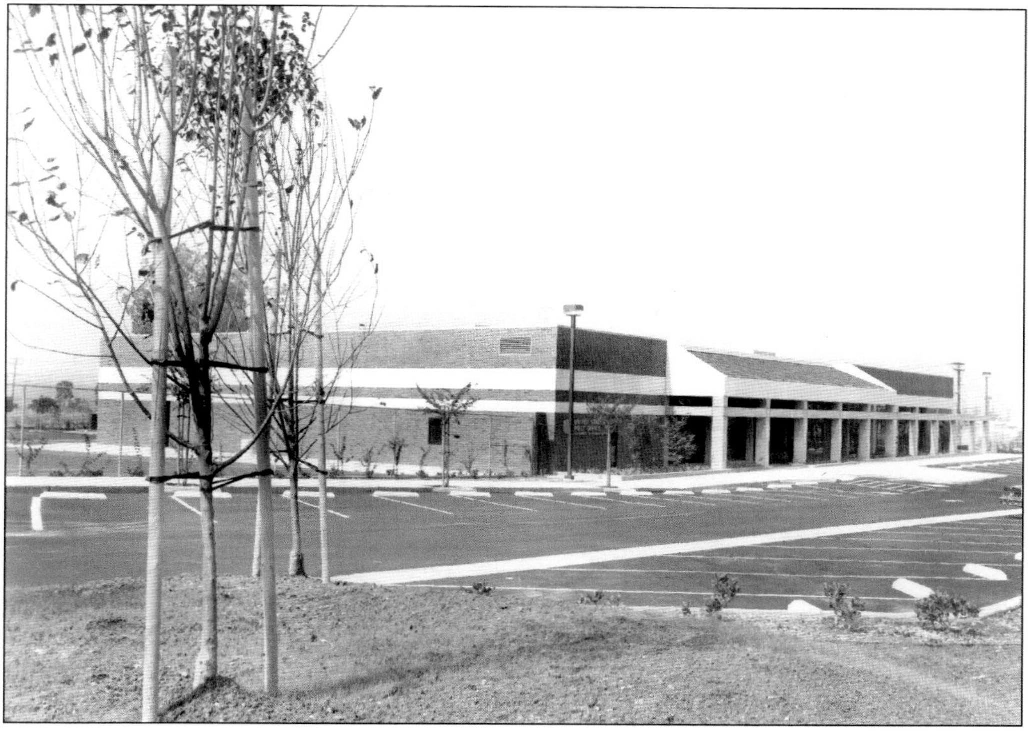

The current San Dimas Post Office was opened in 1988 and serves San Dimas and the surrounding area. The block now contains the post office, Los Angeles County Fire Station 64, and the San Dimas sheriff station.

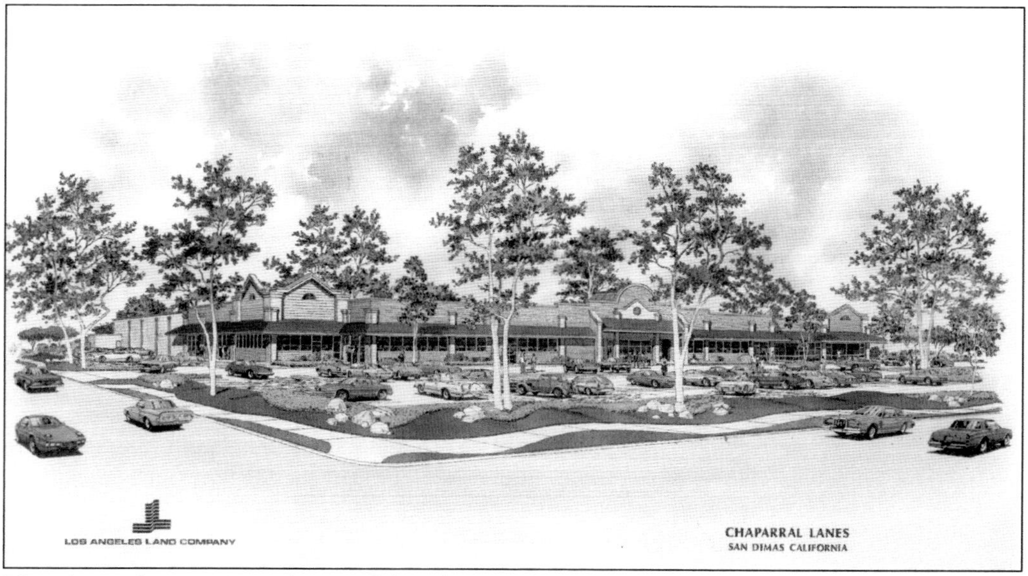

This shows the artist's rendering of the Chaparral Lanes in San Dimas. The bowling center was constructed on the land that once housed the Mexican colony established for Mexican workers of the citrus industry.

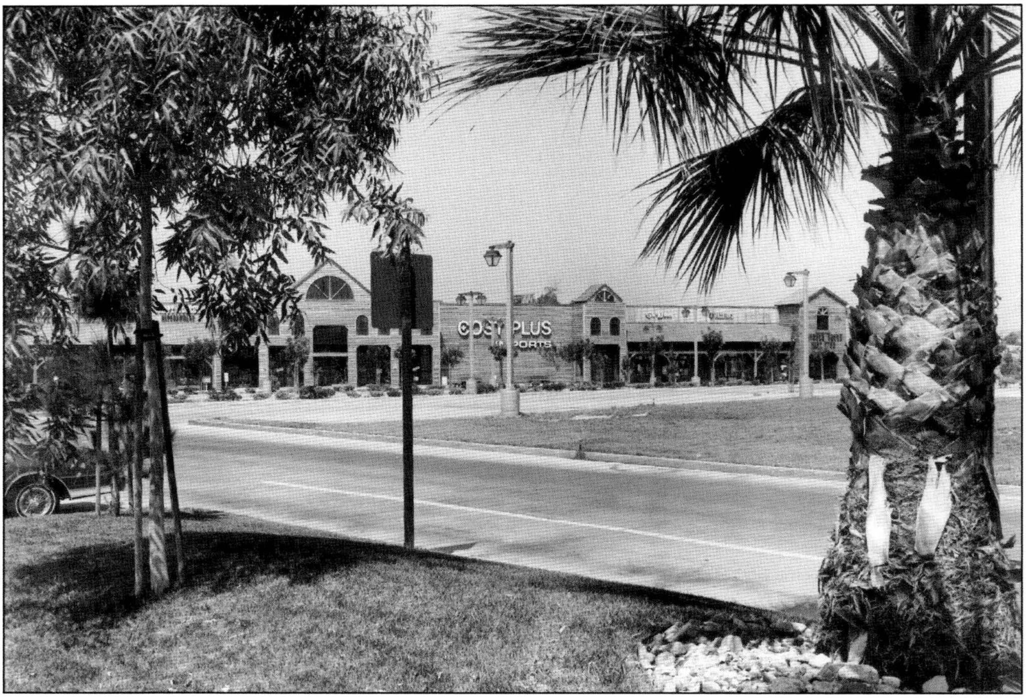

During the 1980s, new construction on the west side of the city offered additional shopping facilities for residents and visitors to the city.

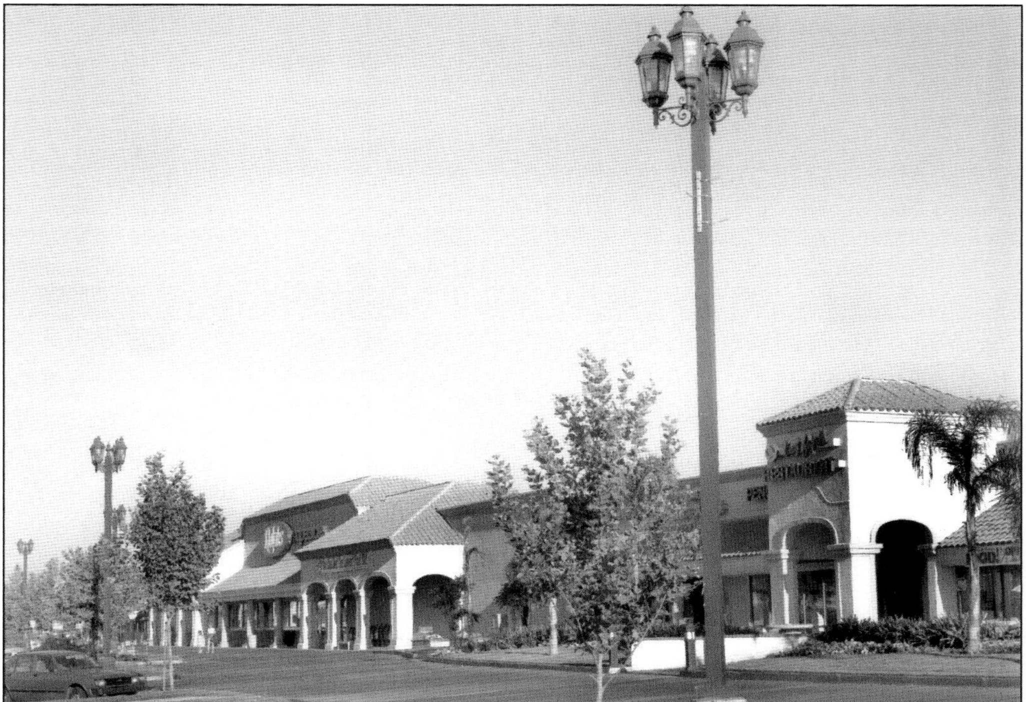

Located on property that was once part of the Dunning Ranch, a new shopping center west of the 57 Freeway added to the shopping abilities for visitors to San Dimas around 1987.

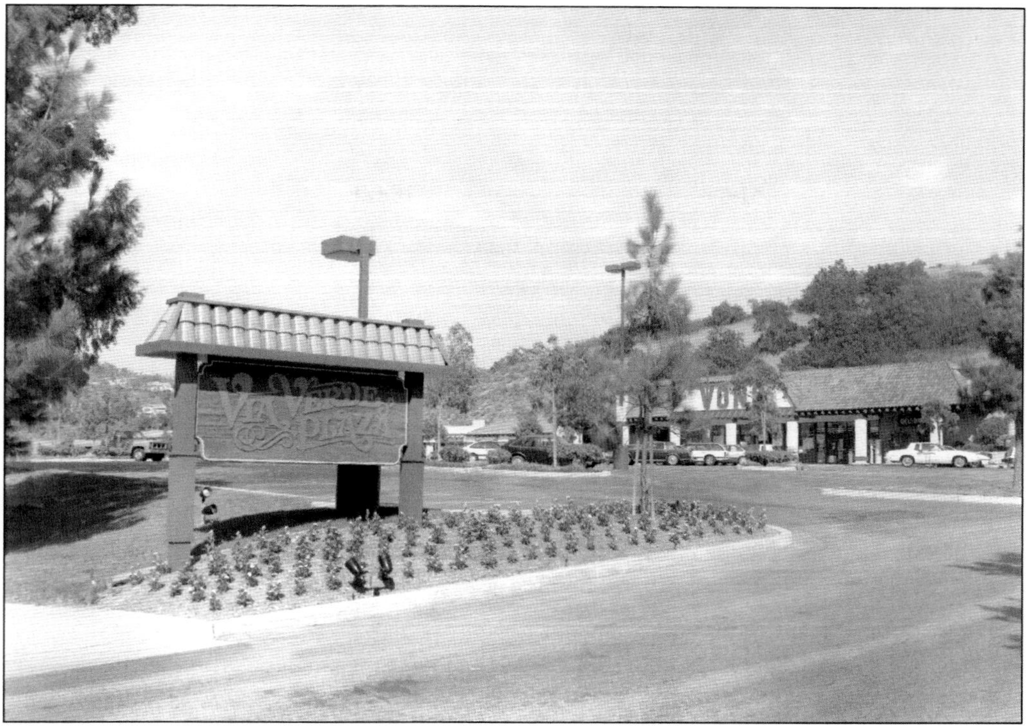

The shopping center in Via Verde includes a grocery store, drugstore, cleaners, bank, and restaurants. The site also features an annual Holiday Celebration and car show each December.

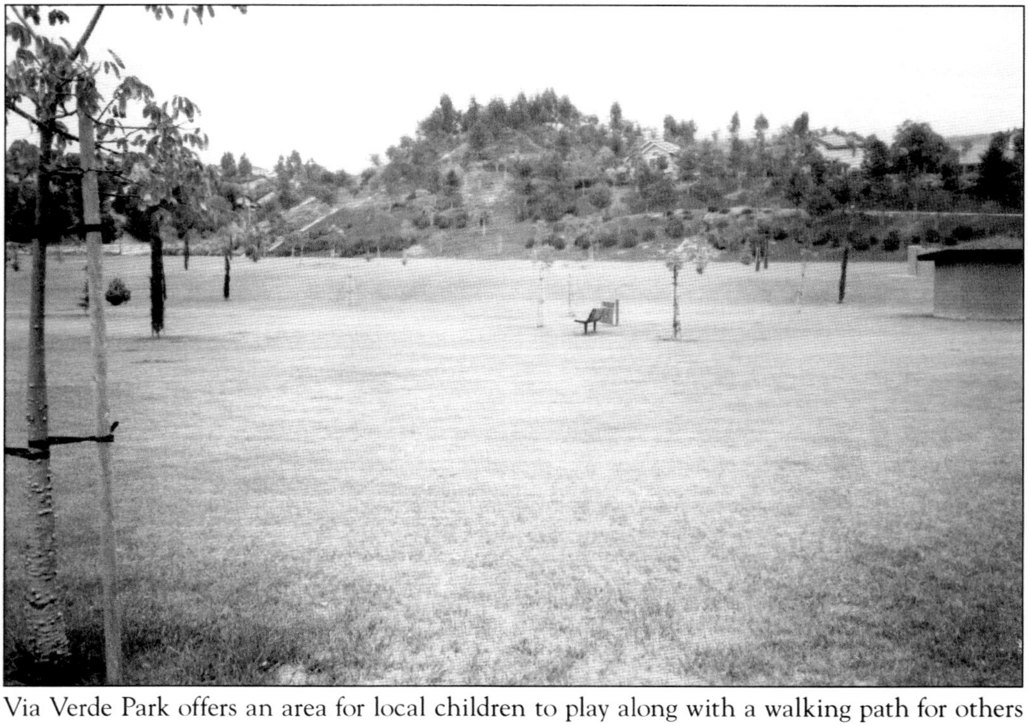

Via Verde Park offers an area for local children to play along with a walking path for others to enjoy.

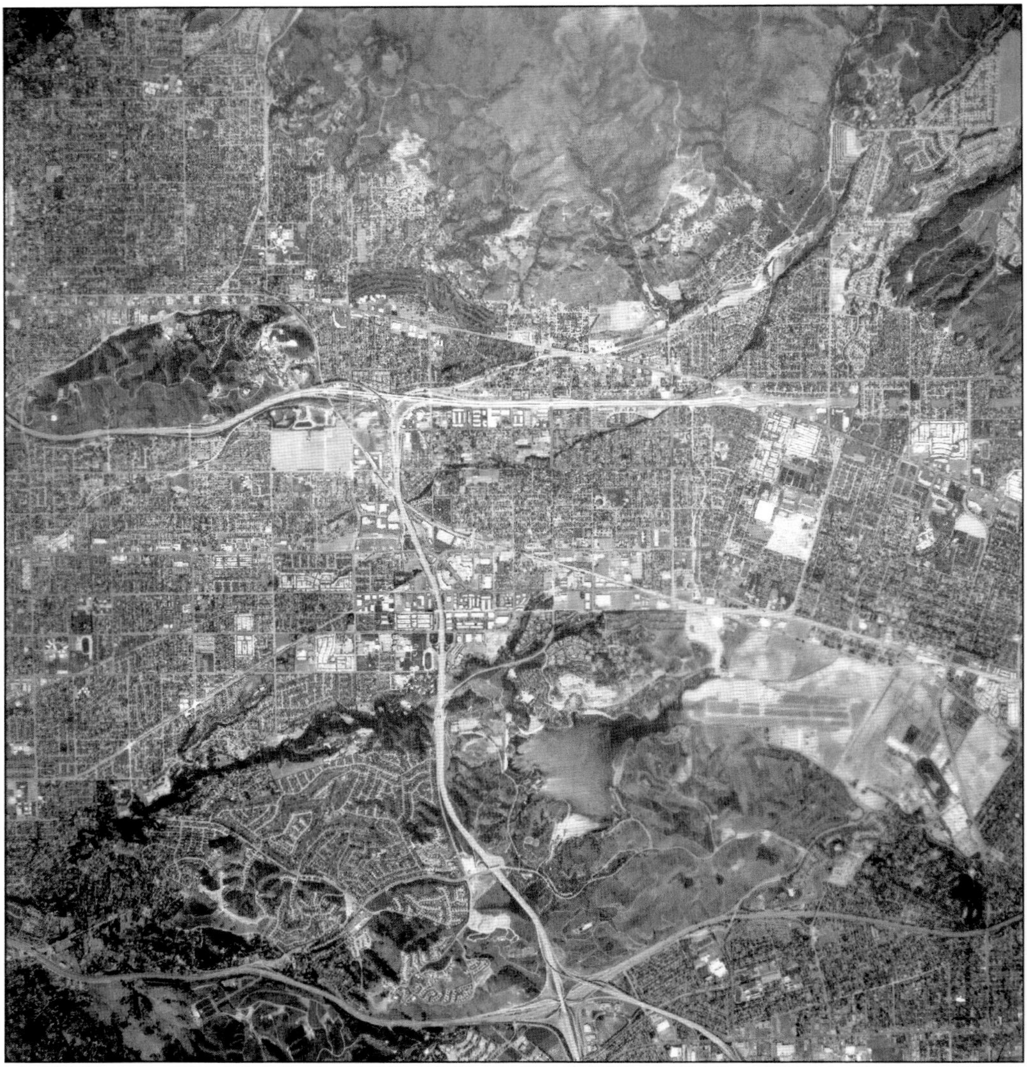

This is an aerial view of San Dimas taken in 1989. The housing in the lower left of the picture is the Via Verde area of San Dimas, with the San Bernardino Freeway (I-10) just below the homes and the Orange Freeway (57) to the east. Toward the lower center of the picture is Puddingstone Reservoir, with Bracket Airport to the east of the lake. In the upper portion of the photograph is the Foothill Freeway (I-210), which now extends farther east.

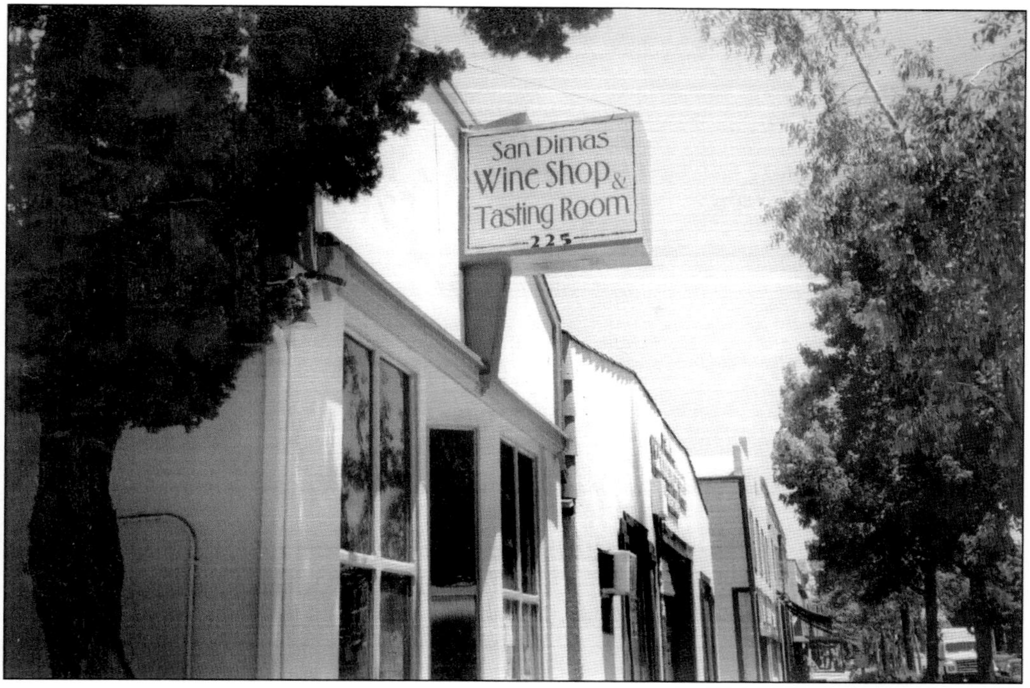

The San Dimas Wine Shop and Tasting Room, a very popular business in San Dimas, is housed in a building that was constructed in 1908 as a small restaurant. The business is another example of the reuse of the older buildings in San Dimas.

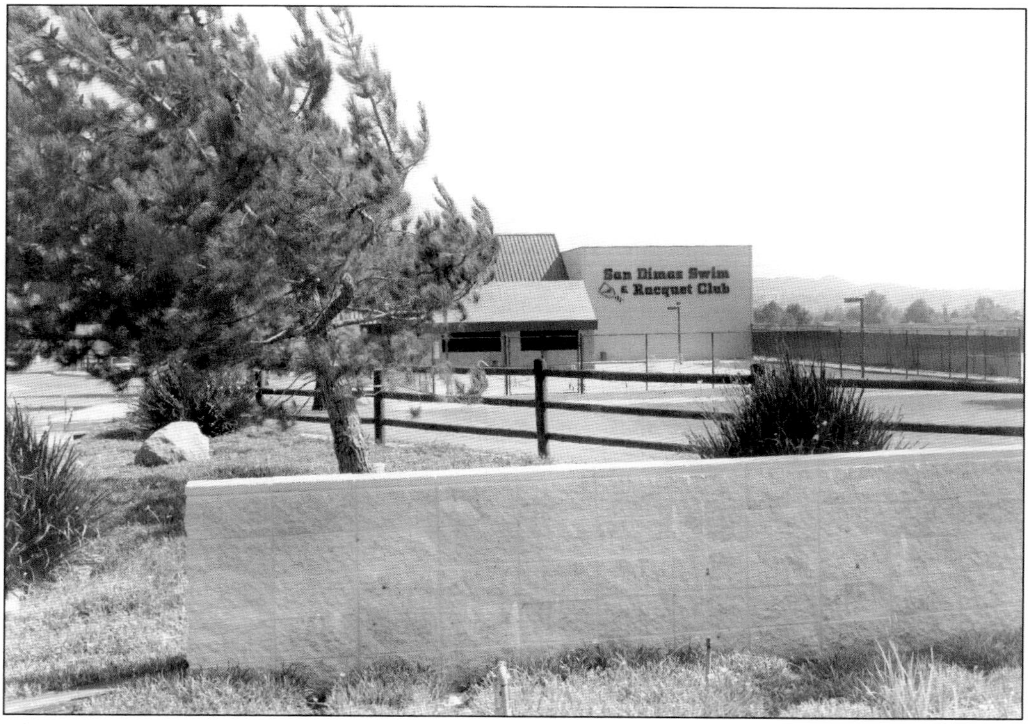

The San Dimas Swim and Racket Club was built next to the high school and serves the community as a place to exercise; it also houses a student union. The building was completed in 1981.

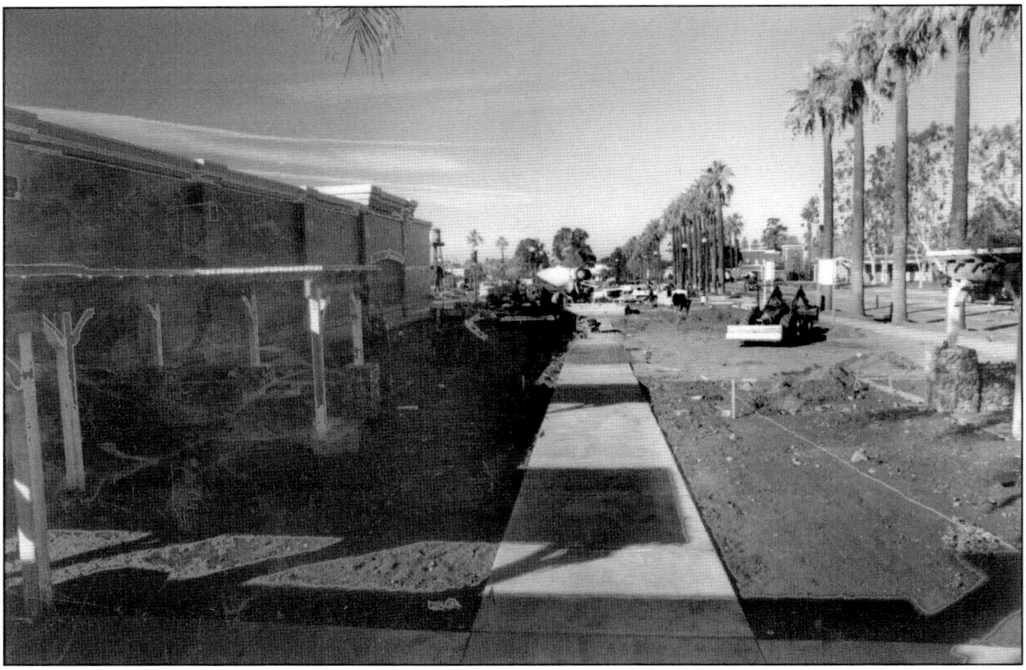

The Albertson's grocery store was under construction in 2003. The building offers the only large market within the historic part of the city. The store and its employees have become good partners with the city and the various civic groups.

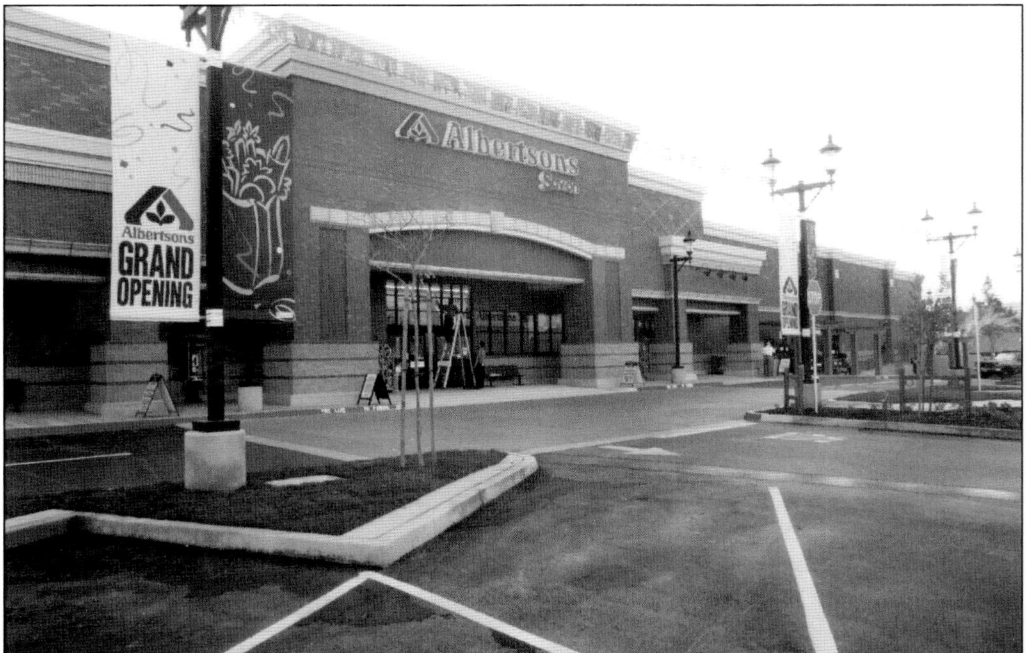

The new Albertson's store is ready for its dedication in February 2003. The market and pharmacy serve a large section of the community that are seniors and do not have the means to travel from the historic part of the city.

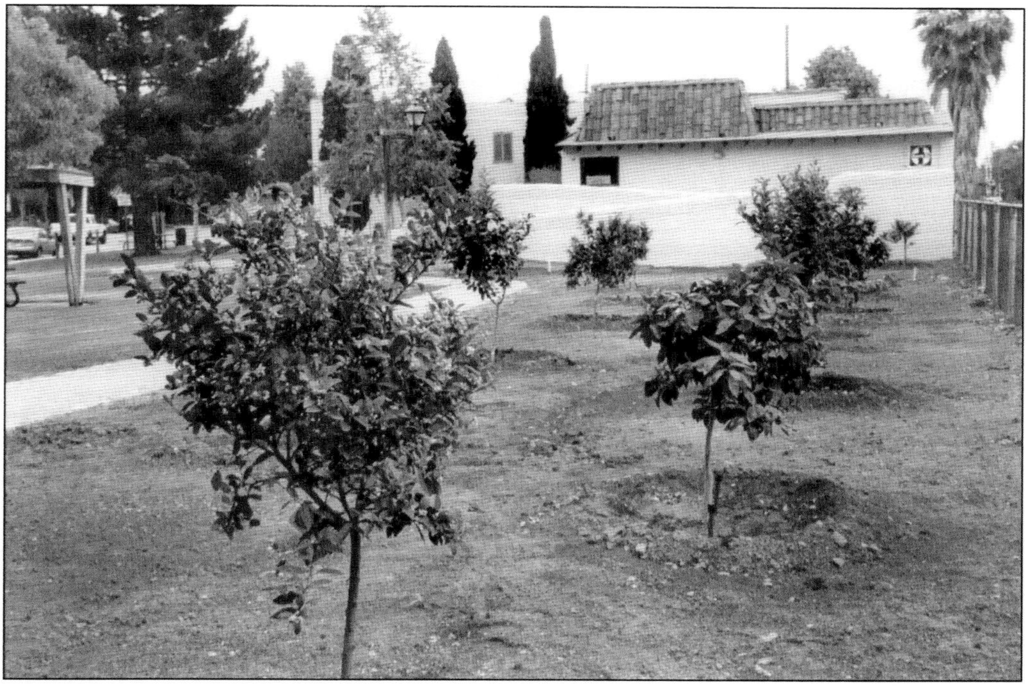

With the construction of the Albertson's store, a small grove of citrus trees indicative of the type of trees grown in San Dimas in the early years had to be removed and replaced by a new grove in Rhodes Park. The grove is a nice addition to the park and the adjacent train station.

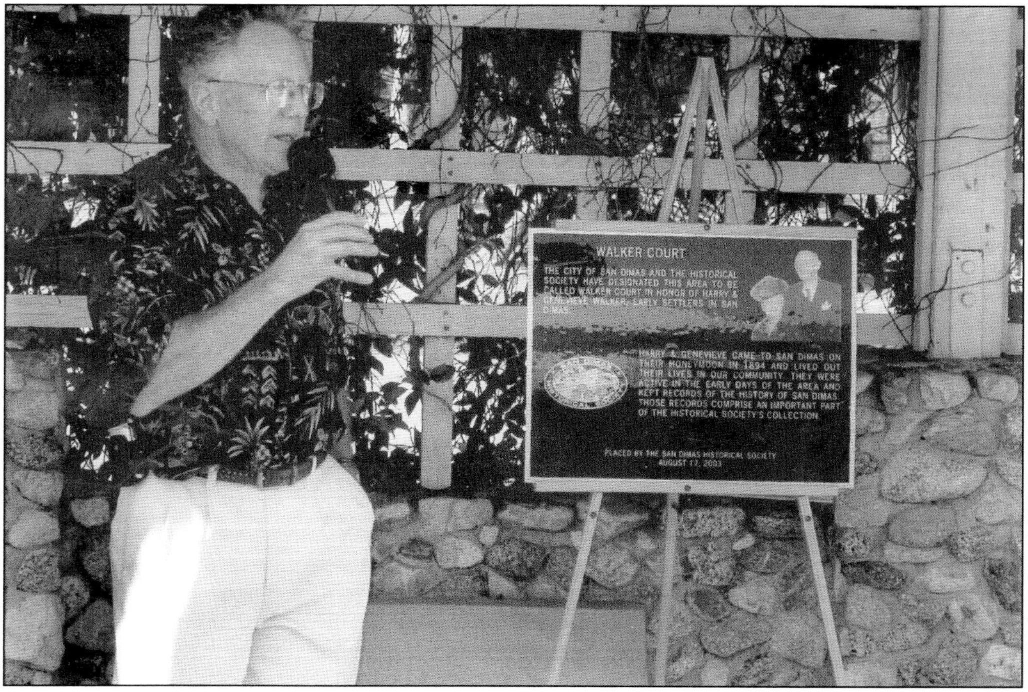

Historical society archivist Paul Rippens speaks at the dedication of Walker Court behind the historic Martin House. The site was named for Harry and Genevieve Walker, who did so much for early San Dimas and who kept the early history of the town and surrounding area.

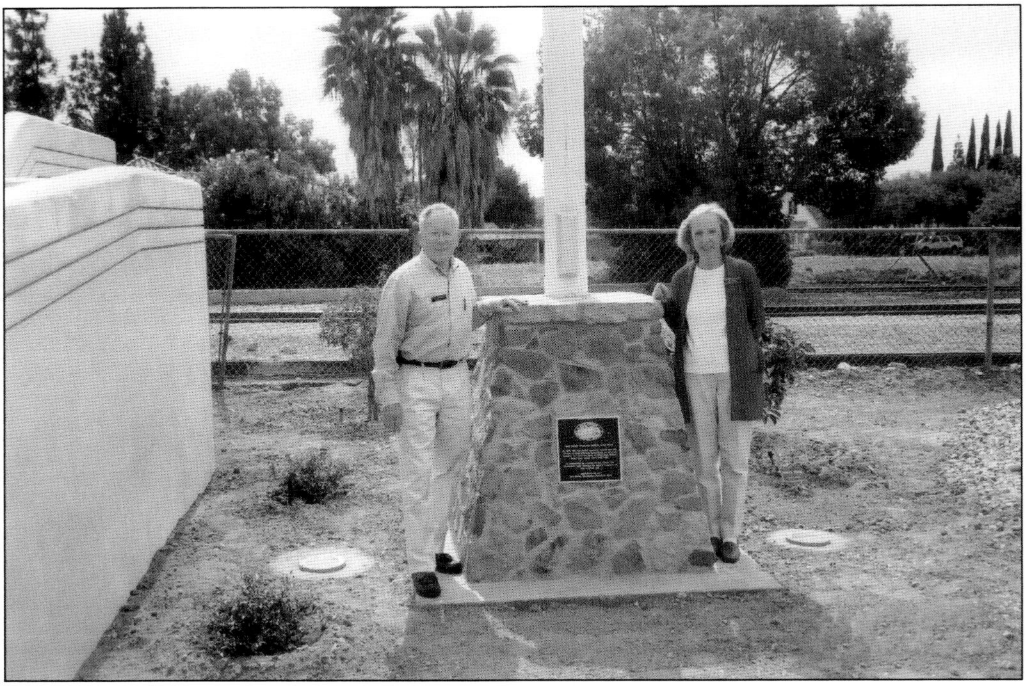

Historical society archivist Paul Rippens and his wife, Pat, stand next to the flagpole that was moved from the site of the early San Dimas Grammar School. The pole was placed in front of the school in 1908 and was noticed by city workers in 2004, long after the school had been torn down. The pole was removed and a portion installed at Rhodes Park as a reminder of the early days of San Dimas.

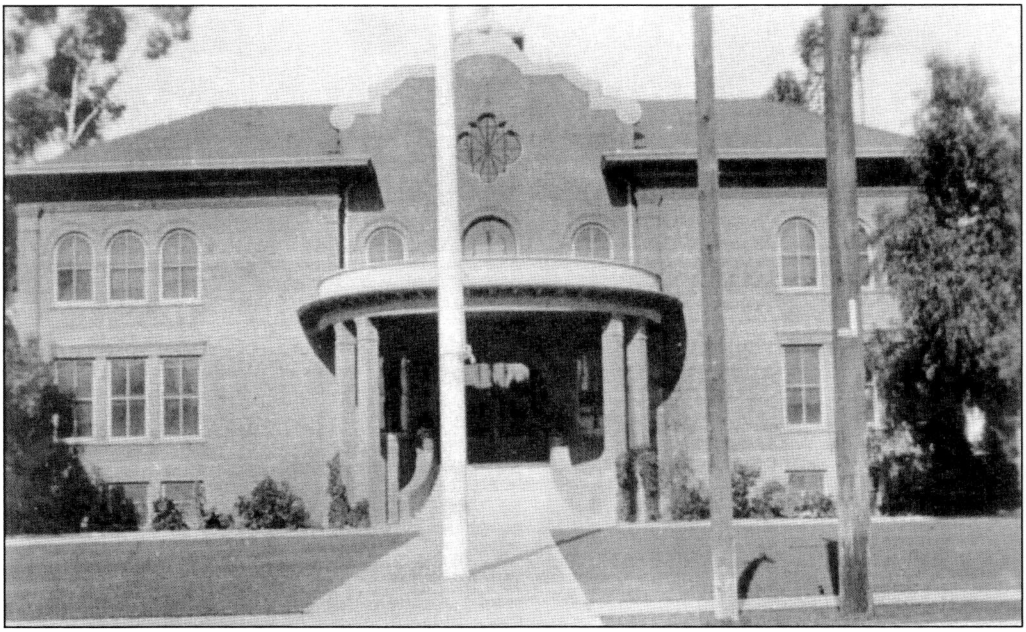

The second of three grammar schools constructed on this site, this building was constructed in 1908 with the "new" flagpole prominent in the foreground. It is this pole that is now in Rhodes Park.

The Technology and Development Center of the U.S. Forest Service, one of only two such centers in the United States, is located in San Dimas. The center was moved here in the 1960s.

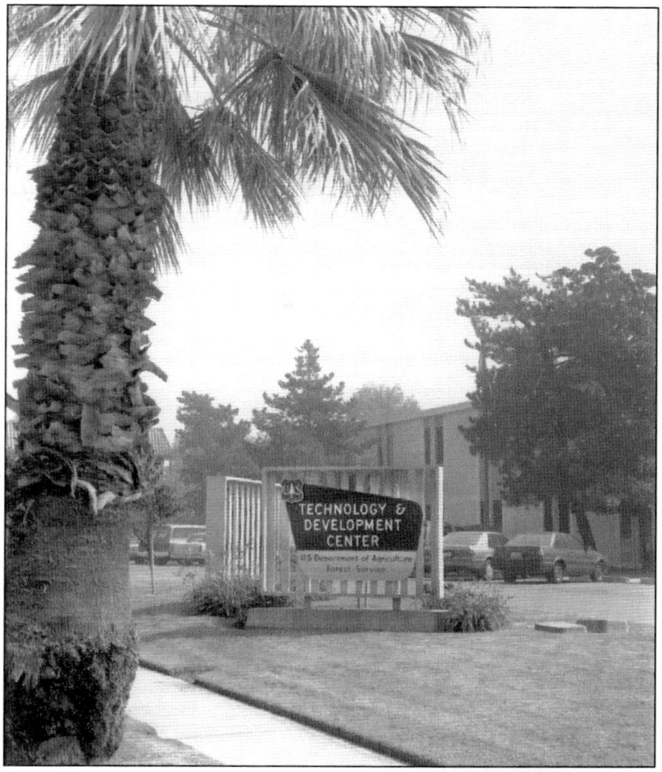

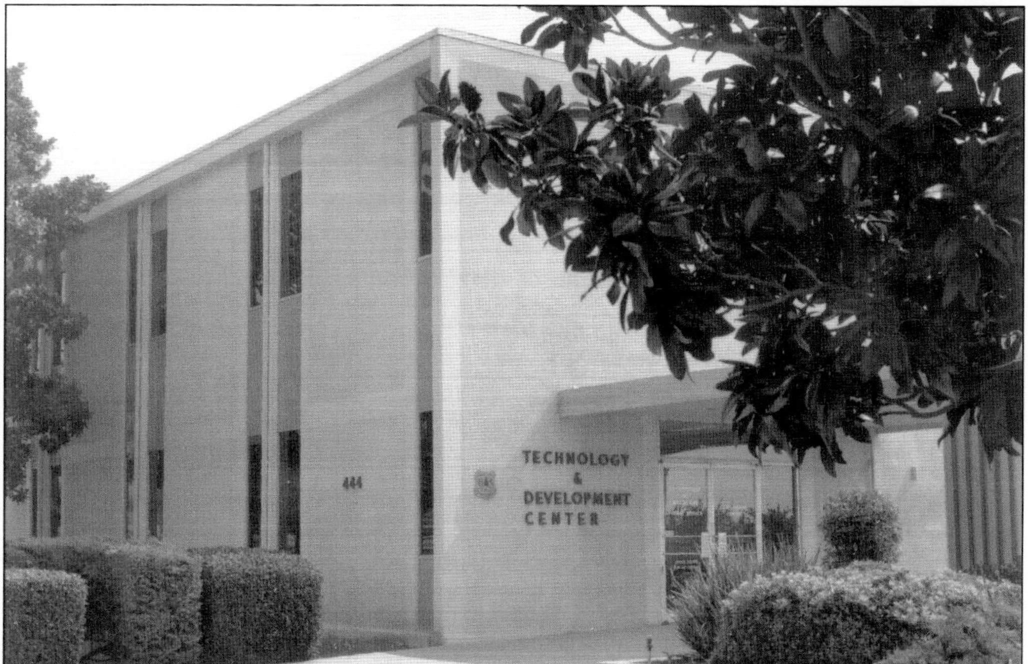

The purpose of the technology and development program is to assist all forest service employees and cooperators with technical solutions to natural resource issues through the application of advanced technology.

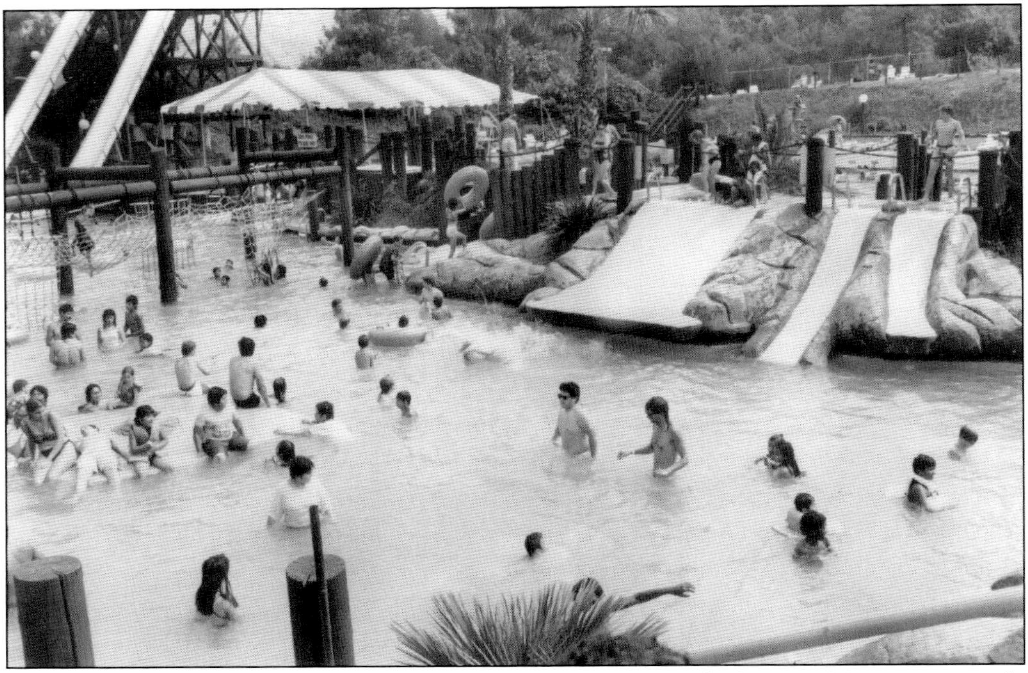

A very popular place in San Dimas during the summertime is the Raging Waters swim park. Constructed by the County of Los Angeles Parks and Recreation, it was later leased to an outside vendor to operate and improve the facility. The park draws thousands of visitors from all over Los Angeles County.

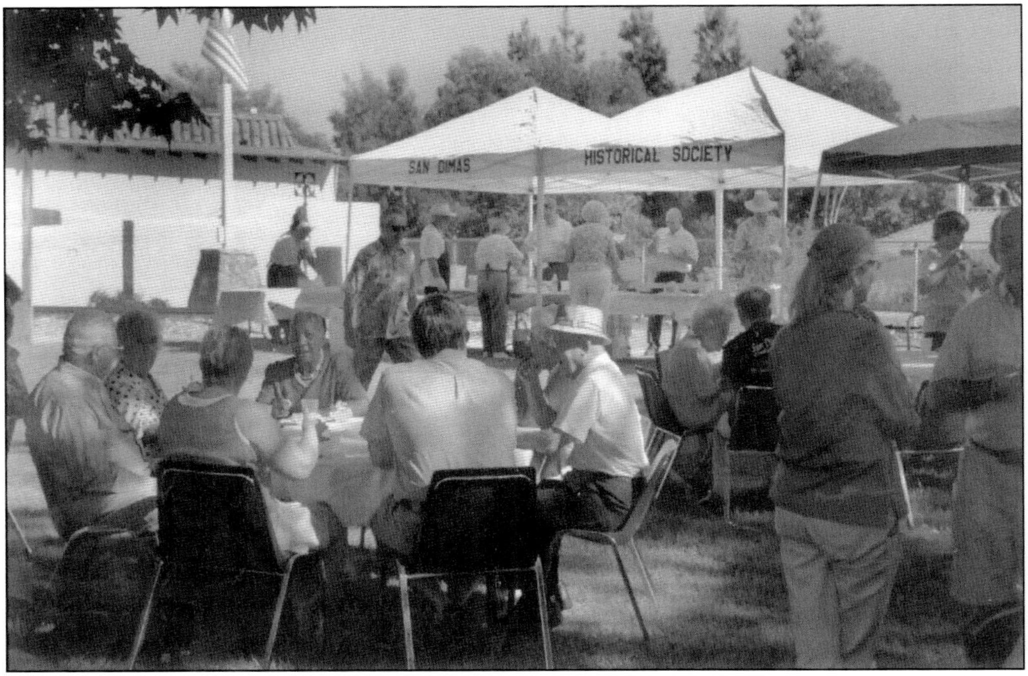

Each summer, members of the San Dimas Historical Society get to enjoy the annual Ice Cream Social. The historical society provides everything for the event, with help from the city and local merchants, to thank their members for their support.

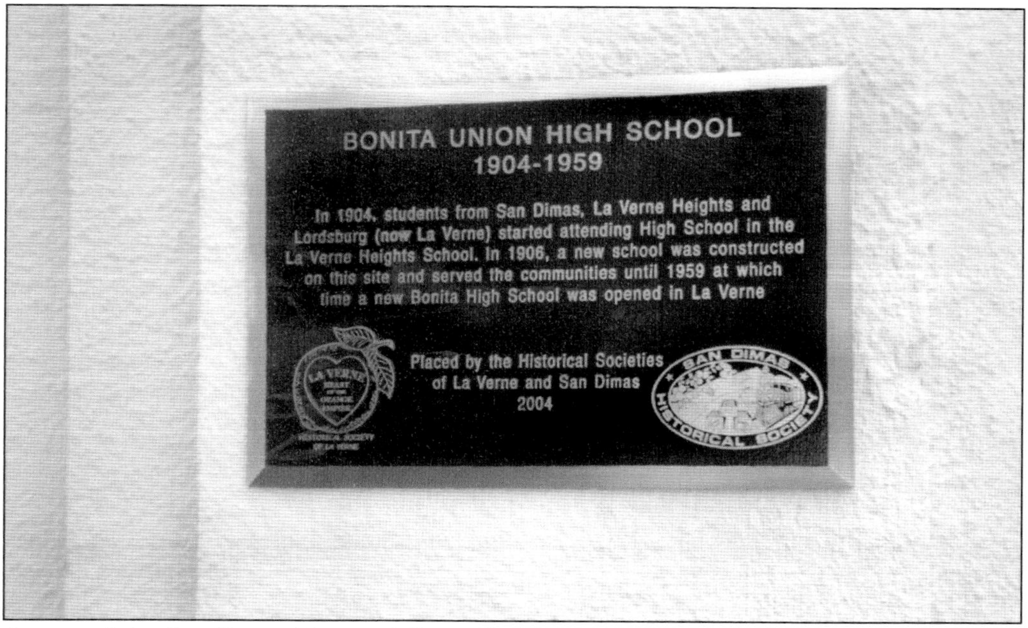

As part of the San Dimas Historical Society's efforts to recognize the history of the city, they have embarked on a project of marking historic sites with bronze plaques. This plaque, posted in cooperation with the La Verne Historical Society, marks the buildings of the old Bonita Union High School used from 1904 to 1959.

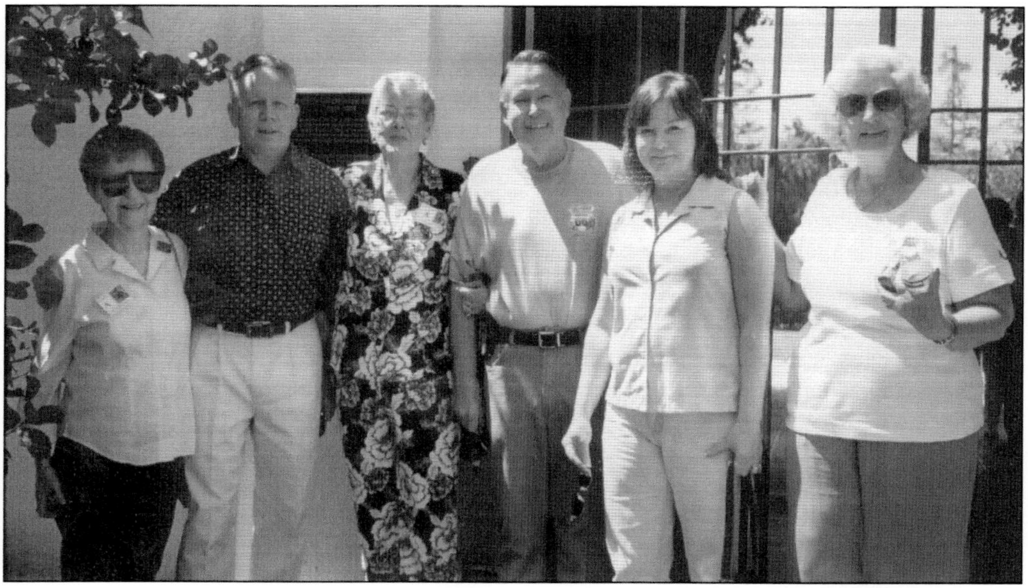

During the Bonita High School plaque dedication, historical society board members, from left to right, Marge Tomkinson, Paul Rippens, Bee Dallas, Bill Emerson, Susan Davis, and Marilyn Angelo pose for a picture.

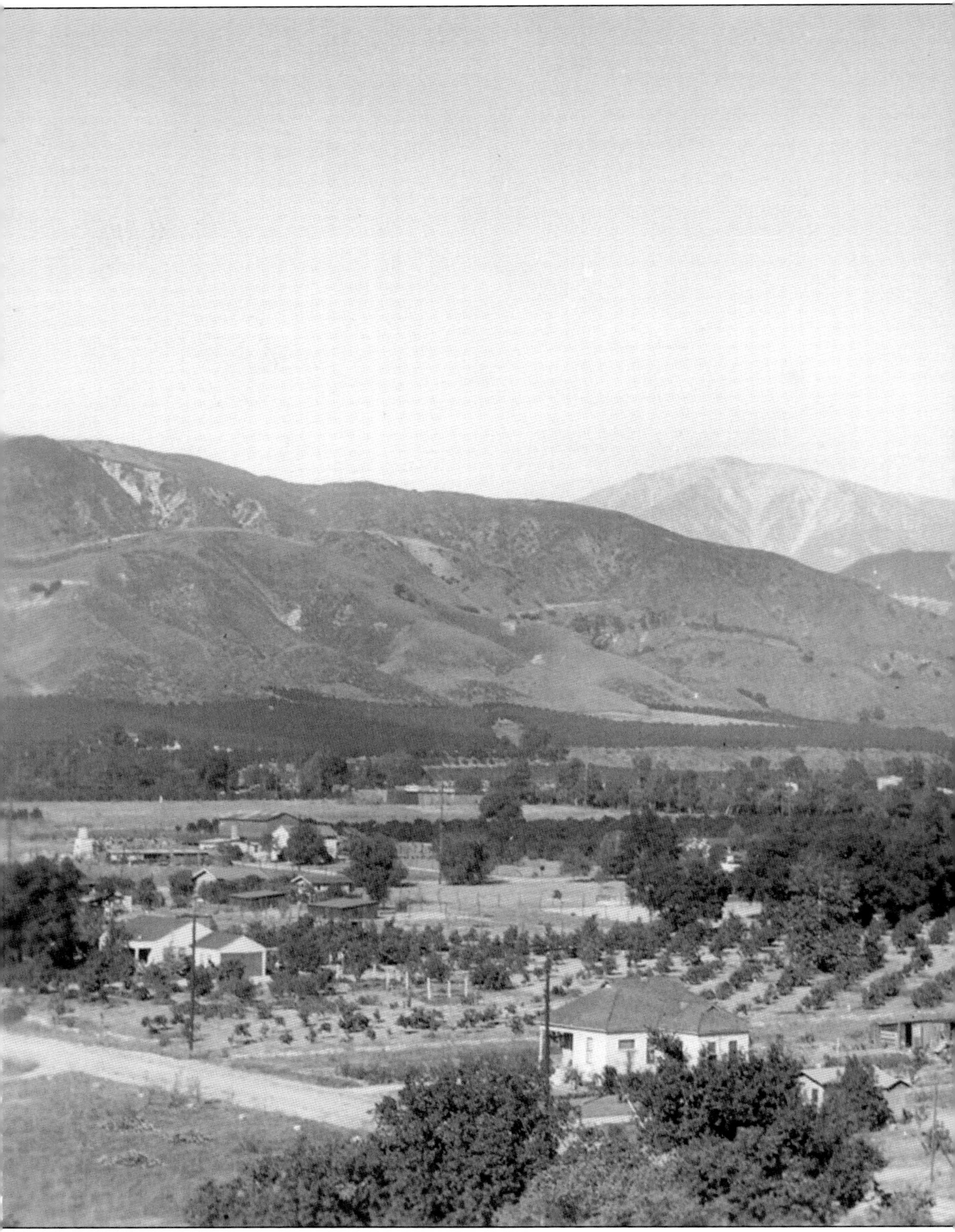

The early days of San Dimas have given way to a busy, vibrant city, crossed by two freeways and home to 35,000 people. The 15.5-square-mile city will never be like it was in this picture; however,

it is a wonderful place to live. Just ask anyone who lives here!

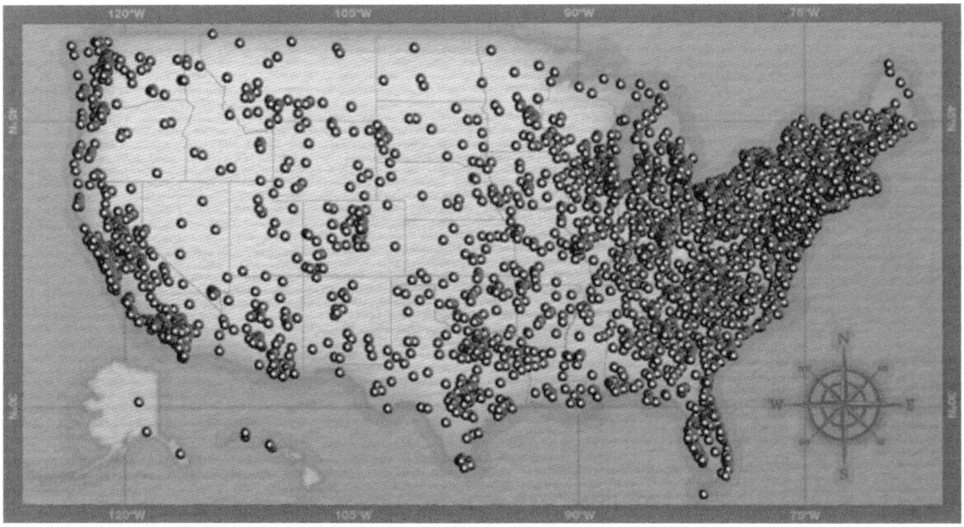